D1518827

The Triumph of the Gun-Rights Argument

The Triumph of the Gun-Rights Argument

Why the Gun Control Debate Is Over

Harry L. Wilson

 PRAEGER

AN IMPRINT OF ABC-CLIO, LLC
Santa Barbara, California • Denver, Colorado • Oxford, England

Library of Congress Cataloging-in-Publication Data

Wilson, Harry L., 1957– author.
   The triumph of the gun-rights argument : why the gun control debate is over / Harry L. Wilson.
       pages cm
   Includes bibliographical references and index.
   ISBN 978–1–4408–3035–8 (cloth : alk. paper) — ISBN 978–1–4408–3036–5 (ebook)
1. Gun control—United States. 2. Firearms ownership—United States. 3. Pressure groups—United States. 4. Lobbying—United States. 5. United States. Constitution. 2nd Amendment 6. Firearms—Law and legislation—United States. I. Title.
   HV7436.W555   2015
   323.4'3—dc23   2014028986

ISBN: 978–1–4408–3035–8
EISBN: 978–1–4408–3036–5

19 18 17 16 15   1 2 3 4 5

This book is also available on the World Wide Web as an eBook.
Visit www.abc-clio.com for details.

Praeger
An Imprint of ABC-CLIO, LLC

ABC-CLIO, LLC
130 Cremona Drive, P.O. Box 1911
Santa Barbara, California 93116-1911

This book is printed on acid-free paper ∞

Manufactured in the United States of America

Contents

Preface

When approached about writing another book on gun control, I was more than excited. The issue seemed to be off the radar for most people, and I was thrilled that someone was still interested in the topic. Perhaps never too far from the front burner, there had been little national discussion about guns in quite some time. The debate among the attentive public, interest groups, and some elected officials had neither abated nor become less intense, but most citizens were focused on other issues.

My interest had been piqued even further by two narrowly decided U.S. Supreme Court cases that had recognized an individual right to possess firearms, but had also made it clear that many types of gun regulations were permissible. Public opinion and public policy had been swinging in the gun-rights direction as well. Fears about what President Obama would do seemed largely unfounded—he was focused on other issues and appeared to be unwilling to fight a losing battle.

My personal interest in the field had grown as well. I was planning an elk hunting trip to Wyoming. I had recently joined a local gun club and gotten involved with target shooting. My collecting interest had shifted from true antique firearms to the realm of milsurps—military firearms ranging in age from 50 years to over 100 years old. I was amazed at how accurate some of them were and intrigued by the challenge of making some others more accurate. It is also interesting to see how the technology evolved over the course of many decades. A friend had convinced me that I should reload my own cartridges for both the elk hunt and for the milsurp rifles to find a "load" that my guns "like."

After more years of frustration than I care to count, I was in the right place at the right time and was successful on the elk hunt. It is difficult to describe the range of emotions that I experienced, but they included both elation with the success and respect for the animal whose life I had taken. Some readers may empathize with that, and others may simply see it as barbaric. All are free to draw their own conclusions.

While virtually all of my personal experiences with guns have been positive, I have known people who have used a firearm to take their own lives, and I knew a person who had been accidentally shot. A former colleague and friend created a Facebook page titled "What Is Your Number?" following the fatal shooting of a close friend. He asked for students, friends, and colleagues to post the number of people they knew who had been a victim of gun violence. He was surprised by the high percentage of his students who knew a person who had been shot.

To understand all of these experiences is to begin to understand the complexities and the layers of how people use and how they view firearms. For all of us, our personal experiences help to shape our perspectives on various issues—that is unavoidable. However, we all need to go beyond those personal experiences and the anecdotes that abound on all sides of the issue of gun control. We need to look at policies as well as proposed regulations and measure and estimate, as objectively and accurately as we can, their actual impacts and likely consequences, intended and unintended. The role of interest groups is to present their point of view; the role of informed citizens is to critically examine those views and make their own decisions.

No policy is perfect. No policy results in only positive outcomes, and no policy is totally ineffective. To argue that restricting firearms would not save any individual lives is absurd. It is equally ludicrous to suggest that those restrictions would not prevent some people from saving their own lives by using a gun in self-defense and impact the recreational uses of guns as well. The questions are which of those sides carries more weight, and how do we balance any restrictions against constitutionally protected rights and what most would see as legitimate uses of firearms. Many of us will have very different answers to those questions, and we will even disagree over how we can save lives. Those answers are elusive.

Those "truths" will not be found in this book, or any other, from my perspective. I hope the reader will find logical, reasoned arguments. Most, if not all, will disagree with some or many of those arguments. There are counterarguments for many of the ideas contained herein. If you at least question some of your preconceived notions regarding guns and gun control, then I will have accomplished my goal, and your time will not have been wasted. Those may be very modest goals, but I think they are logical and reasoned.

Acknowledgments

Roanoke College has shown confidence in me in many ways over many years and enabled me to do my best. President Mike Maxey and Dean Richard Smith have encouraged and supported various endeavors, including expanding the Institute for Policy and Opinion Research (IPOR) and, most important, recognized my strengths in spite of my weaknesses.

A research grant from the college allowed Judi Pinckney to proofread this book several times and to put it in a format that someone other than I can understand. Without her help, meeting deadlines would have been impossible. She is great at reading for typos and reading to see if it makes sense. Even more, she does all of this quite cheerfully.

The staff at IPOR picked up the slack when I was writing. Special thanks to Dave Taylor and Amelia Glaser for holding down the fort. Directing IPOR is the best job I've ever had.

Gregg Carter recommended me to Praeger for this book. Later, he reviewed the manuscript and suggested specific ways to improve it. His insights made it better, and they helped me clarify some points that needed clarification. He not only made suggestions, but he also told me where to find sources to make those points. He encourages and guides. He is a colleague in the best sense of the word.

My editors at Praeger—Beth Ptalis and Jessica Gribble—were supportive and helped keep me on task and on deadline. Rowman & Littlefield Publishers was very gracious in allowing me to use numerous excerpts from *Guns, Gun Control, and Elections*, saving me time and sparing me stress. That work is reprinted with permission from "Constitution," pages

20–30; "Gun Policies," pages 82–104; "Interest Groups and Elections," pages 142–45; and various excerpts on pages 162–70, as found in *Guns, Gun Control, and Elections* by Harry Wilson.

My wife Donna is unfailingly supportive, and she loves me as I am, which is not always an easy task. Whether it is tolerating a very cluttered home office or listening as I incomprehensively explain why I must go elk hunting again, she smiles, rolls her eyes, and lets me be me.

The current pack of canines—Lacey, Stella, and Ivan—drive me crazy when they aren't making me laugh or providing unconditional love. Lacey, at 12 years old and missing a front leg, has taught me much about life and the will to live.

ONE

Introduction

This book was conceptualized in October 2012 with the working title, *The Triumph of the Gun-Rights Argument: Why the Gun Control Debate Is Essentially Over*. At that time, it seemed to be the logical approach to the issue. As it was phrased in the proposal, while small skirmishes will continue to be fought for some time, changing public opinion, Supreme Court decisions, the dominance of gun-rights interest groups, the Democratic Party's virtual withdrawal from the debate, and a declining violent crime rate have formed a perfect storm resulting in the effective ending of the gun control debate.

It appeared as if the Supreme Court decisions in *District of Columbia v. Heller* and *McDonald v. City of Chicago* were the icing on the cake. Public opinion had been trending slowly but surely in the direction of gun rights. Policy at the national level and in most, though certainly not all, states had been moving toward looser gun laws.

Many in the Democratic Party had come to see gun control as the "third rail" of American politics. Even those who supported stronger gun control, including President Barack Obama, were silent on the issue—unwilling to engage in a policy fight they would certainly lose and that could exact a toll on the party as well. National Democrats did not even take up the cause when they controlled both houses of Congress and the White House from 2009 to 2011.

Violent crime declined in the face of a powerful recession, a time when conventional wisdom and most criminologists said that crime rates would increase. Gun sales had soared after Obama's victory in 2008 and again in

2012, making the "more guns, more crime" argument increasingly difficult to make. As one constitutional law scholar expressed it, "Americans
had come to seem almost blasé about the nation's continuing epidemic
of gun violence."[1] However, the politics of gun control was about to
change.

On December 14, 2012, 20-year-old Adam Lanza walked into Sandy
Hook Elementary School in Newtown, Connecticut, where he shot and
killed 20 school children and six teachers and administrators. Earlier that
day, he had shot and killed his mother with her .22 rifle and taken several
of her semiautomatic firearms, which he used in the school shootings. His
actions changed the landscape of the gun control debate in the United
States.

For more than a decade, violent crime had been declining nationally,
and polls showed a gradual but clear shift in favor of gun rights.[2] The
National Rifle Association (NRA) had successfully helped to move laws,
both nationally and in many states, away from stricter regulations on firearms. The Assault Weapons Ban of 1994 expired a decade later with little
impetus in Congress to renew the legislation. The Supreme Court of the
United States had issued two landmark rulings, both in close votes, clearly
stating that the Second Amendment to the Constitution protected an individual right to bear arms for self-defense. While the Court explicitly stated
that some regulations on firearms were constitutionally permissible, gun
bans were found to violate the Constitution, and gun-rights advocates
finally had the Court's imprimatur on their claim of an individual right
to firearms possession.

Even President Barack Obama, who had been a strong supporter of gun
control in the state of Illinois and as a U.S. senator, stated that he supported an individual right in the Second Amendment. "I believe in the
Second Amendment. I believe in people's lawful right to bear arms. I will
not take your shotgun away. I will not take your rifle away. I won't take
your handgun away."[3] In his first term as president, he took no major
action to restrict gun rights, and discussion of gun control was largely
absent from the Presidential campaign in 2012.

While Dan Gross, president of the Brady Campaign to Prevent Gun
Violence, suggested that Obama had done "disappointingly little" in the
area of gun control, NRA chief executive officer Wayne LaPierre somewhat presciently said, "This is the most dangerous election of our life-
times."[4] Despite the dire warnings of LaPierre, there was little evidence
that the second Obama administration was targeting firearms prior to
December 14. All of that changed dramatically with the Newtown
shooting.

This was not the only mass shooting in recent history. Several other shootings had also received significant media attention, including, in recent years, an Aurora, Colorado, movie theater (July 20, 2012; 12 killed; 58 injured), a Safeway grocery store in Tucson, Arizona (January 8, 2012; 6 killed; 13 injured, including Representative Gabrielle Giffords, who was wounded), the Fort Hood, Texas, army base (November 5, 2009; 12 killed; 31 injured), Northern Illinois University (NIU) (February 14, 2008; 6 killed; 21 injured), and the Virginia Tech shootings, the largest in U.S. history (April 16, 2007; 33 killed; 23 injured). One of the first school shootings to receive significant news media coverage occurred at Columbine High School in Colorado on April 20, 1999 (15 killed; 21 injured).

After each of these tragedies, there were calls for stricter gun laws, but little action was taken. In each case there was significant coverage by the news media—often intense for a short period—but media attention usually waned shortly after the funerals for the victims were held. In most cases, the guns were legally purchased, and the shooters were clearly mentally unstable. Many of the shooters took their own lives. Thus, the threat to most people was not viewed as proximate.

George W. Bush, a gun-rights supporter, was president during the earlier shootings, so there was no national figure to push for legislation. President Obama was reluctant to press for gun control in his first term, understanding that he was not likely to be successful in getting legislation passed. He was also heavily invested in dealing with the economic crises and health care reform—two issues that dominated that term. While the Democrats controlled Capitol Hill from 2009 to 2011, there was insufficient time and little congressional support, even among Democrats, for gun control. When the Republicans regained control of the House of Representatives in the midterm elections of 2010, the opportunity for gun-control legislation had passed.

Finally, the timing of the Aurora and Tucson shootings did not coincide with a policy window that might be open.[5] As previously mentioned, violent crime was in decline, support for gun control was down, and the country was focused on economic issues and health care. In short, regardless of his policy preferences, there was no real chance for Obama to shepherd legislation through Congress.

There was some congressional support from those who had pushed for stricter gun laws for years—elected officials such as Senators Dianne Feinstein (D-CA), Charles Schumer (D-NY), and Frank Lautenberg (D-NJ) as well as Representative Carolyn McCarthy (D-NY). But no interest groups that backed stricter laws were a match for the clout of the NRA. The Brady Campaign was still on the scene, but on the periphery;

and New York City mayor Michael Bloomberg's group, Mayors Against Illegal Guns (MAIG), was formed in 2006 but still lacked the political clout to be effective nationally.

But Sandy Hook was different from the other mass shootings. First, the victims were primarily small children and their teachers. This was largely a new experience for America. Even though the shooter had stolen the firearms from his mother, who had them registered in a state with very strict gun laws—making it difficult to envision a law that would have prevented it—this was different. Even though Adam Lanza was clearly mentally unstable, at least at the time of the shooting, like many other mass shooters, this was different. Even though the number of victims was large, we had seen more victims in previous shootings; but this was different. These victims were mostly young children between 5 and 10 years old and the teachers who tried in vain to protect them.

It is painful to imagine a group of college students at Virginia Tech trapped in a classroom, trying to plot an escape from the shooting, which only a few successfully utilized. It gives us all pause to consider people in a dark movie theater with no place to run and no clear path to safety when an individual opens fire. We have difficulty comprehending a shooter in a parking lot, targeting an elected official and many others at a political rally. But none of this comes close to the horror of little children huddled in a corner of a classroom, with only a teacher to protect them, too young to understand what may have been happening and too small and, almost certainly, too frightened to fight back. This was different. The emotional impact was something we had not previously witnessed. The victims at Columbine were teens; those at Virginia Tech and NIU were young adults. Those at Newtown were *children*. The country's response was understandably visceral, and emotion has typically been on the side of gun control.

For those who support stricter gun-control laws, including President Obama, this was their opportunity. The policy window had opened. It is difficult to imagine a political climate more sympathetic to gun laws than that which followed the Newtown tragedy. In the weeks and months following the shootings, gun control remained in the news. While Obama's immediate reaction may have been viewed by some as somewhat muted,[6] his speech at the memorial service for the victims was described as "surprisingly assertive."

No single law, no set of laws can eliminate evil from the world or prevent every senseless act of violence in our society. But that can't be an excuse for inaction ... in the coming weeks I'll use whatever power this office holds in an effort aimed at preventing more tragedies like this.

Because what choice do we have? We can't accept events like this as routine. Are we really prepared to say that we're powerless in the face of such carnage? That the politics are too hard? Are we prepared to say that such violence visited on our children year after year after year is somehow the price of our freedom?[7]

In the following days, there were some signals from pro-gun Democrats in the Senate that they may be open to new firearms regulations.[8] On December 18, the president announced that he was putting Vice President Joe Biden, one of the authors of the original Assault Weapons Ban, in charge of a task force that would investigate gun violence, issue a report, and make specific recommendations for action prior to the State of the Union address in February. This was promised to be a balanced and thorough examination of the gun violence problem, but gun-rights advocates feared that it would focus almost solely on firearms.[9] Early in January 2013, the task force held hearings that included testimony from victims of gun violence as well as advocates from both sides of the debate. On January 16, President Obama announced four legislative proposals and 23 executive actions. Flanked by four young schoolchildren who had written letters to the president regarding gun violence, he called for passage of a strengthened assault weapons ban, a ban on magazines that can hold more than 10 rounds of ammunition, universal background checks to include all private firearms transactions, and legislation banning "armor-piercing" bullets and stronger penalties for straw purchasers, people who legally purchase firearms but then sell or give them to persons prohibited from buying guns themselves.

Four of the 23 executive orders dealt with mental health—three were clarifications of the Affordable Care Act, and one called for a national dialogue on mental health.[10] One provided incentives for schools to hire resource officers. The largest number, six, dealt with background checks, while others included gun safety, law enforcement, gun traces, and clarifications of allowing doctors to ask patients about guns in their homes and reporting violent threats. One somewhat overlooked order mandated that the Centers for Disease Control conduct and support research into the causes and prevention of gun violence.[11]

In an emotional address, the president made it clear that he expected a tough political battle. "I tell you, the only way we can change is if the American people demand it ... We're going to need voices in those areas ... where the tradition of gun ownership is strong, to speak up and to say this is important. It can't just be the usual suspects."[12]

The NRA was silent for nearly a week after the shootings. At a press conference on December 18, 2012, Wayne LaPierre suggested that violent media, "gun-free" zones, lax law enforcement, and a lack of school security put children at risk. Vowing to use the resources of the NRA to create programs to help train and deploy armed security for those schools that want it, he argued that the media and some elected officials perpetuate the problems by misstating the causes of violence and misrepresenting firearms.

> The only thing that stops a bad guy with a gun is a good guy with a gun ... You know, five years ago, after the Virginia Tech tragedy, when I said we should put armed security in every school, the media called me crazy. But what if, when Adam Lanza started shooting his way into Sandy Hook Elementary School last Friday, he had been confronted by qualified, armed security? Will you at least admit it's possible that 26 innocent lives might have been spared? Is that so abhorrent to you that you would rather continue to risk the alternative?[13]

The *Washington Post* described the response as "simplistic" and "crude."[14] The *New York Times* stated, "we were stunned by Mr. LaPierre's mendacious, delusional, almost deranged rant."[15] *USA Today* quoted several Newtown residents, suggesting that LaPierre's remarks were "off the mark," "rude," "completely ludicrous," and "just an awful slap to the face" and suggested that the timing was too soon after the shootings.[16] Other news outlets were equally effusive in their condemnation. In his speech, LaPierre stated, "Now, I can imagine the shocking headlines you'll print tomorrow morning: 'More guns,' you'll claim, 'are the NRA's answer to everything!' " His prediction was not inaccurate.

The president's proposals were generally given a lukewarm reception in the Senate, and their chances of passage in the House of Representatives were seen as slim at best.[17] The focus was on the Senate, where legislation was introduced to ban assault weapons, limit magazine capacity, and expand background checks. It quickly became clear that the only measure that could possibly garner the 60 votes necessary to break a filibuster was expanding background checks.[18] Indeed, a procedural vote received 68 votes, thus temporarily ending a filibuster.

On April 17, 2013, the Senate voted down an amendment that would have expanded background checks to include all firearms transactions at gun shows and Internet sales (which were defined as any firearm that had been advertised in any medium that had an Internet presence). The amendment had been crafted by moderate Democrat Joe Manchin (WV) and conservative Republican Pat Toomey (PA), working with Charles Schumer (D-NY) and Mark Kirk (R-IL). It received 54 votes, falling five short of what was necessary to stall another filibuster.[19] Only four Republicans voted for the amendment, including the two cosponsors, and five Democrats, including Harry Reid, voted against it. In comparison, an amendment to ban assault weapons got 40 votes, while one that would have allowed persons with a concealed-gun carry permit to carry those firearms across state lines—even to states that severely restrict concealed carry—received 57 votes.

Some were quick to blame the White House for not working hard enough to get the necessary votes,[20] but the vote may have been more about geography, politics, and the reluctance of some to take on the issue.[21] In addition, the nature of the Senate—in which smaller states, which tend to be more rural, more Republican, and more pro-gun, have disproportionate power because each state has two votes—was also critical. In essence, the two votes from Alaska canceled out the two from California. At the same time, the red-state/blue-state divide was clearly evident in the vote.[22]

While the White House, Michael Bloomberg, and MAIG, as well as Mark Kelly and Gabrielle Giffords, and Americans for Responsible Solutions (ARS), all vowed to continue the fight, it was not clear how they could persuade five senators to change their vote or how they could then get a majority of members in the House of Representatives to support the bill.

Six months after the shooting, Michael Bloomberg wrote a letter to prominent Democratic supporters in New York, asking them to withhold contributions to the four U.S. senators who voted against the Manchin-Toomey amendment. In a nod to electoral politics, a Bloomberg aide suggested that they were targeting the Democrats because none of the Republicans who voted against the amendment were facing serious challenges in 2014. Many national Democrats, including Senator Schumer, a close friend of Bloomberg, questioned the value of a strategy that could cost the Democrats seats in the Senate, particularly if those seats were lost to Republicans even more hostile to gun control.[23]

Then, on September 16, 2013, Aaron Alexis, a mentally unstable veteran who worked for an independent contractor, gained entrance to the Washington Navy Yard, assembled a shotgun he had legally purchased days before, and opened fire, killing 12 before he was killed by police. Despite several violent incidents with firearms and documented mental health issues, he managed both to gain clearance to a secure facility and to pass a background check.

The immediate response to this event was muted from both sides. President Obama noted the sorrow and frustration of dealing with another mass shooting, and the White House attempted to shift responsibility for action to Congress. Gun-rights groups were largely quiet, as is the norm after such events. However, gun-control groups were also mostly silent following the shooting. Initial media reports, later proven to be inaccurate, suggested that Alexis had an AR-15—an "assault rifle"—which brought some immediate calls for gun control. Within a day, though, it was reported that he only had a shotgun and obtained a semiautomatic pistol from a guard he killed inside the facility. In short, the only weapon he carried with him was a shotgun—ironically, the same type of firearm that Vice President Biden had suggested people use for self-defense only a few months prior. Similar to the Sandy Hook tragedy, it is difficult to see what specific gun control regulation would have prevented the tragedy.

The response from gun-control groups was best expressed by Matt Bennett, who worked for the Third Way, a Washington, D.C. think tank that advocates for enhanced background checks: "I think there's a sense of resignation that has taken hold. People in our community believe that these types of tragedies are going to continue and some of them may spur some progress, but it's a very, very long slog to get to new federal gun safety laws."[24]

President Obama and the NRA responded in very predictable ways. During his eulogy at the Navy Yard, Obama said:

[Gun violence] ought to be a shock to all of us ... it ought to obsess us. It ought to lead to some sort of transformation. That's what happened in other countries when they experienced similar tragedies. In the United Kingdom and Australia ... when just a single mass shooting occurred ... they understood that there was nothing ordinary about this kind of carnage. They endured heartbreak, but then they mobilized and changed ... Our tears are not enough. Our words and our prayers are not enough. If we really want to honor these twelve men and women ... we are going to have to change. We are going to have to change.[25]

Reflecting on the stalemate in Washington, Obama reiterated that change would have to originate with the American people. On the same day, on *Meet the Press*, the NRA's Wayne LaPierre suggested that the answer was more armed guards, noting that most military personnel are not armed while on base.[26] "The problem is, there weren't enough good guys with guns," he said. "When the good guys with guns got there, it stopped."[27] Meanwhile, on *Face the Nation*, Senator Joe Manchin was asked if he would attempt to revive his failed background check bill. He replied that he would only push when there was sufficient support for the legislation to pass. "You know, I'm not going to go out there and just beat the drum for the sake of beating the drum. There has to be people willing to move off the position they've taken. They've got to come to that conclusion themselves."[28]

The public's reaction did not reflect strong support for more gun control, either. In a Gallup poll that asked why they thought mass shootings occur, 48 percent of respondents blamed a failure of the mental health system to identify individuals who are a danger to others, while 40 percent blamed easy access to guns, and 37 percent said that drug use was most to blame.[29] When combining blaming a great deal and blaming a fair amount, access to guns dropped to third on the list of causes. In that same poll, support for stricter gun laws had declined to 49 percent from the 58 percent recorded shortly after the Newtown shootings. Lydia Saad summarized the poll's major findings:

> As long ago as 2007, in reference to the Virginia Tech shootings, Americans' unaided responses to how such events could be prevented included many more references to screening and monitoring students for mental health problems than to changing the gun laws. In the same vein, today Americans are more likely to believe the mental health system is to blame than gun laws, a slight shift from 2011, and support for stricter gun laws is down from the surge of support seen right after Newtown.[30]

Public opinion polls taken a year after the Newtown shootings found that support for stronger gun-control measures had receded back to where it was prior to the shootings.[31] At the same time, other events had replaced gun violence on the national agenda as well as on legislative agendas. Immigration reform, continuing budgetary issues, and, most important, a problem-plagued rollout of national health care replaced gun control as important priorities for both elected officials and the public. By January 2014, even President Obama had backed off on his push for gun control. It merited one brief, generic paragraph more than halfway through his State of the Union speech. "Citizenship means standing up for the lives that gun violence steals from us each day. I have seen the courage of parents, students, pastors, and police officers all over this country who say 'we are not afraid,' and I intend to keep trying, with or without Congress, to help stop more tragedies from visiting innocent Americans in our movie theaters, shopping malls, or schools like Sandy Hook."[32]

Still, gun control is never more than a tragic event away from being back on the front burner.

THE STATES AND GUN CONTROL

While the focus of most of the nation is on Washington, much of what happens with regard to gun control takes place in the 50 states. It is there that we see evidence of the strong differences of opinion regarding how to deal with gun violence and the rights of gun owners. Policy responses vary tremendously, reflecting regional as well as urban/rural differences. The events of 2013 served to intensify both the attitudinal differences and policy responses.

Despite the legislative failures at the national level, several states passed very strict laws in the wake of the Newtown shootings. Most prominent among them were Connecticut, New York, Maryland, and Colorado. At the same time, more than a dozen states loosened gun restrictions, mostly dealing with concealed-carry laws, although Kansas declared that no federal gun laws could be enforced in the state, a law that realistically could not be enforced or pass constitutional muster.[33]

Much of the national focus on state activity centered on Colorado, a western state that had become more urban and more liberal over the past several decades. The state passed several regulations, including comprehensive background checks for private sales and limiting magazine capacity to 15. It was a hard-fought battle that left harsh feelings. Citizen-led recall initiatives placed two key Democratic state legislators on the ballot for recall in special elections. John Morse, the Senate president who was instrumental in pushing the laws, and Angela Giron of Pueblo were both defeated in elections that would not typically draw national media attention.

Both the reason for the recall—passage of stricter gun-control laws—and the involvement of outside interests created an atmosphere in which the elections became much more than a simple recall for two state-level officials. Michael Bloomberg personally gave $350,000 to help defend the legislators, and their total contributions from pro-control groups and individuals totaled more than $3 million. The NRA and others, meanwhile, countered that with more than $500,000. Despite the spending disparity, both legislators were recalled. One journalist described the importance of the vote as follows: "The vote, which came five months after the United States Senate defeated several gun restrictions, handed another loss to gun-control supporters and gave moderate lawmakers across the country a warning about the political risks of voting for tougher gun laws."[34]

A year after the shootings, a *New York Times* analysis found that states had enacted a collective 109 new gun laws, 70 of which were judged to loosen restrictions on firearms. Most of the laws that tightened restrictions were passed in states in which the legislatures and the governorships were controlled by Democrats. Conversely, states that loosened restrictions were generally controlled by Republicans.[35] It is also true that the states that adopted stricter laws were more urbanized states with tougher existing laws, while states that favored gun rights tended to be more rural states with laws that were less strict prior to Newtown. It appeared that existing trends continued in the states and a national stalemate was reached.

THE GUN CULTURE AND THE ANTI-GUN CULTURE

There is much discussion about a "gun culture." It is difficult, if not impossible, to define the term. In reality, there may be several different threads that comprise the gun culture. Most people who study gun control agree that the gun culture has roots in American history, dating back to colonial times and the American Revolution, running through the settlement of the frontier West; and that it embodies the rugged individualism admired by many Americans and revered in movies, television programs, and books. Some suggest that those accounts are mythologized ideals that never existed, while others maintain there is more than a kernel of truth in those portrayals.

Most also agree that there is more than one strand of that culture. Different aspects of the culture may be reflected in the varying reasons owners offer for having guns. For collectors, it may be the aesthetic appeal of firearms. For history buffs, it may be the allure of owning a piece of America's past or holding a weapon that may have been used in battle. Hunters are more likely to see the gun as a tool. Sport shooters see their guns as part of an activity they enjoy. For many, firearms offer personal protection for themselves and their families.

Spitzer suggests there are two major traditions in the gun culture—the hunting/sporting ethos and the militia/frontier ethos.[36] For Hawley, the branches of the culture are numerous, running from urban minority street culture to Civil War reenactors, from deer hunters to collectors to survivalists.[37]

Intertwined with the gun culture is a distrust of government that has a long history in the United States, dating back to the nation's founding. While that distrust may be found in many areas even today, it is particularly prevalent among gun owners. An attachment to individualism suggests that one be more self-reliant and less dependent upon other individuals or society, and it also brings with it a healthy skepticism of government. Gun-rights advocates, for example, are more likely to cite incidents such as Ruby Ridge, in which federal agents shot and killed two people in 1992; and the siege of the Branch Davidian compound in Waco, Texas, in 1993, during which six members of a religious cult were shot and killed while another 76 men, women, and children perished in a botched attempt to remove them from the compound.

More recent incidents involving the Bureau of Alcohol, Tobacco, Firearms, and Explosives (BATF) also fuel this fire. Among them are Operation "Fast and Furious," in which illegally purchased firearms were "allowed" to be taken to Mexico as part of a sting and were subsequently "lost" between 2009 and 2011. One of the guns was found at the scene of a shootout in which a Border Patrol agent was killed. An investigation by the *Milwaukee Journal Sentinel* in 2013 found that several ATF sting operation across the country employed questionable tactics that may have crossed the line into entrapment, creating illegal gun traffic where none had existed, and using mentally challenged individuals to locate drugs and guns and to encourage others to do business with undercover agents.[38] Needless to say, incidents such as these create and exacerbate distrust of the government.

Much less has been written about an "anti-gun culture." An Internet search for the term reveals that most of the references are to right-wing blogs. If, however, we assume that a gun culture exits in the United States, then it is equally plausible that there is an anti-gun culture. And, as there is some stereotyping in describing the gun culture, there is some in describing the anti-gun culture as well. "Gun control diehards . . . hope that the United States can become more like the United Kingdom, where all handguns are banned and long guns . . . are uncommon. 'The time has come for us to disarm the individual citizen,' said former New York City Police commissioner Patrick Murphy."[39]

Adherents of this philosophy almost universally do not own guns and do not see the *need* for the vast majority of people to own guns. Use of the word "need" has several implications. First, it minimizes or denies the possibility that a firearm can be used in self-defense or to prevent crime. That is the job of law enforcement officials, not the individual. Second, it suggests that only those who have a demonstrable need to own a gun should have one. This denies or minimizes the idea that gun ownership is a constitutionally protected right—a right with limitations, to be sure, but a right nonetheless.

Not surprisingly, the anti-gun culture is more prevalent among those who live in urban areas and who have limited or no knowledge of or experience with firearms. Some research has suggested that familiarity with firearms may be as strong a predictor of attitudes toward guns as political party, gender, or whether one lives in a rural or urban area.[40]

For many people, guns are almost inherently evil. They see guns as the harbinger of death and injury. They look at the statistics on gun-related deaths and see the lives that could have been saved. Indeed, many of the leaders in the gun-control movement have relatives who were killed by gun violence (Representative Carolyn McCarthy) or are survivors of gun violence themselves (former White House press secretary Jim Brady, Representative Gabrielle Giffords, Virginia Tech shooting survivor Colin Goddard).

Expressions of these anti-gun sentiments enacted into policies may be found in zero-tolerance policies in schools where some students have been suspended for allegedly chewing a pastry into the shape of a gun, pointing a finger, and saying "pow" to another student, or a young girl "threatening" to shoot another with a plastic toy that "shoots" bubbles. In other incidents, a school refused to serve birthday cupcakes to a third-grade class because they had World War II toy soldiers on them; and another threatened suspension if an eighth-grade student did not remove his T-shirt featuring the insignia of the U.S. Marine Corps, which includes interlocking guns.[41] In June 2013, an elementary school in Hayward, California, sponsored a toy gun buyback event in which children received a book and a chance to win a bike in return for their toy guns. The school principal said that such toys desensitized children and made it easier for them to use real guns.[42]

Gun-control advocates rejoiced at the 2000 publication of *Arming America*, written by acclaimed historian Michael Bellesiles. In the book, Bellesiles argued that gun possession and ownership were, in fact, rare in early America, and that many of those that existed were not in good working order. His book was based on the review of large numbers of probate records, in which all the possessions of a deceased person were listed. He found that only a small percentage of those records from the late eighteenth and early nineteenth centuries contained any reference to firearms. In short, the gun culture was a myth.

Bellesiles's work won accolades from academics and from gun-control groups. It was awarded the Bancroft Prize, given annually by Columbia University to the most distinguished academic works in American history. This exposition of the lies told by the NRA and other gun rights supporters was music to the ears of those who do not like guns. There was only one problem with the heavily footnoted tome and the research that backed it up: It wasn't true.

Some of the facts seemed a little too convenient for a Northwestern University law professor, who began to check Bellesiles's work. When he discovered discrepancies, and more questions arose, Bellesiles's home institution, Emory University, assembled a panel of distinguished scholars to review his work. Their report stated there was evidence of falsification and serious failures and carelessness in the research and presentation. Bellesiles resigned; Columbia rescinded the Bancroft award; and the gun-culture concept was restored. "Bellesiles went wrong where so many anti-gun people go wrong: by hoping that appearances are all that matter ... Bellesiles may have thought that if he made his book look authoritative ... he could change the gun debate in America."[43]

This cultural divide is evident in public opinion polls and in congressional debates. A recent Pew Center poll found that while 31 percent of those who are consistently liberal would be unhappy if a family member married a gun owner (more than a born-again Christian, an atheist, or a Republican), only 1 percent of those who are consistently conservative would be unhappy.[44] The areas of consensus are few; disagreements are plentiful.[45] While some see guns as the problem, others see guns as the solution. Many people are in the middle, but significant numbers are at opposite ends of the opinion spectrum. Just as some descriptions of the gun culture are disparaging, so are some references to the anti-gun culture.[46]

OUTLINE OF THE BOOK

It is against this backdrop that we will consider the place of firearms in the United States. Although the shootings in Newtown brought the issue back to the forefront of national politics, guns and gun control have been seriously debated in America for more than half a century.

At their core, the arguments are relatively simple. Advocates of stricter regulations on firearms believe that government regulation can reduce the number of people killed by guns—more than 30,000 each year. They suggest that most gun regulations are permissible under the Constitution and that wise public policy dictates that we address gun violence by controlling both who may possess firearms and the types of guns they may own.

Opponents argue that few restrictions are permissible under the Constitution. Further, they believe that guns make people safer. Guns can be and are used to protect citizens against crime. They are also used for sporting purposes. Gun-rights advocates further argue that more regulation of firearms will only impact law-abiding citizens, while those who cannot obtain a gun legally will always find a way to get one.

Gun control can take several forms. Laws may restrict the types of guns that may be legally purchased or owned. They may prevent some types of people, such as convicted criminals and those who have been adjudicated as mentally unstable, from possessing firearms. They may also regulate how guns are transferred or sold. Finally, firearm possession may require some type of government permission, such as a license or permit, or require that the gun be registered with the government. There are logical arguments on both sides of this issue. The only thing that is certain in this debate is that some type of middle ground or compromise has been and is likely to continue to be extremely difficult to achieve. While everyone wants to reduce gun violence and keep guns away from those who should not have them, the means to achieving those ends are not easily agreed upon.

This book will examine the Second Amendment of the Constitution, a source of much debate. Although the Supreme Court has finally ruled on the nature of the right, those two decisions were very narrowly decided and narrowly written. There are many issues left to be clarified, and those decisions could be overturned or, more likely, reinterpreted with one or two key replacements of justices on the Court. While those decisions established, at least for the short term, an individual right to self-defense and to possess firearms, they did not preclude firearms regulations. On the contrary, Justice Antonin Scalia's majority opinion in the *Heller* case recognized the constitutionality of numerous regulations.

We will then look at some basic facts of firearms in the United States and examine the events that often cause us to debate gun control. Important gun-control legislation has been passed in the wake of a tragedy or as a proposed solution to a long-term problem. Gun laws tend to be loosened when crime is low and most citizens are less likely to feel a threat from firearms. The politics of the issue are more favorable to those who support stricter gun laws when gun violence is high; that is, when there are more murders or mass shootings, citizens tend to be more supportive of gun regulations.

The news media play a key role in increasing our awareness of these events. Through their continuing coverage, they keep the attention of both the public and policy makers on gun control. Often the coverage subsides a short time after the event, and the fervor of gun control supporters typically wanes with the decreased media attention.

Public opinion and elections are two important ways in which citizens express their preferences to policy makers. We will examine how we view guns and gun control, both at the present time and in retrospect. Gun control is rarely a decisive factor in national or even statewide elections, but the issue is certainly more important in some elections than in others. Several elections have been heavily influenced by the candidates' positions on firearms, and gun control is an issue frequently considered by those running for elected office. While the issue is often cast in partisan terms—Democrat versus Republican—it may be more useful to look at the issue as one that separates those of us who live in urban areas from those who live in more rural settings.

Interest groups influence how issues are framed and understood. They also impact elections and the policy-making process through lobbying and electoral activities, including, but not exclusively through, campaign contributions. While the NRA has been the dominant interest group focusing on firearms, it is not alone. Other groups represent the interests of gun rights, and several groups push for stricter gun control. In the wake of the Newtown shootings, former representative Gabrielle Giffords and her husband, former astronaut Mark Kelly, formed Americans for Responsible Solutions and immediately gained credibility in the gun-control debate; and Michael Bloomberg's group, Mayors Against Illegal Guns, gained some clout, but later merged with Moms Demand Action for Gun Sense in America to form Everytown for Gun Safety. At that time, Bloomberg pledged $50 million to fund Everytown and fight the NRA. This book will examine the role of interest groups in the debate and suggest how we might put that activity into proper perspective.

We will analyze the influence of the NRA and its sources of strength. We will also explore why many Americans seem to view the NRA differently from other interest groups. There are many calls for the NRA to "moderate" its views and accept "common-sense gun reforms." There are few voices suggesting that the American Civil Liberties Union accept discrimination against *some* groups because their views are particularly heinous or repulsive. Likewise, no one suggests that the National Organization for Women accept *some* policies that might discriminate against women because they might be in the best interest of other people. Why are our expectations of the NRA different?

After reading this book, you will probably have the same position on gun control that you hold now. You may have as many questions about this issue as you do now. You should, however, have an increased awareness of guns and gun control, from the perspectives of citizens, policy advocates, and the elected officials who set policy for the states and the nation. Therefore, it is hoped that those questions you might have and your position on this issue will be better informed.

NOTES

1. Adam Winkler, *Gunfight: The Battle over the Right to Bear Arms in America* (New York: W. W. Norton & Company, 2013), x. This author will take issue with the "continuing epidemic" description of gun violence. In fact, violent crime and homicides had been declining for a decade or more. Still, the description of American attitudes is apt.

2. Michael Planty and Jennifer L. Truman, "Firearm Violence, 1993–2011," *Bureau of Justice Statistics*, May 2013, http://bjs.gov/content/pub/pdf/fv9311.pdf; Mark Blumenthal, "Gun Control Polls Show Longterm Decline in Support, Despite Columbine Bump," *Huffington Post*, July 20, 2012, http://www.huffingtonpost.com/2012/07/20/gun-control-polls-aurora-shooting_n_1690169.html.

3. "Obama in 2008: 'I Am Not Going to Take Your Guns Away,' " RealClearPolitics video, posted December 27, 2012, http://www.realclearpolitics.com/video/2012/12/27/obama_2008_i_am_not_going_to_take_your_guns_away.html.

4. Eileen Sullivan and Jack Gillum, "US Gun Industry Is Thriving during Obama's Term," Associated Press, October 19, 2012, http://bigstory.ap.org/article/us-gun-industry-thriving-during-obamas-term.

5. For a discussion of policy windows, see John Kingdon, *Agendas, Alternatives, and Public Policies*, updated ed. (New York: Longman Publishing Group, 2011), 166–72.

6. Mark Landler and Erica Goode, "Obama's Cautious Call for Action Sets Stage to Revive Gun Debate," *New York Times*, December 12, 2012, http://www.nytimes.com/2012/12/15/us/politics/obamas-reaction-to-connecticut-shooting-sets-stage-for-gun-debate.html?pagewanted=1&_r=0.

7. Mark Landler and Peter Baker, " 'These Tragedies Must End,' Obama Says," *New York Times*, December 16, 2012, http://www.nytimes.com/2012/12/17/us/politics/bloomberg-urges-obama-to-take-action-on-gun-control.html?pagewanted=all.

8. Jennifer Steinhauer and Charlie Savage, "Pro-Gun Democrats Signaling Openness to Limits," *New York Times*, December 17, 2012, http://www.nytimes.com/2012/12/18/us/politics/pro-gun-democrats-signal-openness-to-limits.html?ref=todayspaper&pagewanted=all&_r=0.

9. Julie Pace, "Obama Announces Gun Violence Task Force, Presses for Policy Changes after Shooting," *Huffington Post*, December 19, 2012, http://www

.huffingtonpost.com/2012/12/19/obama-gun-violence-task-force_n_2331238
.html.

10. Rick Ungar, "Here Are the 23 Executive Orders on Gun Safety Signed
Today by the President," Forbes.com, January 16, 2013, http://www.forbes
.com/sites/rickungar/2013/01/16/here-are-the-23-executive-orders-on-gun-safety
-signed-today-by-the-president/.

11. Julie Rovner, "Debate Rages on Even as Research Ban on Gun Violence
Ends," NPR, February 6, 2013, http://www.npr.org/blogs/health/2013/02/06/
170844926/debate-rages-on-even-as-research-ban-on-gun-violence-ends. This last
order may be very important given that past CDC research has found that the costs
of firearms ownership far exceed the benefits. These findings have been disputed,
but it is reasonable to expect that future research will reach similar conclusions.

12. Peter Baker and Michael D. Shear, "Obama to Put 'Everything I've Got'
Into Gun Control," *New York Times*, January 16, 2013, http://www.nytimes.com/
2013/01/17/us/politics/obama-to-ask-congress-to-toughen-gun-laws.html?page
wanted=all.

13. Wayne LaPierre, "NRA: Full Statement by Wayne LaPierre in Response
to Newtown shootings," *Guardian*, December 21, 2012, http://www.theguardian
.com/world/2012/dec/21/nra-full-statement-lapierre-newtown.

14. Editorial Board, "The NRA's Simplistic Response to Newtown: 'Good
Guy with a Gun,' " *Washington Post*, December 21, 2012, http://articles.washington
post.com/2012-12-21/opinions/36017867_1_gun-violence-gun-owners-and
-manufacturers-wayne-lapierre.

15. "The N.R.A. Crawls from Its Hidey Hole" (editorial), *New York Times*,
December 21, 2012, http://www.nytimes.com/2012/12/22/opinion/the-nra
-crawls-from-its-hidey-hole.html.

16. Rick Jervis, "Newtown on NRA Speech: 'Completely Off the Mark,' "
USA Today, December 21, 2012, http://www.usatoday.com/story/news/nation/
2012/12/21/nra-guns-newtown-reaction/1784957/.

17. Michael O'Brien, "Obama's Gun Plans Spark Little Enthusiasm with
Key Lawmakers," First Read, NBCNews.com, January 16, 2013, http://
firstread.nbcnews.com/_news/2013/01/16/16546691-obamas-gun-plans-spark
-little-enthusiasm-with-key-lawmakers?lite; "Senate Dems Hesitant on Obama's
Gun Control Plan," Fox News, January 18, 2013, http://www.foxnews.com/
politics/2013/01/18/senate-dems-noncommittal-on-obama-gun-control-plan/?
test=latestnews.

18. Associated Press, "Pro-Gun Voters Put Heat on Democratic Senators,"
Fox News, March 9, 2013, http://www.foxnews.com/politics/2013/03/09/
pro-gun-voters-put-heat-on-democratic-senators/?intcmp=related.

19. Senate Majority Leader Harry Reid (D-NV) voted against the amendment in a procedural move so he could bring it up again at a future date. In effect,
the amendment had the support of 55 senators.

20. Pablo Eisenberg, "On Gun Control, White House Fails to Tap Power of
(Its Own and Other) Nonprofits," *Huffington Post*, April 2, 2013, http://www

.huffingtonpost.com/pablo-eisenberg/post_4592_b_2999416.html; Michael D. Shear and Peter Baker, "In Gun Bill Defeat, a President's Distaste for Twisting Arms," *New York Times*, April 22, 2013, http://www.nytimes.com/2013/04/23/us/politics/in-gun-bill-defeat-a-president-who-hesitates-to-twist-arms.html?nl=todaysheadlines&emc=edit_th_20130423&_r=0.

21. Jennifer Steinhauer, "Gun Control Effort Had No Real Chance, Despite Pleas," *New York Times*, April 17, 2013, http://www.nytimes.com/2013/04/18/us/politics/despite-tearful-pleas-no-real-chance.html?nl=todaysheadlines&emc=edit_th_20130418&_r=0.

22. Chuck Todd et al., "First Thoughts: Why the Gun Measure Went Down to Defeat," First Read, NBCNews.com, April 18, 2013, http://firstread.nbcnews.com/_news/2013/04/18/17809775-first-thoughts-why-the-gun-measure-went-down-to-defeat.

23. Nicholas Confessore and Jeremy W. Peters, "Bloomberg Asks Donors to Withhold Gifts over Gun Votes," *New York Times*, June 12, 2013, http://www.nytimes.com/2013/06/12/nyregion/bloomberg-urges-no-gifts-to-democrats-who-blocked-gun-bill.html?pagewanted=1&tntemail0=y&emc=tnt.

24. Don Gonyea, "Gun Control Advocates Say Little After Navy Yard Shootings." NPR, September 18, 2013, http://www.wbur.org/npr/223627238.

25. "President Obama's Remarks at the Memorial Service for Navy Yard Victims," September 22, 2013, http://www.wjla.com/articles/2013/09/full-text-president-obama-s-remarks-at-the-memorial-service-for-navy-yard-victims-94350.html.

26. The debate over arming military personnel on base while in the United States was reignited by the Fort Hood, Texas, shootings on April 2, 2014, when a gunman killed three and wounded 16.

27. Wayne LaPierre, appearance on *Meet the Press*, September 22, 2013.

28. Joe Manchin, appearance on *Face the Nation*, September 22, 2013.

29. Lydia Saad, "Americans Fault Mental Health System Most for Gun Violence," Gallup Politics, September 20, 2013, http://www.gallup.com/poll/164507/americans-fault-mental-health-system-gun-violence.aspxU.

30. Ibid.

31. "CNN Poll: Support for Stricter Gun Control Fades," CNN, December 4, 2013, http://politicalticker.blogs.cnn.com/2013/12/04/cnn-poll-support-for-stricter-gun-control-fades/?iref=allsearch; Carroll Doherty, "Did Newtown Really Change Public Opinion about Gun Control?" CNN, December 6, 2013, http://globalpublicsquare.blogs.cnn.com/2013/12/06/did-newtown-really-change-public-opinion-about-gun-control/?iref=allsearch.

32. Barack Obama, State of the Union address, January 28, 2014.

33. Wayne Drash and Toby Lyles, "States Tighten, Loosen Gun Laws after Newtown," CNN, June 8, 2013, http://www.cnn.com/2013/06/08/us/gun-laws-states/index.html?hpt=hp_t1.

34. Jack Healy, "Colorado Lawmakers Ousted in Recall Vote over Gun Law," *New York Times*, September 11, 2013, http://www.nytimes.com/2013/09/

11/us/colorado-lawmaker-concedes-defeat-in-recall-over-gun-law.html? emc=edit_tnt_20130911&tntemail0=y.

35. Karen Yourish et al., "State Gun Laws Enacted in the Year since New-town," *New York Times*, December 10, 2013, http://www.nytimes.com/ interactive/2013/12/10/us/state-gun-laws-enacted-in-the-year-since-newtown .html?emc=edit_tnt_20131211&tntemail0=y.

36. Robert J. Spitzer, *The Politics of Gun Control*, 5th ed. (Boulder, CO: Paradigm Publishers, 2012), 9–12.

37. Francis Frederick Hawley, "Gun Culture," in *Guns in American Society: An Encyclopedia of History Politics, Culture, and the Law*, ed. Gregg Lee Carter, 2nd ed. (Santa Barbara, CA: ABC-CLIO, 2012), 343.

38. John Diedrich and Raquel Rutledge, "ATF Uses Rogue Tactics in Storefront Stings across Nation," *Milwaukee Journal Sentinel*, December 7, 2013, http://www.jsonline.com/watchdog/watchdogreports/atf-uses-rogue -tactics-in-storefront-stings-across-the-nation-b99146765z1-234916641.html.

39. Winkler, *Gunfight,* 19.

40. Harry Wilson, *Guns, Gun Control, and Elections* (Lanham, MD: Rowman & Littlefield Publishers, 2007), 125–27.

41. "School Confiscates Third-Graders Cupcakes Topped with Toy Soldiers," *Daily Caller*, March 8, 2013, http://news.yahoo.com/school-confiscates-third -grader-cupcakes-topped-toy-soldiers-215018982.html.

42. Jessica Chasmar, "Calif. Elementary School Offers Toy Gun Buyback," *Washington Times*, June 10, 2013, http://www.washingtontimes.com/news/ 2013/jun/10/calif-elementary-school-offers-toy-gun-buyback/.

43. Winkler, *Gunfight*, 31.

44. Pew Research Center for the People and the Press, "Political Polarization in the American Public," June 12, 2014, http://www.people-press.org/2014/06/ 12/section-3-political-polarization-and-personal-life/.

45. Pew Research Center for the People and the Press, "In Gun Control Debate, Several Options Draw Majority Support," January 14, 2013, http:// www.people-press.org/2013/01/14/in-gun-control-debate-several-options-draw -majority-support/.

46. Ray Stern, "The Anti-Gun Culture: Irresponsible, Phobia-Driven, and Just Plain Wrong on the Facts," *Phoenix New Times Blogs*, January 14, 2011, http://blogs.phoenixnewtimes.com/valleyfever/2011/01/the_anti_gun_culture _irrespons.php.

TWO

The Second Amendment, the Supreme Court, and Firearms

A well-regulated Militia, being necessary to the security of a free State, the right of the people to keep and bear Arms, shall not be infringed.

—Second Amendment, U.S. Constitution

The language of the Second Amendment to the U.S. Constitution appears to be relatively simple, but its meaning is often contested. The amendment's interpretation has been disputed in two different ways. One deals with the meaning of the amendment at the nation's founding and focuses on the term "militia" and the preamble to determine if the right is an individual or collective right. The second area of contention is if technological developments in weaponry and the country's evolution have changed how the amendment should be applied today.

The former is exclusive to the Second Amendment. The latter deals with the broader scope of constitutional interpretation. Does the meaning of the Constitution evolve over time to fit the current social and political climate, or can it be found by determining what it meant when it was adopted? These conflicting ideas are commonly referred to as a "living Constitution" versus "originalism."

Many of the questions dealing with the nature of the right conferred in the Second Amendment were answered by the U.S. Supreme Court in two relatively recent decisions. In *District of Columbia v. Heller*, the Court ruled that the federal right applies to the individual, and in *McDonald v. City of Chicago*, it extended the scope of the right to include the states. The right has yet to be more fully defined, and that process may take decades.

In this chapter we will first examine various perspectives on the meaning of the Second Amendment. We will then discuss the few Supreme Court precedents in the field. Most of our attention will be given to those two recent decisions that have transformed the way we view the right to bear arms.

PHILOSOPHICAL BACKGROUND OF THE RIGHT

The primary arguments in favor of an individual right to bear arms include the right of self-defense, the need to be able to overthrow a tyrannical government, and to defend the nation against foreign invasion. There are counterarguments for the first two of these. The last argument, defense of country, is the basis of the collective right interpretation as well.

The right to self-defense is described in the ancient writings of the Roman orator Cicero. "[T]here exists a law ... inborn in our hearts; a law which comes to us ... from nature itself ... if our lives are endangered by ... violence or armed robbers or enemies, each and every method of protecting ourselves is morally right."[1] Social contract theorists argue, to the contrary, that an ordered society requires that this right rests with the society and not the individual. Even today, there are differences of opinion regarding the existence of the right to self-defense and its extent.

There are both practical and moral considerations when discussing the right of self-defense. Practically, the issue turns on one's ability and willingness to defend themselves and others, if necessary. Some people are obviously more willing and physically capable of offering resistance against an attacker. A firearm can help even the odds, so to speak, if one is physically overmatched, but one must be willing to fight and have the requisite knowledge to use the gun. Those who argue in favor of self-defense note that many victims who fight back suffer fewer injuries, while those who argue against self-defense point to victims who have their weapons seized and used against them by the perpetrator.[2]

There is also the moral issue of whether we have the right to physically injure or kill another person, even if they wish to do us harm. While not a view held by the majority of Americans, many individuals and some religions morally object to all violence. The government has recognized these beliefs, for example, by assigning those who qualified for conscientious objector status to noncombat roles during times when a military draft existed.

A reference to the potential crime-reducing benefit of an armed citizenry was supplied by Beccaria, who suggested, "[T]he laws which forbid men to bear arms are of this sort [a false idea of utility]. They only disarm those who are neither inclined nor determined to commit crimes."[3] While Aristotle seems to believe that an armed citizen is a good citizen, Machiavelli argues that only the state can exercise the war power.[4] Some philosophers have warned that despots and their regimes have a tendency to disarm the citizenry, while others have disagreed.

In British history, King James II of England used two acts of Parliament to disarm the citizenry in the late seventeenth century. James was a Catholic king in the largely Protestant and anti-Catholic Britain. Having escaped two rebellions designed to topple him from the throne in the early weeks of his reign, he determined to prevent further threats. The Militia Act of 1664 gave the king the power to seize weapons of those who were "dangerous to the peace of the Kingdom," and the Game Act of 1671 limited gun ownership to protect wild animals from overhunting. These gave James the opportunity to seize the weapons of many Protestants and commoners, whom he deemed to be threats to the Crown. He ordered gunsmiths to provide lists of gun purchasers, and he set out to disarm them.

James was overthrown by his daughter Mary, who had been replaced as heir by a newborn son of questionable parentage, and her husband William of Orange, who aspired to the throne, in the "Glorious Revolution." The bloodless coup resulted in William and Mary being joint sovereigns, agreeing to limited power and to respect the individual rights of Englishmen. The English Bill of Rights, adopted in 1689, stated that James had trampled on many rights in many ways. "By causing several good subjects, being Protestants, to be disarmed," he had ignored "true, ancient, and indubitable rights." The Bill of Rights included a statement protecting at least some private ownership of weapons. "Subjects which are Protestants may have Arms of their Defence suitable to their Conditions and as allowed by Law." William Blackstone, recognized by many as the authority of old English law, cited the Bill of Rights as protecting a right to have guns for self-defense. The 1744 case of *Malloch v. Eastly* recognized it was settled law that guns could be possessed for defense of home and family.[5]

As the American colonies became increasingly problematic for the Crown, King George III ordered that exports of firearms and ammunition to the colonies be stopped and that British troops disarm several provinces, especially in the North. The British military conducted searches of ships and carriages, seeking guns. When Boston was placed under military occupation, citizens who wanted to leave were required to surrender their weapons when they departed. The soldiers began seizing the weapons and powder that had been stockpiled by the American militia.

Many of the Founding Fathers owned and used guns. George Washington reportedly owned 50 of them. John Adams regarded guns as a means of personal self-defense in addition to their obvious utility in warfare. Thomas Jefferson owned many firearms and even recommended shooting as a means of self-improvement. Clearly, independence would not have been won without the private arms of the Americans.

In the American colonial experience, Thomas Paine suggested that citizens should be reluctant to surrender their arms to the government.[6] James Madison, in Federalist No. 46, stated, "To these (the regular army) would be opposed a militia ... with arms in their hands ... the advantage of being armed, which the Americans possess over the people of almost every other nation."[7] On the other hand, Alexander Hamilton, Madison's *Federalist Papers* coauthor, argued that, "If a well-regulated militia be the most natural defense of a free country, it certainly ought to be under the regulation and at the disposal of that body which is constituted the guardian of the national security."[8] In Federalist No. 28, Hamilton wrote, "if the representatives of the people betray their constituents, there is then no recourse left but in the exertion of that original right to self-defense which is paramount to all positive forms of government"; and in Federalist No. 29, he said, "little more can be reasonably aimed at, with respect to the people at large than to have them properly armed and equipped."[9]

During the discussions prior to ratification of the Constitution, supporters of ratification "promised all individuals that the right to keep and bear arms would be more than a paper right."[10] Gallia argues that the individual right to keep and bear arms was generally accepted throughout the ratification debates.[11]

Perhaps the strongest argument in favor of the historical antecedent of an individual right to bear arms is offered by Shalhope.[12] He argues that the belief system that emerged in colonial America reflected classical philosophy and a tradition of republicanism that joined the themes of personal right and communal responsibility. In this way, the collective right to bear arms does not preclude the individual right to own firearms, but rather it is a derivative of the individual right.

THE SECOND AMENDMENT

Background

The history of the Second Amendment is inextricably linked with several of the important debates that faced the Founding Fathers. The relationship between the government and its citizens, as well as the relationship between the federal and state governments, are closely tied to the right to bear arms. Did a citizen's right to rebel against a government end when the Revolutionary War concluded? How were states to defend their sovereignty against possible incursions from the federal government? When, if ever, does the nation's need for a citizen-militia disappear?

The ideal of a citizen-militia has deep roots in the American political culture and colonial history. Part-time citizen-soldiers were largely responsible for the local defense. There was a strong distrust of standing armies, given the experience of European armies that often served more to tyrannize than to free citizens. Therefore, both citizens and local authorities often relied on the militia.[13]

Despite the somewhat spotty record of the militia in the Revolutionary War, many Americans continued to hold the militia in high esteem. Seven of the former colonies adopted state constitutions that included a formal declaration on rights of the militia. Each prohibited a standing peacetime army and asserted civilian control of the military. Three explicitly protected the right to bear arms.[14] While there is ample evidence that the intent of many of the Framers was to create an individual right to possess firearms, it is also clear that this freedom was not without limits.[15] Still, other scholars place the emphasis on the role of the militia in society and suggest that the constitutional right is limited to that context.[16]

Various forms of gun control existed in the colonies and during the Revolution. The militia was essential to the success of the fight for independence, and measures were taken to ensure that the militia would be as well armed as possible. Members of the militia were required to assemble periodically at musters, gun in hand, for the weapon to be inspected by government officials and entered on the public roll—a form of gun registration. In some states, there were door-to-door canvasses to search for guns, and, if they were deemed to be needed for the public defense, then they may be temporarily taken from their owner as part of the war effort. They would ultimately be returned, but the family may have been temporarily, at least, unable to defend themselves. There were numerous laws regulating who could own firearms, excluding at different times and in different colonies: slaves; free blacks; people of mixed race; Catholics; those who were *not* loyal to Britain; and then later, those who *were* loyal to Britain.

The Revolutionary-era militia laws alone amount to a set of onerous gun laws that few modern-day gun rights advocates would ever accept ... The founders believed that ordinary people should have guns and that government shouldn't be allowed to completely disarm the citizenry. Yet their vision was certainly not that of today's gun rights hard-liners, who dismiss nearly any gun regulation as an infringement on individual liberty. Although the fact is rarely discussed in the individual-rights literature, the founding generation had many forms of gun control. They might not have termed it "gun control," but the founders understood that gun rights had to be balanced with public safety needs.[17]

The question of the necessity of an armed citizenry to keep the government in check is still debated. One side argues that disarming the citizenry can have disastrous implications. "Where Hitler or Stalin ruled, gun control was an essential step toward genocide. Gun registration lists were used to confiscate guns from the prospective victims. Once the victims were helpless, the exterminations began . . . *Every* episode of genocide in the past century has been preceded by assiduous efforts to disarm the victims [emphasis in original]."[18] In another text, two sections entitled "The Propensity of Absolute Rulers to Disarm Their Subjects" and "The Citizen Militia as Dual Safeguard against Tyranny and Foreign Invasion" contain excerpts from classical theorists from Plato, Aristotle, and Machiavelli to Thomas Paine and James Madison that help to reinforce those ideas.[19]

Arguments opposing this idea point to the necessity of legitimate governments controlling the use of domestic force. Horwitz and Anderson point to the examples of Yugoslavia, Afghanistan, Somalia, and the Democratic Republic of Congo, among others, in which governments have failed and wars have ensued when arms fell into the wrong hands. "The monopoly on the legitimate use of force is one requirement of a successful state . . . Threatening that monopoly by arming citizens with enough firepower to counter the government has been tried and failed, with disastrous results all over the world."[20] To them the "Insurrectionist idea" is one to be feared.

The Meaning of the Second Amendment

While the original intent of the Framers is still debated, the discussion regarding the contemporary meaning of the right to bear arms is no more settled. The Second Amendment has emerged as an important topic of discussion within the academic community in the past several decades.

In what is perhaps the most frequently cited discussion of the history of the Second Amendment, Shalhope examined several historical principles related to the formation of the right to bear arms. These included the individual right to bear arms, the fear of standing armies, the concomitant reliance upon citizen-formed militias, and civilian control of the military.[21]

A few years later, the article that reinvigorated the debate, "The Embarrassing Second Amendment," spawned a new school of thought referred to as the Standard Model.[22] While not insisting that an individual right is the only reasonable way to interpret the Second Amendment, Levinson suggests that to dismiss it out of hand, as many constitutional scholars have done, is equally incorrect. He argues that the right conferred is indeed an individual right, but it is not absolute.[23]

Levinson's article generated a great deal of scholarship on both sides of the debate, and it helped push the Standard Model into the mainstream of academic writing.[24] While those who subscribe to the Standard Model differ in the degree to which they would hold various, or any, gun-control statutes to be unconstitutional, they all agree that there is an individual right conferred on the people by the Second Amendment.

In further explaining this line of thought, Volokh suggests that the Second Amendment has been viewed differently by some scholars because it contains both an operative clause, which protects the right to bear arms, and a justifications clause, which explains why this right is important.[25] While no other amendment in the Bill of Rights contains such language, Volokh points out that many state constitutions use similar language, and it does not limit the rights only to that instance or situation. Echoing a point raised by Levinson, he notes that the First, Fourth, and Ninth Amendments also refer to "the right of the people," and they have been consistently interpreted to confer an individual right.[26]

Williams argues that this right refers not to individuals, but to the "Body of the People."[27] If the people 200 years ago were somewhat homogeneous, those similarities have dissipated to the extent that today's society is much more diverse and that this "Body of the People" no longer exists. As such, the Second Amendment's meaning has changed, and to look to the Framers for guidance in interpretation is misguided. The Second Amendment must be interpreted in light of the situation that exists today. That would include both changes in how we provide for national defense and the nature of crime and criminals. Citizen militias are obsolete, and violent crime has become both more common and more lethal. We might also consider the technological changes that have made firearms much more dangerous in modern times. Taking all of that into consideration clearly suggests that the Second Amendment's interpretation should evolve to fit the reality of twenty-first-century America.

While the response of Williams might be described as challenging the basis for the Standard Model, Cornell's might be called an attack. "Indeed, recent writing on the Second Amendment [Standard Model] more closely resembles the intellectual equivalent of a check kiting scheme than it does solidly researched history."[28] Cornell argues that the Standard Model misinterprets history, misreads the text of the Constitution, and recycles the ideas of its adherents until they become accepted as legitimate. Cornell suggests that there is little, if any, evidence that even the states were unwilling to disarm the citizenry at the time the Constitution was written. In addition, the term "the people" was applied in a much more restrictive fashion 200 years ago. Writing in advance of the *Heller* decision, Cornell was no more kindly disposed toward an individual right.

> Gun rights supporters ... made the Second Amendment a rallying cry, and lavished resources on generating new scholarship and mobilizing popular support for their theory of the right to bear arms. Having effectively ceded the Second Amendment to their opponents, gun control supporters were ill-prepared to deal with the revisionist campaign waged by their opponents to transform popular and scholarly discourse on the Second Amendment. This campaign has been hugely successful and the future of the Second Amendment is very much up for grabs.[29]

Dorf argues that the Second Amendment is best interpreted to mean only that the federal government may not abolish state militias.[30] Because this prohibition is largely meaningless in America today, the amendment itself is largely meaningless in the contemporary context.[31] Thus, any regulation regarding firearms would be constitutionally permissible.

Yet, even if one adopts the Standard Model, it does not imply an unfettered right to own, possess, carry, or use firearms. There is no absolute right guaranteed by the Constitution. All rights must be balanced against others. This is evident from even a cursory examination of the history of Supreme Court decisions with regard to any of the other Amendments in the Bill of Rights as well as that of the Fourteenth Amendment. Neither freedom of speech, freedom of the press, freedom of religion, nor any of our guarantees of due process or equal protection is absolute. There are times we may constitutionally be constrained from speaking or practicing our faith, and the government may infringe on other fundamental rights as well when it has a compelling reason to do so.

To argue that the Second Amendment would not be subject to these same potential restrictions would imply that it is *the primary* right and the only one that enjoys absolute protection. Few, if any, mainstream scholars would make this argument. Kates, one of the strongest proponents of the individual-rights theory, clearly states that "the amendment does not forbid gun *control* [emphasis in original], as opposed to wholesale prohibition. Registration, licensing and other regulations are permissible if, but only if, they do not unreasonably hinder the freedom of law-abiding adults to choose to acquire firearms."[32] A one-day waiting period to conduct a background check would likely pass constitutional muster, while an eight-month waiting period would not.

It is reasonable to conclude that the Second Amendment does indeed confer an individual right as well as one that protects state militias. It is, however, clearly not an absolute right. Not every citizen will enjoy the right. Various types of regulations, wise or unwise, effective or ineffective, are permissible even if they impact law-abiding citizens to some degree. How far these regulations may go before they infringe too far on the Second Amendment right is an issue for the courts to decide.[33]

THE SUPREME COURT AND THE SECOND AMENDMENT

For most of the nation's history, the U.S. Supreme Court was largely silent regarding its meaning. Two nineteenth-century cases deal, at least indirectly, with the right to bear arms. In *United States v. Cruikshank*, Chief Justice Waite wrote: "The right there specified is that of 'bearing arms for a lawful purpose.' This is not a right granted by the Constitution. Neither is it in any manner dependent upon that instrument for its existence. The second amendment declares that it shall not be infringed; but this, as has been seen, means no more than that it shall not be infringed by Congress."[34]

The Second Amendment claim in this case was one of many, and this is all the attention it received in the Court's opinion. This passage seems to indicate that the states were free to infringe upon the right although the national government could not. This is not surprising, given that the Supreme Court did not begin to incorporate the Bill of Rights—that is, make them applicable to the state governments—until 1897, nearly 30 years after the decision in *Cruikshank*.

In *Presser v. Illinois*, Justice Woods reasserted the statement from *Cruikshank* that the Second Amendment did not apply to the states. Justice Woods clearly stated that the defendant did not have a right to parade while armed if not part of an organized militia, but he offered some support for an individual right interpretation and addressed the right to bear arms as follows: "It is undoubtedly true that all citizens capable of bearing arms constitute the reserved military force or reserve militia of the United States as well as of the states, and ... the states cannot, even laying the constitutional provision in question out of view, prohibit the people from keeping and bearing arms."[35]

The opinion in *Presser* concludes that the Illinois law which prohibited Presser from parading, drilling, and forming a citizen militia without state authorization did not violate the Second Amendment. It is not clear from the opinion if the law is constitutional because the right is not an individual right, or because it was the state and not the national government that was infringing upon the right. The opinion does state, however, that the government, both national and state, has the power to regulate and control military organizations and that citizens do not enjoy the right of association as a military company or organization.

UNITED STATES v. MILLER, 307 U.S. 174 (1939)

"Both sides of the gun control debate draw support from this ambiguous decision,"[36] and they like to claim the decision in *Miller* as their own. "[T]he Court stated that citizens could possess a constitutional right to bear arms only in connection with service in a government-organized and regulated militia."[37] An alternative interpretation suggests that the Supreme Court held that the Second Amendment "protects possession of only military type and quality weapons. If so, then the amendment covers high-quality handguns and other firearms, but not poor-quality or gangster-type weapons."[38] A closer examination may help shed some light on this confusing case.

The facts of the case are fairly straightforward. Jack Miller and Frank Layton were charged with violating the National Firearms Act by transporting a sawed-off shotgun across state lines. The act required that the men had to pay a $200 tax and register the gun.

Justice McReynolds's opinion for the unanimous Supreme Court in its review of the District Court's decision stated, in part:

In the absence of any evidence tending to show that possession or use of a 'shotgun having a barrel of less than eighteen inches in length' at this time has some reasonable relationship to the preservation or efficiency of a well regulated militia, we cannot say that the Second Amendment guarantees the right to keep and bear such an instrument.

Certainly it is not within judicial notice that this weapon is any part of the ordinary military equipment or that its use could contribute to the common defense.[39]

The Court continued to discuss the role and the history of the militia in the United States at great length while saying little about the Second Amendment itself. The opinion stated that the amendment was adopted "to assure the continuation and render possible the effectiveness of such forces [the militia]" and "it must be interpreted and applied with that end in view."

While this provides comfort to the collective right argument, the logic of these passages and the rest of the opinion indicate that firearms which can be effectively used in a military context may be protected under the Second Amendment. "Ironically, *Miller* can be read to support some of the most extreme anti-gun control arguments, that the individual citizen has a right to keep and bear bazookas, rocket launchers, and other armaments . . . including, of course, assault weapons."[40]

DISTRICT OF COLUMBIA v. HELLER, 554 U.S. 570 (2008)

The central meaning of the Second Amendment was neither fully addressed nor adequately explained in the *Miller* decision. Was the right intended to apply to the states and their militias, assuming that the members would arm themselves, or did it guarantee an individual right to keep and bear arms? The Supreme Court declined to answer that question for nearly 70 years. In *District of Columbia v. Heller*, the U.S. Supreme Court recognized a constitutional right to self-defense and a right to keep firearms in the home for that purpose.

The case began when a small group of Libertarian lawyers, who thought that a recent change in position on the Second Amendment announced by the Department of Justice and Attorney General John Ashcroft might suggest that courts would adopt a more "gun rights"–friendly view, went in search of an appropriate attorney and appropriate case to litigate.[41] They decided to challenge the Washington, D.C., gun ban because that would be a pure Second Amendment case, with no Fourteenth Amendment implications. Robert Levy, a wealthy attorney, agreed to help locate a true litigator to argue the case and to fund the effort. Alan Gura, a young but experienced attorney, was convinced to take the case for a salary that was less than that commanded by higher-profile lawyers because the case was likely to take several years.

The case would not be a sure bet because no one could predict how a majority of the justices on the Supreme Court would ultimately rule. The Court had not ruled on the Second Amendment in almost 50 years, and that case (*United States v. Miller*) was ambiguous. Both sides of the gun-control debate may have been more than a little nervous about the outcome.[42] Law professor Nelson Lund and attorney Charles Cooper, both with NRA connections, attempted to dissuade Levy from pursuing the case. They expressed concerns about several of the Court's conservative justices, who were more law-and-order types rather than libertarian types. Nevertheless, Levy and Gura pushed onward. They even rebuffed some NRA suggestions that the suit include some possible "end runs" so the Court could decide the case on other than Second Amendment grounds. They feared that if they did not pursue a case now with a "good" plaintiff, then someone else would bring a complaint with a less-than-savory character who wanted to assert his gun rights. Gura selected Shelley Parker, an elderly black woman who had been fighting with drug dealers in her Capitol Hill neighborhood. When the NRA was unable to convince them to delay or modify their suit, they filed their own suit and attempted to get legislation passed by Congress to make the suit a moot point. After much maneuvering by both sets of attorneys, the cases were dismissed by the District of Columbia Circuit Court of Appeals for lack of standing by the plaintiffs. Gura and Levy were left with Dick Heller, the only plaintiff who passed the standing test.[43]

The Washington, D.C., "gun ban" essentially prohibited the possession of handguns. It was illegal to own or carry an unregistered firearm, and handgun registration was prohibited. Lawfully owned guns, such as long arms, had to be stored in the home and secured, unloaded, and disassembled or equipped with a trigger lock. Even those handguns purchased prior to the ban could not be moved from room to room within the home without a license.

Dick Heller was a special police officer at the Federal Judicial Center in Washington, D.C., who was required to carry a gun while on duty. His request for a license to keep a handgun at home for personal protection was denied. He was a white antigovernment ideologue who wanted to be able to fight off government tyranny as much as, if not more than, potential intruders to his house. He was not as sympathetic as Shelley Parker, but he was now the heart of the case.[44]

The scope of the legal challenge was limited. According to Levy, the case "will not be about machine guns and assault weapons. It will be about the right to own ordinary, garden-variety handguns. Nor will the plaintiffs argue for the right to carry a gun outside the home. That's another question for another day."[45]

The federal district court dismissed the suit, thus upholding the law.[46] The District of Columbia Circuit Court of Appeals reversed that ruling, holding that the gun ban and storage requirement violated Heller's Second Amendment rights.[47] The U.S. Supreme Court granted certiorari and handed down its landmark decision on June 26, 2008. The 5–4 decision was split largely along ideological lines, with Chief Justice Roberts and Justices Scalia, Kennedy, Thomas, and Alito comprising the majority.

Majority Opinion—Justice Scalia

The majority opinion, written by Justice Antonin Scalia, generally relies on his "originalist" theory of interpretation and examines the history and legal antecedents of the Second Amendment. He begins by noting that the prefatory clause or preamble "A well-regulated Militia, being necessary to the security of a free State" neither limits nor expands the scope of the operative clause, but rather serves to clarify one purpose of the amendment. He also suggests the language of the amendment should be interpreted in the common meaning of the words to voters at the time of its adoption.

Scalia first finds that the right applies to the individual, not the community. In other instances when the Constitution refers to "right of the people"—the First and Fourth Amendments—the right is an individual right. The language of the Ninth Amendment is similar, and, it too, refers to the individual. Similarly, when the Constitution refers to "the people," it refers to everyone, not a particular group of persons. In contrast, the militia consisted of able-bodied males in a particular age range. The militia and the people were two distinct groups.

Scalia follows with a lengthy discussion of the meaning of "keep and bear arms." This section is largely a response to the Justice Stevens dissent, which argues that the phrase applies only in the military context to the militia.[48] Scalia holds that the phrase applies to everyone, and that "bear" means to carry while "keep" means to possess. "Arms" refers to anything that may be used for defense, not exclusively to weapons used by the military. The majority opinion looks to sources such as eighteenth-century dictionaries, British legal scholar William Blackstone, and state constitutional provisions to reach its conclusions. Several contemporary state constitutions included explicit protections to keep arms for both military and self-defense purposes.

Scalia does not deny that the phrase "to bear arms" was often used in a military context. Rather, he argues that using the idiom in that fashion does not mean it was exclusively used in that context. Many of the sources quoted in the dissent, he argues, often refer to the military, so they would naturally use the phrase in a military context. Broadening the scope of inquiry to include other federal sources, though, reveals that it was also frequently used in a nonmilitary fashion. Going even further to look at nongovernmental sources, the phrase was also applied beyond an exclusively military context.

Regarding Stevens's argument that the grammatically singular use of the word "right" suggests that "keep" and "bear" are tied together as a single right, Scalia refers to the First Amendment "right" of the people to assemble and petition the government for redress of grievances. Use of the singular was not uncommon at that time. The right to defend oneself predates the Constitution. The Second Amendment did not confer that right; rather, it simply states that it shall not be infringed.

The majority opinion then turns its attention to the prefatory clause. For Scalia, the militia existed prior to the Second Amendment, as the Constitution refers to "the" militia rather than "a" militia (if it had to be created by the new government). The federal militia was a subset of the larger militia of all able-bodied men. "Well-regulated" simply means to be trained, and "state" in this clause refers to the polity at large, not an individual state. The majority spends much less time on this section, and it is less convincing than its discussion regarding the operative clause.

Turning his attention to the ratification debates, Scalia notes briefly the conflicts between Anti-Federalists, who were concerned that a standing army or militia would disarm the citizenry, and Federalists, who assured them that would not happen because Congress had no authority to disarm the people. "It was understood across the political spectrum that the right helped to secure the ideal of a citizen militia, *which might be necessary to oppose an oppressive military force if the constitutional order broke down* [emphasis added]."[49] The prefatory clause, then, was designed to prevent disbanding the citizen militia.[50]

Although Scalia quickly applies the Second Amendment right to self-defense, he states that "self-defense had little to do with the right's *codification*; it was the *central component* of the right itself [emphasis in original],"[51] and it could be interpreted more broadly than most people today conceptualize self-defense. Four states had arms-related clauses in their state constitutions prior to adoption of the Second Amendment, and nine other states added them prior to 1820. Several of them, but not all, explicitly referenced self-defense as one of the purposes; none excluded it.

The majority of legal commentaries of the nineteenth century mentioned an individual right, and several state court cases did as well, although none focused solely on the Second Amendment. In *Houston v. Moore*,[52] Justice Story's dissent suggested that the Second Amendment conferred an individual right, but the case was not decided on Second Amendment grounds. After the Civil War, there was much discussion about preventing freed slaves from keeping firearms. While Scalia finds this too late to be instructive regarding original intent, it does suggest that concern was centered not on a militia right, but on an individual right. Commentaries from the late nineteenth century also discuss an individual right.

Precedents

Not surprisingly, the majority argues that the *Cruikshank* decision supports, "if anything," an individual-right interpretation, although it did hold that the Second Amendment did not prevent any state restrictions on the right. The right in question was clearly not a militia-oriented right.

According to the majority, *Presser* had very little do with the Second Amendment other than its holding that the state may prohibit membership in private paramilitary groups, a holding that no one disputes. And, for Scalia, the mention later in *Presser* that the defendant was not a member of the militia was relevant for his Fourteenth Amendment rights, not Second Amendment rights. Stevens's dissent relies strongly on that association.

As one might expect, the *Miller* decision provides fodder for both sides. The majority reads it as supporting an individual right, the dissenters see it as strong evidence for a collective right. Scalia, not known for mincing words, unleashes some of his harshest criticism of the dissent in this section.

JUSTICE STEVENS places overwhelming reliance upon this Court's decision in *United States v. Miller*, 307 U. S. 174 (1939). "[H]undreds of judges," we are told, "have relied on the view of the amendment we endorsed there," *post*, at 2, and "[e]ven if the textual and historical arguments on both side of the issue were evenly balanced, respect for the well-settled views of all of our predecessors on this Court, and for the rule of law itself ... would prevent most jurists from endorsing such a dramatic upheaval in the law," *post*, at 4. And what is, according to JUSTICE STEVENS, the holding of *Miller* that demands such obeisance? That the Second Amendment "protects the right to keep and bear arms for certain military purposes, but that it does not curtail the legislature's power to regulate the nonmilitary use and ownership of weapons." *post*, at 2.

Nothing so clearly demonstrates the weakness of JUSTICE STEVENS' case. *Miller* did not hold that and cannot possibly be read to have held that ... Rather, it was that the *type of weapon at issue* was not eligible for Second Amendment protection ...

This holding is not only consistent with, but positively suggests, that the Second Amendment confers an individual right to keep and bear arms (though only arms that "have some reasonable relationship to the preservation or efficiency of a well-regulated militia") ... JUSTICE STEVENS can say again and again that *Miller* did "not turn on the difference between muskets and sawed-off shotguns, it turned, rather, on the basic difference between the military and nonmilitary use and possession of guns," *post*, at 42–43, but the words of the opinion prove otherwise ... *Miller* stands only for the proposition that the Second Amendment right, whatever its nature, extends only to certain types of weapons [references and emphasis in original].[53]

Regarding the types of weapons protected by *Miller*, the majority concludes:

Read in isolation, *Miller*'s phrase "part of ordinary military equipment" could mean that only those weapons useful in warfare are protected. That would be a startling reading of the opinion, since it would mean that the National Firearms Act's restrictions on machineguns (not challenged in *Miller*) might be unconstitutional, machineguns being useful in warfare in 1939. We think that *Miller*'s "ordinary military equipment" language must be read in tandem with what comes after: "[O]rdinarily when called for [militia] service [able-bodied] men were expected to appear bearing arms supplied by themselves and of the kind in common use at the time." 307 U. S., at 179.[54]

The operative phrase here is "common use at the time," which precludes those weapons not commonly possessed by law-abiding citizens. The majority finds no precedent that precludes their individual-rights interpretation. Given that for most of American history, the federal government has not been involved in the regulation of firearms, it is not surprising that so few precedents exist. Additionally, incorporation is a relatively recent phenomenon, so states were free to regulate firearms largely as they chose.

The majority clearly and explicitly recognizes limitations of the Second Amendment rights, however. "Nothing in our opinion should be taken to cast doubt on longstanding prohibitions on the possession of firearms by felons and the mentally ill, or laws forbidding the carrying of firearms in sensitive places such as schools and government buildings."[55] Later, the opinion mentions that the M16 rifle, the fully automatic military version of the AR-15 "assault rifle," may be banned even if more advanced weaponry may be necessary to fight a true war.

The majority concludes that the D.C. handgun ban is unconstitutional because handguns are the most popular firearm to be kept in the home for personal defense. Likewise, safe-storage laws that prevent a person from accessing a firearm for self-defense are invalidated. *Heller* did not challenge the licensing requirement, and the Court did not address it.

Finally, Scalia defends the majority's refusal to establish a level of judicial scrutiny to evaluate firearms laws or to discuss all types of restrictions that may be permissible by stating that the Supreme Court's first foray into a right is never designed to be the final word on the subject. He does, however, reject the "interest-balancing" approach to evaluating gun restrictions suggested in Justice Breyer's dissent. The level of scrutiny applied to Second Amendment cases is crucial in determining whether a regulation will be upheld or struck down.

Dissenting Opinion—Justice Stevens

In his dissent, Justice Stevens argues that the debate is not about an individual or collective right, but the scope of the individual right, which he concedes does exist. Yet, while the right is an individual one, its implementation is essentially collective. It does not include nonmilitary purposes such as hunting and self-defense. It was designed to protect the integrity of the state militias. "Neither the text of the Amendment nor the arguments advanced by its proponents evidenced the slightest interest in limiting any legislature's authority to regulate private civilian uses of firearms."[56]

Stevens relies on the *Miller* decision, arguing that it affirmed a military-use right and that the majority's "feeble attempt" to read *Miller* in any other fashion contradicts both the opinion in that case and the Framers' intent. For Stevens, the preamble of the Second Amendment describes the intent and purpose of the amendment. The reference to the militia underlines the overriding concern with protecting the states from federal encroachment at that time. The absence of any mention of self-defense or hunting, when they were included in contemporaneous state constitutions, indicates that the Framers intended to exclude nonmilitary uses of firearms from constitutional protection.

Some of the individual rights protected explicitly in the First Amendment—to assemble and petition for redress of grievances—are rights that can only be effectively utilized in a collective manner. Likewise, the right to keep and bear arms is a unitary right that applies to military purposes exclusively. "Indeed, not a word in the constitutional text even arguably supports the Court's overwrought and novel description of the Second Amendment."[57]

Numerous proposed amendments to the Constitution that would have protected the rights to hunt and self-defense failed to pass in state ratifying conventions. Still, the primary concern of all at the time, particularly those opposed to the Constitution, was the ability of the states to prevent incursions from the federal government. With all those available additional sources, James Madison chose to rely more heavily on the Virginia proposal, which is more military-related and initially included a conscientious-objector exemption, further suggesting a military application.

Stevens also objects to the majority's use and misreading of legal commentaries both prior to and after ratification and the sparse discussion of the drafting debates. In addition, he is concerned that the majority opinion ignores Blackstone's admonition to give appropriate weight to preambles when interpreting clauses of such documents. Beyond that, Stevens argues that the writings of Joseph Story, both prior and subsequent to his service on the Supreme Court, suggest that he viewed the Second Amendment as protecting the militia, not self-defense. And he dismisses any commentary after the Civil War as being too far removed from the amendment's adoption to be instructive with regard to its meaning.

Not surprisingly, Stevens reads both *Cruikshank* and *Presser* as supporting a collective right. To bolster his similar reading of *Miller*, he quotes liberally from that opinion:

> With obvious purpose to assure the continuation and render possible the effectiveness of such forces [the militia] the declaration and guarantee of the Second Amendment were made. It must be interpreted and applied with that end in view ... the common view was that adequate defense of country and laws could be secured through the Militia—civilians primarily, soldiers on occasion. The signification attributed to the term Militia appears from the debates in the Convention, the history and legislation of Colonies and States, and the writings of approved commentators. *Miller,* 307 U. S., at 178–179.[58]

Finally, Stevens suggests that precedents should be overturned only when a new piece of historical evidence is found or there is a new line of argument not considered in the precedents. Neither is applicable in *Heller*.

Dissenting Opinion—Justice Breyer

Justice Breyer takes up the second point for the dissenters: that even if there is a Second Amendment protection for self-defense, that protection is not absolute, and the state may impose regulations that are not "unreasonable or inappropriate." Colonial laws regulated the use of firearms in nonmilitary situations, and a wide variety of laws have been implemented since those times.

Assuming there is a right to self-defense, the Washington, D.C., statute would not be unconstitutional under a "rational basis" standard of scrutiny, which only requires that a regulation bears a "rational relationship" to a "legitimate governmental purpose." Clearly, the majority rejects a "strict scrutiny" standard by virtue of the numerous types of regulations it explicitly exempts from its consideration. Thus, Breyer suggests that the Court adopt an "interest-balancing" approach, under which the D.C. law is permissible. This approach, which has been adopted in other cases, requires significant deference to legislatures.

Given the stated purpose of the law is to save lives, gun regulations are clearly a reasonable means to that end. Breyer examines statistics regarding the number of gun-related deaths, both nationally and in the District of Columbia, and the prevalence of handguns in those deaths. He notes that the urban experience is different from the rural experience. Even after considering social science evidence that stricter gun laws may *increase* violent crime, Breyer concludes that the evidence is not sufficient for a court to override the judgment of a legislative body. This is particularly true since other studies suggest that stricter gun laws are effective in reducing violence. The regulations may be controversial, but they are not unconstitutional. Finally, there are no other equally effective but less restrictive measures that may be taken, so under "interest balancing," the District's law is constitutional.

McDONALD v. CITY OF CHICAGO, 561 U.S. 742 (2010)

McDonald v. City of Chicago extended the Second Amendment protections grounded in *Heller* to the states through incorporation.[59] While the five-justice majority uses different means to reach the same conclusion, they agree that the protections afforded in *Heller* apply to individuals across the country.

The Chicago ordinance at issue was very similar to the Washington, D.C., regulation. The city required that all firearms be licensed, and prohibited most handguns from being licensed, creating, essentially, a handgun ban. Oak Park, Illinois, had similar ordinances, and that case was consolidated with *McDonald*. Otis McDonald, in his seventies when the suit was filed, lived in a high-crime area, and co-plaintiff Colleen Lawson, whose home had been burglarized, sought to keep handguns in their homes for personal protection.

Majority Opinion—Justice Alito

Justice Samuel Alito begins by tracing the history of incorporation doctrine. Alito chooses to incorporate the Second Amendment by using the Due Process Clause of the Fourteenth Amendment, the common method for incorporation. The question regarding whether to incorporate a right turns on "whether a particular Bill of Rights guarantee is fundamental to *our* scheme of ordered liberty and system of justice [emphasis in original]," not as the city argued that any civilized society might not afford the right.[60] In its brief, the city of Chicago argued that because strict gun laws are common among modern democracies, an individual right to possess firearms was not a fundamental right. Alito responded that it is the experience of the United States that holds sway here, not the experience of other nations. Relying heavily on and repeating many of the assertions of the majority opinion in *Heller*, Alito concludes that the Second Amendment right to self-defense meets that standard. He highlights the attempts to disarm freed slaves after the Civil War and protections afforded by the Civil Rights Act of 1866 as well as the debates surrounding adoption of the Fourteenth Amendment. He rejects the claim that the post–Civil War Congress intended only to outlaw discrimination, meaning a gun ban is permissible so long as it is nondiscriminatory.

Alito addresses Justice Breyer's dissent, which argues against incorporation for four reasons. First, Alito points to an amicus brief supporting incorporation signed by 58 senators and 251 members of the House of Representatives as evidence that a consensus exists that holds the right to be fundamental. Additionally, 38 state attorneys general signed a similar brief. Second, the right does protect minorities in so far as they are disproportionately victims of violent crimes and need protection not currently provided. Third, incorporation does, to some extent, limit the responses of various states, but that is inevitable. Finally, judges will not be required to balance interests because that reasoning was rejected in *Heller*.

Concurring Opinions—Justice Scalia and Justice Thomas

Justice Scalia writes a somewhat lengthy concurrence in which he takes Justice Stevens to task for his dissent, which Scalia finds relies too heavily on a "living Constitution" argument and provides little guidance to judges in determining which rights should be incorporated. Thomas's lengthy and history-laden concurrence uses the Privileges and Immunities Clause of the Fourteenth Amendment, eschewing the Due Process Clause.[61] Thomas pays special attention to the historical plight of African Americans and their need for self-defense when the state did not protect them.[62]

Dissenting Opinion—Justice Stevens

Justice Stevens argues that this case is substantive due process[63] and that incorporation has never been complete or mirror images of the right being defined. The issue for Stevens is if a fundamental right to possess a firearm in the home exists and is enforceable against the states. For Stevens, "personal liberty" is the right protected by the Fourteenth Amendment. Thus, rights guaranteed by the first eight amendments may or may not be protected, and others not named therein may also qualify for protection. "Rather than seek a categorical understanding of the liberty clause, our precedents have thus elucidated a conceptual core ... Self-determination, bodily integrity, freedom of conscience, intimate relationships, political equality, dignity and respect—these are the central values we have found implicit in the concept of ordered liberty."[64]

While he finds the utility of handguns for personal defense to be a consideration, they are not essential to the concept of self-defense. Thus, the question still hinges on whether keeping a handgun in the home is part of the "liberty" interest that is fundamental. For Stevens, the answer is no. "First, firearms have a fundamentally ambivalent relationship to liberty. Just as they can help homeowners defend their families and property from intruders, they can help thugs and insurrectionists murder innocent victims."[65] Further, guns may be transported outside the home, and the state can take action to preempt that possibility. Under the Chicago ordinance, other guns are permitted, so the right to self-defense is protected. There is no right to the weapon of your choice.

Borrowing from the city's argument, Stevens notes that other democracies' experience is to restrict firearms, suggesting that the right is not fundamental to liberty. Those nations are, of course, different, but their experiences should not be ignored. He reiterates his concerns from *Heller*, that the Second Amendment protects the states' militias, not an individual right. There is a long history of state regulation of firearms. Stevens concludes with a plea to allow federalism to flourish by not preempting the states from adopting their own policy responses, although it is not clear that the majority opinion entirely prevents this as it does allow for numerous regulations, which states may or may not chose to adopt. He also argues that Scalia's methodology makes subjective judgments regarding which rights are worthy of constitutional protection.

Dissenting Opinion—Justice Breyer

For Justice Breyer, the Second Amendment does not protect an individual right to own firearms for self-defense; therefore it is not fundamental. He recounts the criticism of some legal scholars and historians regarding Scalia's reading of history in *Heller*. To qualify for incorporation, a right must remain fundamental over time with little dissent. "Any contemporary disagreement about whether the right is fundamental" can indicate a lack of consensus.[66]

> Further, there is no popular consensus that the private self-defense right described in *Heller* is fundamental ... every State regulates firearms extensively, and public opinion is sharply divided on the appropriate level of regulation ... One side believes the right essential to protect the lives of those attacked in the home; the other side believes it essential to regulate the right in order to protect the lives of others attacked with guns. It seems unlikely that definitive evidence will develop one way or the other.[67]

Employing this standard can be problematic, however. For example, a strong argument could be made that *Roe v. Wade* should be overturned. Public opinion remains divided on the abortion question even 40 years after the decision was handed down. While the Court may decline to grant certiorari in cases dealing with very controversial issues, there are few, if any, precedents that decline to define a right as fundamental because the citizenry is split regarding its inherent value.

LEGAL COMMENTARY ON *HELLER* AND *MCDONALD*

There has been much debate among constitutional law scholars regarding the jurisprudential impact and appropriateness of the *Heller* and

McDonald decisions. While important analyses, they are largely beyond the scope of this book, so they will be discussed only briefly here. The fact is that an individual right based largely on self-defense was recognized in *Heller* and extended in *McDonald*. The deference given to precedents by the Supreme Court makes it unlikely that a future Court would overturn either ruling, although the scope of the right could be severely limited without technically overruling the precedent.

While there are often competing camps with regard to constitutional interpretation—the originalists versus those who argue for an "evolving" meaning—both those in the majority and the dissenters in *Heller* looked to history for their reasoning. According to Second Amendment scholar Joyce Lee Malcolm, "History is essential to revealing that meaning ["the people"], and all the justices tried their hands at employing historical inquiry . . . The majority opinion is a model of rigorous historical inquiry, while the dissenters fall short."[68]

Malcolm is particularly critical of Stevens's analysis, but she also takes Scalia to task for not grounding his discussion of the drafting of the Second Amendment more in history. Citing James Madison and the Senate's rejection of a motion to add "for the common defense" after "to keep and bear arms," Malcolm suggests that history again is on the side of an individual right.[69]

Akhil Reed Amar is not enamored of the reasoning by either side in this case, but he gives credit to Scalia for referencing the text of the Constitution, something that Amar suggests rarely happens in modern jurisprudence. He is particularly critical of Stevens's dissent and its deference to precedent. First, Amar notes that the Supreme Court is certainly not bound by the precedents of lower courts. He then argues that the *Miller* opinion is muddled, at best, and its discussion of the Second Amendment was only five pages and was "long on quotation and citation, but short on analysis."[70]

He reserves his strongest criticism, though, for the Stevens argument that precedent can only be overruled with new historical evidence or a new line of reasoning. First, he suggests that the Constitution is the supreme law, not the Court's previous rulings. Second, he argues that Stevens's adoption of this principle seems to be "in tension" with many of his previous opinions.

Reva Siegel argues that the *Heller* decision represents the triumph of the gun-rights movement. The important debates over the meaning of the Second Amendment that shaped Scalia's opinion occurred primarily in the 1980s and 1990s, not at the nation's founding.

> [T]his Comment looks beyond the text of the *Heller* opinion itself
> to the decades of the social movement conflict that preceded the

decision. This history illustrates how contests over the Constitution's meaning can endow courts with authority to change the way they interpret its provisions. The effort to persuade—and to capture institutions that can authoritatively pronounce law—can prompt . . . a process that can forge and discipline new understandings.[71]

Allen Rostron, former staff attorney for the Brady Campaign and now a law professor, states that much of Scalia's reasoning in *Heller* is "a solid presentation of textual arguments and historical evidence . . . to protect non-military use of guns."[72] He finds that the regulatory exceptions noted by Scalia, however, are much more political in nature than historical interpretations of the Second Amendment. "The fact that the majority endorses these measures in a cursory bit of dicta, without engaging in any real analysis, undermines the pretense that their originalist methodology truly drives their decision-making."[73] In a similar vein, Mark Tushnet views the *Heller* decision, particularly the Scalia opinion, as a compromise. He sees the regulations exceptions noted in the opinion as "transparent add-ons . . . clearly tacked on to the opinion to secure a fifth vote (presumably Justice Anthony Kennedy's)."[74]

One important technical aspect of the rulings of great importance is the level of scrutiny that future Courts will apply when examining gun laws. There are typically three levels of scrutiny possible. In the lowest level of scrutiny—the rational basis test—the government must demonstrate that the regulation is rationally related to a legitimate state interest. Under this test, few laws are judged unconstitutional. Under strict scrutiny, which is reserved for rights that are thought to be fundamental, the state interest must be compelling and the regulation "narrowly tailored" with no less intrusive method available to achieve the interest. Many regulations are unconstitutional under this standard. With intermediate scrutiny, there must be an important state interest, and the law must be substantially related to serving that interest. This standard often results in less predictable outcomes, and it is more easily molded to fit the predilections of the decision makers.

Although the majority opinion in *Heller* did not specify a level of scrutiny, it did explicitly reject a rational basis test as well as the interest-balancing approach suggested by Justice Breyer's dissent. It is not clear if interest balancing is related to intermediate or strict scrutiny, or if it is completely separate from the levels of scrutiny. As Rosenthal and Malcolm suggest, some interest-balancing may be required in order to uphold the regulations specifically referenced in *Heller*.[75] Alternatively, the majority may have simply relied on the long-standing nature of those regulations. The majority also appears to have rejected a strict scrutiny standard under which some of the regulations specifically referenced in the opinion would almost certainly be unconstitutional.

Defining the limits of protected rights may require some form of balancing even if it goes by a different name. For example, Tushnet suggests that the Court might employ the "inside-out" model of the First Amendment. In this way, the Court would define the core (inside) of what is protected by the Second Amendment. That might be firearm possession for home defense. That would then allow prohibitions for carrying firearms outside the home. While this is a somewhat neat package, it is not clear how personal defense outside the home would be "outside" the parameters outlined in *Heller*. It would be difficult to argue that one has a right to self-defense in the home but that right is totally relinquished as soon as one steps outside the house, although it could be diminished.

Volokh suggests that rather than concerning themselves with trying to apply a particular level of scrutiny to a law, courts should "recognize that there are four different categories of justifications for a restriction on the right to bear arms." First is the scope of the restriction, which may not be covered by the Constitution itself, its original meaning, traditional views of what the text means, or background legal principles. Second, the extent of the burden may be so small that it does not rise to the level of infringement. Third, a restriction may reduce other dangers—specifically crime and injury—to such an extent that even a substantial burden may be justified. Finally, the government may have the "authority as proprietor, employer or subsidizer to control behavior on its property or behavior by the recipients of its property."[76]

Volokh recognizes that under his categories, as well as under different levels of scrutiny, some restrictions that he does not favor or believes will be ineffective or even harmful, will be constitutional. "But not all unwise laws are unconstitutional; and, conversely, not all that is constitutionally permitted should in fact be implemented."[77]

IMPACT OF *HELLER* AND *MCDONALD*

Shortly after the *Heller* decision, Cass Sunstein suggested there were three possible interpretations of the Court's actions. The first sees the case as a "modern incarnation of *Marbury v. Madison*," a landmark case that honestly and in a neutral fashion uncovers the true original meaning of the Second Amendment. It explicates the individual right intended by the Founders and grounds it contextually in history. A second view judges *Heller* as "a modern incarnation of *Lochner v. New York*," a case that overruled the decisions of democratic legislatures in order to impose its own misinterpretation of the Constitution. A third view, supported by Sunstein, sees *Heller* more like *Griswold v. Connecticut*, a case that tries to ground its reasoning in originalist constitutional interpretation, but one that relies as much on contemporary arguments and values. "*Heller* is a narrow ruling with minimalist features ... the development of the gun right, as it is specified over time, will have close parallels to the development of the privacy right. As the law emerges through case-by-case judgments, the scope of the right will have as much to do with contemporary understandings as with historical ones."[78]

Sunstein was accurate in so far as the limits of the rights contained in the Second Amendment were not fleshed out by *Heller*, and *McDonald* did little to clarify them. The full impact of the *Heller* and *McDonald* decisions is likely to be debated and determined over several decades at least. What we can say at present is that the fundamental finding in *Heller* allowed that debate to continue. The existence of an individual right to self-defense and to keep firearms in the home means that legislatures and the courts can continue to define the limits of the right. Had the dissenters prevailed, the discussion would have ended. With only a collective right, any and all gun regulations would have been constitutional. Whether that debate will be continued more in lower courts or at the Supreme Court level remains to be seen. Some fear a deluge of cases, while others hope for the flood. "[T]he Second Amendment involves questions and issues that inspire fierce passion in large numbers of Americans, and in well-funded organizations both equipped and inclined to pursue follow-up litigation in both state and lower federal courts."[79]

The majority opinion in *Heller* explicitly recognizes the constitutionality of several types of regulations and does not rule out others. In fact, it only negates the most stringent of regulations—gun bans. *Heller* can and has been claimed, then, as a victory by both sides. It seems more accurate to see it as a limited victory for the advocates of gun rights and a setback, but not a rout, for gun-control proponents.

The decision in *McDonald* is clearly important in so far as it applied the protections afforded by the Second Amendment, however they are ultimately defined, to the states. In terms of striking down what was essentially a gun ban, *McDonald* created no new rights other than those recognized by the Court in *Heller*. It simply, and not surprisingly, extended those rights to residents of the 50 states.

In an analysis of lower-court cases since *McDonald*, Sobel found that a majority had employed an intermediate-level scrutiny test in their decisions.[80] A few had relied on a rational basis test and, not surprisingly, found gun laws to be constitutional. Only one had used strict scrutiny, and it found the regulation to violate the Constitution. As suggested above, employing intermediate scrutiny, the courts generally evaluate the level of intrusiveness on the Second Amendment right.

Sobel would prefer that courts use the "undue burden" test, which has been employed as an alternative to intermediate or strict scrutiny in reproductive rights cases. As explicated by Justice O'Connor in *City of Akron v. Akron Center for Reproductive Health*, "If the particular regulation does not 'unduly burden' the fundamental right, then our evaluation of that regulation is limited to our determination that the regulation rationally relates to a legitimate state purpose."[81] For Sobel, this would protect gun rights but give the state the ability to regulate firearms.

Regardless of how the courts decide future cases, the psychological impact of the decisions in *Heller* and *McDonald* should not be underestimated. While supporters of gun control rarely, if ever, refer to the Second Amendment, it is present in virtually all the arguments and communications from groups that support gun rights. For example, election fliers mailed by the NRA and the National Shooting Sports Foundation (NSSF) in the 2012 presidential election both referenced the Second Amendment. "The actions of President Barack Obama have harmed the Second Amendment for generations to come . . . They [Romney and Ryan] will appoint Supreme Court justices who will uphold the rulings . . . which held that the Second Amendment guarantees a fundamental, individual Right to Keep and Bear Arms for all Americans."[82] "Barack Obama's nominees to the Supreme Court don't believe the Second Amendment guarantees an individual right to keep and bear arms."[83]

Having Supreme Court precedents to point to in defense of one's argument provides an immeasurable boost to the weight of the argument. Whereas those groups have always clearly stated that the Second Amendment right was an individual right, they now have judicial rulings to buttress that contention. While that will not convince many of their opponents, it offers support to gun-rights advocates.

Conversely, it has been suggested that the Court's rulings may simply move the battle back to the legislative arena. Rostron speculated, "In the long run, the Supreme Court's decision [*Heller*] may help to drive the nation away from unproductive bickering over guns and toward reasonable compromises and real progress on the issue."[84] Recent legislative battles at both the national and state levels suggest that the *Heller* and *McDonald* decisions did not end the discussion of gun control. However, Rostron's view that compromise might be found appears to be more optimistic than realistic.

Writing prior to the *Heller* decision, Bennett suggested that the sky would not fall regardless of the outcome and that little would change.

> The alarmists on both sides are wrong because they envision a United States in which gun rights could be established for the first time or utterly abolished. Both sides ignore reality—we live in a nation in which gun rights already exist and they are not going away. But we also live in a land of gun laws, and those are not going away either. The balance we have achieved is one of the rights that come with responsibilities. The equipoise is not perfect, but it is strong and enduring.[85]

He examines some facts—the number of guns in private hands, the belief of most citizens and many political leaders that the Second Amendment confers an individual right that can be balanced with responsible gun laws, and that most gun laws would survive legal challenges—and concludes that the status quo will survive. "Many Americans like guns, and almost all Americans like gun laws, and no judges, politicians or even law professors are going to take either of them away."[86]

Those ideas are echoed by Adam Winkler, writing a year after the decision in *Heller*. While very critical of Scalia's analysis as relying on modern theories of gun rights as opposed to originalism, Winkler wrote:

> *Heller* is more likely to be accepted precisely because Scalia's opinion departed from the original meaning of the Second Amendment. Moreover, this celebrated landmark decision has had almost no effect on the constitutionality of gun control ... While some laws are sure to be invalidated in time, the new Second Amendment's bark is far worse than its right. The greatest irony is that *Heller's* logical flaws and inconsistencies improve the decision, making it more likely to endure and helping cement a reasonable, not radical, right to bear arms.[87]

Winkler's assessment and prediction that few gun laws would fall as a result of *Heller* was correct. The status quo largely remained, even after the *McDonald* decision. However, it is critically important to bear in mind that had *Heller* been decided in favor of the District's gun ban, then the door would have been opened to numerous other restrictions, which will not be enacted at all, or will fall under judicial scrutiny. To be sure, other laws have been enacted since their decision by several states, and, if tested, they are likely to be held to be constitutional. Outright bans of all firearms are, however, now off the table.

The major impact of *Heller* and *McDonald* may still be determined in legislative battles in which the lines of permissible gun regulations are drawn within the parameters of an individual right to ownership and self-defense. "Culture wars produce repeated battles in the courts and symbolic victories and defeats there, but permanent victory comes from developments elsewhere, which then yield real rather than symbolic decisions by the courts."[88] With a largely divided public, those "real decisions" may be some time in the making and prove quite difficult to reach.

NOTES

1. Cicero, "In Defense of Titus Annius Milo," in *Selected Political Speeches of Cicero,* ed. and trans. Michael Grant (New York: Penguin Books, 1969), 234.

2. See, for example, Gary Kleck and Miriam A. DeLone, "Victim Resistance and Offender Weapon Effects in Robbery," *Journal of Quantitative Criminology* 9, no. 1 (1993): 55–81; and Lawrence Southwick Jr., "Self-Defense with Guns: The Consequences," *Journal of Criminal Justice* 28, no. 5 (2000) 351–70; and contrast with the discussion in David Hemenway, *Private Guns, Public Health* (Ann Arbor: University of Michigan Press, 2004), 75–77.

3. Cesare Beccaria, "On Crimes and Punishment," in *On Crimes and Punishment and Other Essays,* ed. Richard Bellamy (New York: Cambridge University Press, 1995), 101.

4. Andrew J. McClurg, David B. Kopel, and Brannon P. Denning, *Gun Control and Gun Rights* (New York: New York University Press, 2002), 122–25.

5. Adam Winkler, *Gunfight: The Battle over the Right to Bear Arms in America* (New York: W. W. Norton & Company, 2013), 99–103.

6. McClurg, Kopel, and Denning, *Gun Control,* 136. A more detailed discussion of the philosophical background of the right to bear arms may be found in Don B. Kates, "The Second Amendment: A Right to Personal Self-Protection," in Gary Kleck and Don B. Kates, *Armed: New Perspectives on Gun Control* (Amherst, NY: Prometheus Books, 2001), 343–56.

7. James Madison, "The Federalist No. 46," in *The Federalist,* ed. Sherman F. Mittell (Washington, DC: National Home Library Foundation, 1938), 299–300.

8. Alexander Hamilton, "The Federalist No. 29," in *The Federalist,* ed. Sherman F. Mittell (Washington, DC: National Home Library Foundation, 1938), 176.

9. Alexander Hamilton, "The Federalist No. 28," in *The Federalist,* ed. Sherman F. Mittell (Washington, DC: National Home Library Foundation, 1938), 173; Hamilton, "The Federalist No. 29," 178–79.

10. Stephen P. Halbrook, *That Every Man Be Armed: The Evolution of a Constitutional Right* (Oakland, CA: The Independent Institute, 1994), 150, cited in Anthony Gallia, " 'Your Weapons, You Will Not Need Them,' Comment on the Supreme Court's Sixty-Year Silence on the Right to Keep and Bear Arms," *Akron Law Review* 33 (1999): 131–62.

11. Gallia, *Your Weapons*, 150.

12. Robert E. Shalhope, "The Armed Citizen in the Early Republic," *Law and Contemporary Problems* 49 (1986): 125–41.

13. For a discussion of the history of the militia in the United States, see Don Higginbotham, "The Federalized Militia Debate: A Neglected Aspect of Second Amendment Scholarship," *William and Mary Quarterly* 55 (1998): 39–58.

14. Saul Cornell, Introduction, in *Whose Right to Bear Arms Did the Second Amendment Protect?* (Boston: Bedford/St. Martin's, 2000), 10. Even Robert Spitzer agrees that there was a widespread and strong bias against a standing army and in favor of an armed citizen militia in the colonial era and in the early years of the republic. Robert J. Spitzer, *The Politics of Gun Control,* 5th ed. (Chatham, NJ: Chatham House Publishers, 2004), 22–24.

15. Shalhope, "Armed Citizen."

16. Lawrence Delbert Cress, "An Armed Community: The Origins and Meaning of the Right to Bear Arms," *Journal of American History* 71 (June 1984): 22–42.

17. Winkler, *Gunfight,* 114.

18. David B. Kopel, *The Truth about Gun Control* (New York: Encounter Books, 2013), 21.

19. McClurg, Kopel, and Denning, *Gun Control,* chap. 3.

20. Joshua Horwitz and Casey Anderson, "Public Policy Approach: The Insurrectionist Idea and Its Consequences," Symposium on Firearms, the Militia and Safe Cities: Merging History, Constitutional Law and Public Policy, *Albany Government Law Review* 1, no. 2 (2008): 510.

21. Robert E. Shalhope, "The Ideological Origins of the Second Amendment," *Journal of American History* 69 (December 1982): 599–614.

22. Sanford Levinson, "The Embarrassing Second Amendment," *Yale Law Journal* 99 (1989): 637–59. The term Standard Model originated in Glenn H. Reynolds, "A Critical Guide to the Second Amendment," *Tennessee Law Review* 62 (1995): 461–512.

23. For most Supreme Court justices and legal scholars, there is no such thing as an absolute right. All rights must be balanced against other rights, and governmental restrictions are, in some circumstances, permissible.

24. Wills has identified the "inner circle of Standard Modelers" as including Robert J. Cottrol, Stephen P. Halbrook, Don B. Kates, Joyce Lee Malcolm, and Robert E. Shalhope. Garry Wills, "To Keep and Bear Arms," in Saul Cornell, *Whose Right to Bear Arms Did the Second Amendment Protect?* (Boston: Bedford/St. Martin's, 2000), 65.

25. Eugene Volokh, "The Commonplace Second Amendment," *New York University Law Review* 73, no. 3 (1998): 793–821.

26. Ibid., 810.

27. David C. Williams, "The Unitary Second Amendment," *New York University Law Review* 73, no. 3 (1998): 822–30.

28. Saul Cornell, "Commonplace or Anachronism: The Standard Model, the Second Amendment, and the Problem of History in Contemporary Constitutional Theory," *Constitutional Commentary* 16 (1999): 223.

29. Saul Cornell, "Historical Approach: The Ironic Second Amendment," Symposium on Firearms, the Militia and Safe Cities: Merging History, Constitutional Law and Public Policy, *Albany Government Law Review* 292 (2008): 293–94.

30. Michael C. Dorf, "What Does the Second Amendment Mean Today?" Symposium on the Second Amendment: Fresh Looks, *Chicago-Kent Law Review* 76 (2000): 291–347.

31. Whether or not we retain a right to revolution is more than just an academic question to many. Ruhl, Rizer, and Wiel write, "no matter how farfetched the need to take arms against the government might seem, America was founded on the principle that professional soldiers and police should not have a monopoly on the legitimate use of force. And, at the very least, the people have the right to take back power when the government becomes abusive." Jesse Matthew Ruhl, Arthur L. Rizer, and Mikel J. Weir, "Gun Control: Targeting Rationality in a Loaded Debate," *Kansas Journal of Law and Public Policy* 13 (Winter 2004): 49. More practically, they suggest that many modern governments have killed a larger number of citizens than those of the eighteenth century. On the other hand, Hardaway, Gormley, and Taylor point out that the Constitution itself prevents insurrection through its definition of treason, which is to make war on the United States. Also, one of the functions of the militia is to suppress insurrection, i.e., Shays' Rebellion. Robert Hardaway, Elizabeth Gormley, and Bryan Taylor, "The Inconvenient Militia Clause of the Second Amendment: Why the Supreme Court Declines to Resolve the Debate over the Right to Bear Arms," *St. John's Journal of Legal Commentary* 16 (Winter 2002): 99–102.

32. Don B. Kates, "Introduction, The Second Amendment: A Right to Personal Self-Protection," in *Armed: New Perspectives on Gun Control,* ed. Gary Kleck and Don B. Kates (Amherst, NY: Prometheus Books, 2001), 24.

33. This interpretation fits well with the conclusions of Shalhope, who argues that the "people" did enjoy a personal right to own and possess firearms, but he recognizes a much more limited definition of the people and the power of the states to restrict the rights of citizens for the common good. Robert E. Shalhope, "To Keep and Bear Arms in the Early Republic," *Constitutional Commentary* 16 (Summer 1999): 269.

34. *United States v. Cruikshank,* 92 U.S. 542 (1876).

35. *Presser v. Illinois,* 116 U.S. 252 (1886).

36. McClurg, Kopel and Denning, *Gun Control,* 155.

37. Spitzer, *Politics of Gun Control,* 35.

38. Kates, "Introduction," 24.

39. *United States v. Miller,* 307 U.S. 174 (1939).

40. Levinson, "Embarrassing," 655–56.

41. For a discussion of the Ashcroft memo, see Harry Wilson, *Guns, Gun Control, and Elections* (Lanham, MD: Rowman & Littlefield Publishers), 27.

42. The silence of the Supreme Court regarding the Second Amendment is discussed in Wilson, *Guns, Gun Control,* 36–37.

43. Winkler, *Gunfight,* 60–63, 88–92.

44. Ibid., 92.

45. Robert A. Levy, "Challenging the D.C. Gun Ban," Cato Institute, http://www.cato.org/publications/commentary/challenging-dc-gun-ban.

46. *Parker v. District of Columbia,* 311 F.Supp. 2d 103, 109 (2004).

47. *Parker v. District of Columbia,* 478 F.3d 370, 401 (2007).

48. Much of the majority opinion is devoted to responding to points raised by the dissents. This back-and-forth allows the justices to debate the points openly and, perhaps, to openly criticize one another.

49. 554 U.S. 570 at 599 (emphasis added).

50. This section is comparatively brief, but the sentence seems to confirm a "right to insurrection," which is scarcely mentioned in most analyses of this decision. This is an important consideration for many rank-and-file supporters of gun rights, and its mention in the majority opinion should not be overlooked nor its consequences underestimated. This argument underlies many of the objections to firearm registration and background checks that may necessitate more comprehensive record-keeping by the BATF or some other government agency. Knowledge of gun ownership is thought by some to be the first step toward gun confiscation and tyranny.

51. 554 U.S. 570 at 599 (emphasis in original).

52. *Houston v. Moore,* 5 Wheat. 1, 24 (1820).

53. 554 U.S. 570 at 621–23.

54. Ibid., 624.

55. Ibid., 626.

56. Ibid., 637.

57. Ibid., 652.

58. Ibid., 678–79.

59. Incorporation is the method by which the Supreme Court makes the Bill of Rights applicable to the states. Typically, using the Fourteenth Amendment as its justification, the Court holds that various rights that are protected from infringement by Congress are also protected against incursions from the state. For a discussion of the theory of incorporation, see Craig R. Ducat, *Constitutional Interpretation*, 7th ed. (Belmont, CA: West, 2000), 495–500.

60. Slip opinion, 16.

61. For a discussion of the merits of using the Privileges and Immunities Clause or the Due Process Clause in order to incorporate the Second Amendment, see Michael Nieto, "The Changing Landscape of Firearm Legislation in the Wake of *McDonald v. City of Chicago,* 130 S.CT. 3020 (2010)," *Harvard Journal of Law and Public Policy* 34 (2011): 1117–30.

62. This is an interesting constitutional law argument that recognizes the historical problems with substantive due process, but it is not pertinent to the focus of this book.

63. Substantive due process refers to a series of Supreme Court cases that are now commonly thought to have been decided on policy merits rather than constitutional arguments. Applications of substantive due process range from decisions that struck down minimum wage laws because they violated a "right of contract" to those that struck down abortion laws as violative of a "right to privacy."

64. Slip opinion, 23.

65. Slip opinion, 35.

66. Slip opinion, 7.

67. Slip opinion, 9.

68. Joyce Lee Malcolm, "The Supreme Court and the Uses of History: *District of Columbia v. Heller*," *UCLA Law Review* 56 (2009): 1377.

69. Ibid., 1392.

70. Akhil Reed Amar, "Comment: *Heller*, HLR, and Holistic Legal Reasoning," 122 *Harvard Law Review* 122, no. 1 (2008): 151.

71. Reva B. Siegel, "Comment: Dead or Alive: Originalism as Popular Constitutionalism in *Heller*," *Harvard Law Review* 122, no. 1 (2008): 193–94.

72. Allen Rostron, "Protecting Gun Rights and Improving Gun Control after *District of Columbia v. Heller*," *Lewis and Clark Law Review* 13, no. 2 (2009): 386.

73. Ibid., 387.

74. Mark Tushnet, "*Heller* and the Perils of Compromise," *Lewis and Clark Law Review* 13, no. 2 (2009): 420.

75. Lawrence Rosenthal and Joyce Lee Malcolm, "*McDonald v. Chicago*: Which Standard of Scrutiny Should Apply to Gun Control Laws?" *Northwestern University Law Review* 105 (2011): 437.

76. Eugene Volokh, "Implementing the Right to Keep and Bear Arms for Self-Defense: An Analytical Framework and a Research Agenda," Symposium: The Second Amendment and the Right to Bear Arms after *D.C. v. Heller*, *UCLA Law Review* 56 (2009): 1446–47.

77. Ibid., 1448.

78. Cass R. Sunstein, "Comment: Second Amendment Minimalism: *Heller* as *Griswold*," *Harvard Law Review* 122 (2008): 248.

79. Brannon P. Denning and Glenn H. Reynolds, "Five Takes on *McDonald v. Chicago*," *Journal of Law and Politics* 26 (Winter 2011): 303.

80. Stacey L. Sobel, "The Tsunami of Legal Uncertainty: What's a Court to Do Post-*McDonald*?" *Cornell Journal of Law and Public Policy* 21 (2012): 489–524.

81. *City of Akron v. Akron Center for Reproductive Health*, 462 U.S. 453 (1983).

82. NRA-ILA, "Who's the Right Team to Restore Our Freedoms—and Rebuild Our Future?" election flier, 2012.

83. National Shooting Sports Foundation, "Our Freedoms Face Serious Challenges," election flier, 2012.

84. Rostron, "Protecting Gun Rights," 385.

85. Matthew Bennett, "Public Policy Approach: Misfire: How the Debate over Gun Rights Ignores Reality," Symposium on Firearms, the Militia and Safe Cities: Merging History, Constitutional Law and Public Policy, *Albany Government Law Review* 482 (2008): 485.

86. Ibid., 495.

87. Winkler, *Gunfight,* 1551.

88. Tushnet, "*Heller* and the Perils," 432. Tushnet provides a detailed discussion of the possible approaches that future courts may use to define the limits of the rights found in the *Heller* decision. This analysis is strongly recommended for those more interested in legal critiques of the decision and the Scalia opinion.

THREE

Violence, Public Policy, and Firearms

Violence is a multifaceted and deeply entrenched phenomenon in American society. Violence implicates our history, including slavery and the near genocide of Native Americans; our economic system, including the widening gap between the wealthy and the poor; our social organization including a multiplicity of ethnic, racial and religious groups; our culture, including extreme emphasis on individual achievement and material success; our family values, including extremely high rates of teenage pregnancy and families without fathers; our patterns of drug use, including a tremendous amount of alcohol and drug abuse and a close relationship between alcohol, drugs, and violence; our mental health, including high levels of anxiety, stress, depression, and serious pathology; and our criminal justice system, especially penal institutions that breed and amplify violence ... There is no single type of violence and no single remedy ... In any event, gun control can only be one part, probably only a small part, of remedying the multifaceted violence problem. The broader effort must involve individuals, families, schools, churches, media, corporations, and political institutions and especially those neighborhoods that are the locus of the most intense violence. To change the patterns of violence in a violent society will require more than a better gun policy; it will require changing society.[1]

There are three conditions prominently associated with lethal violence in the United States that must be addressed by any agenda for the control of life-threatening violence. These are handgun availability and use, high rates of lethal violence among African-Americans, and the high incidence of homicides where victim and offender were previously unacquainted ... No program for the prevention of lethal violence can possess even superficial credibility without paying sustained attention to guns ... Anything short of drastic change in gun policy is either an acceptance of very high death rates or a gamble on very sharp reductions in violent assault.[2]

What are the causes of homicide and violent behavior? Must the solutions to violence be rooted in the causes, or can policies not directly related to the cause help reduce violence? Is gun control an end in itself, or must it result in fewer deaths in order to be successful?

As we can see in the quotes above, even those well versed in the study of violence do not agree on either causes or solutions. Jacobs argues that the causes of violence are numerous and have little to do with firearms. He does not argue that guns should be unregulated. Rather, he suggests that stronger regulation of guns will not solve the violence problem in the United States. If we want to solve the violence problem, then we need to deal with the causes of violent behavior.

Zimring and Hawkins argue that we do not have to address the root causes of violence in order to reduce it. In fact, they do not define the problem as "violence" or "crime," but rather as "lethal violence." "[L]ethal violence rather than high rates of crime is the disabling problem that sets the United States apart from other developed countries."[3] "We need "to shift the subject from crime to life-threatening violence ... the mislabeling of violence as a crime problem can only perpetuate a cycle of failure and frustration."[4] Reducing lethal violence to violence that does not result in death is feasible, they say, through better regulation of the instruments that escalate the violence.

Winkler argues that the focus on the tragic events such as Newtown is misplaced. Even countries with very strict gun laws, such as Norway and France, have suffered serious mass shootings in the past few years. If we incorrectly identify the problem, then the proposed solutions will not work.

Perhaps the mistake begins with the goal of preventing mass killings. Although it takes a high-profile incident like that at Newtown to finally begin discussion about guns and gun control, such shootings cannot be prevented ... In America, however, guns are everywhere and easy for someone with a criminal intent to acquire. Those guns are here to stay, which means—awful as it is to admit—that mass shootings are here to stay as well. Gun control resources would be better spent trying to reduce the daily, routine death toll from guns.[5]

Suicides account for about 60 percent of all firearm-related deaths, and their numbers have not declined as has the number of Americans who are murdered. Perhaps we should devise strategies to reduce the number of Americans who take their own lives. As we will see, much of the public health literature focuses on suicides in addition to homicides.

Each of the authors raises important points. We must define the problem before we can find a solution. We have not done that as a nation. Citizens, elected officials, interest groups, and media have similar but different definitions of the problem and, of course, the solution. Is the problem a high violent-crime rate, a high murder rate, too many accidental deaths, or too many suicides? If it is crime or homicide, then how do we tackle those problems? Are they problems of violence from strangers? From those we know? Is it mass shootings, or is it the much more common individual homicide? How many accidental shootings and suicides can we actually prevent?

And is the root cause of all of this human nature or instrumentality? Is it the "evil" in humans and society, an entertainment media that glorifies violence, mental illness, and drugs, or is it a "gun problem?" One thing is almost certain—opposite sides of the gun control debate define the cause of the problem in different terms, which leads them to very different solutions.

About 30,000 deaths each year are firearm-related, more than half of them suicides, while slightly more people are killed each year in automobiles—the vast majority of which are accidental.[6] It is a fact, not just a slogan, that guns do not kill people. Neither do automobiles. That is not to say that gun control cannot save lives any more than traffic laws cannot save lives. And just like cars, guns are typically used responsibly and provide their owners with useful tools and, yes, enjoyment. Again, like vehicles, firearms can also be used to save lives. Ambulances can transport patients to hospitals in time to save their lives, and guns can be used to defend their owners and others from attack, injury, and death. Of course, both can also be used irresponsibly and result in injury or death.

Clearly, guns do not cause people to become violent.[7] With the most conservative estimate that one-third of American households have at least one firearm, it is obvious that the vast majority of those households do not contain a person who uses those guns for violence. But guns do make it easier to injure or kill another person. Removing them from all households would save lives, but it is not politically possible or practically feasible, and it also would be unconstitutional. Similarly, a national speed limit of 40 miles per hour with zero tolerance for alcohol or drugs while driving and a minimum one-year prison term for anyone in violation of those laws would also save lives but would be politically impossible to pass, though they would be constitutional.

So, what causes us to be violent? A multitude of variables are related to violence, including physiological, psychological, and environmental factors. Some brain anomalies may impact violent behavior. Some psychological/behavioral traits may also be related to violence. A host of environmental factors may predispose one to violence. Everything from poverty to eating Twinkies to playing violent video games or watching violent entertainment programming to mental illness to being a victim of violence to drug abuse to access to firearms have been blamed for violent behavior. Disentangling all those possible causes is far beyond the scope of this book and, perhaps, beyond our current analytical capabilities. After decades of research, we are, at best, only moderately successful at predicting violent behavior.[8] It appears that there are many "causes" of violence, which vary from person to person. We are not much better at predicting suicide, although, again, many risk factors have been identified.[9]

In order to "treat" the violent tendencies, we must know their root cause. We may not, however, need to isolate causal factors in order to reduce violence. Obviously, we can prevent any person from injuring or killing another with a firearm if we can stop that person from accessing a gun.[10] In the same way, we can prevent a person from harming others if we isolate them. If incarcerated or detained, an individual can only harm those with whom they have contact; if isolated, then they cannot harm anyone, regardless of the source of their violent behavior. Selective incapacitation underlies much of the justification for lengthy prison sentences. Of course, this is implemented *after* the person has been convicted of a criminal act. Predicting who will be a criminal or who will be violent is very imprecise, and preventive incarceration or civil commitment of even sexual predators—who have high recidivism rates—violates our general sense of justice and, perhaps, the Constitution.

Similarly, preventing a person from accessing some means to commit suicide may reduce the number of suicides, although there is likely to be some method substitution. Again, we are only somewhat effective in predicting suicide attempts, typically *after* the individual has been in a treatment facility.

Few, if any, of us do not agree that those who have been convicted of a violent felony[11] or have been adjudicated as being a danger to themselves or others should be denied access to firearms. There may be disagreements regarding if, when, or how the right to possess a gun should be restored, but no one wants "dangerous people" to possess firearms.

Theoretically, we can put those people we identify as dangerous on a list and, through the use of comprehensive background checks, prevent them from gaining access to a gun. Practically, that is not a simple or easy task. Record keeping and reporting, particularly for mental health, is very poor, and many people who need help do not seek it or get it. In addition, privacy laws prevent many of their records from being made public, so many of the people who are dangerous do not appear on any list anywhere.

If we wish to reduce the death toll from mass shooters, then we may adopt policies that restrict the size of magazines, and we may ban various types of firearms that permit rapid fire. Such semiautomatic firearms are quite popular today, both long guns and handguns, so those bans produce protracted and difficult legislative struggles. We must also bear in mind that mass shootings constitute only a very small percentage of gun-related deaths. Therefore, even if we were able to eliminate all "assault rifles" and the deaths they cause, we would barely make a dent in the number of annual deaths in the United States.

Of course, there is no policy that will eliminate crime, suicide, or lethal violence, but that does not mean that no policy will reduce crime or violence. We should evaluate existing and potential policies by examining their feasibility, impact, cost, unintended consequences, and their ability to withstand constitutional challenges. Whether a policy makes people *feel good*, in this analysis, is of some but very little consequence.

In that context, several facts and basic assumptions underlie what follows. There are over 300 million firearms in the United States today. Any policy enacted today may impact future production and sales, but the existing cache of firearms is unlikely to be impacted. It is inconceivable that a mandatory gun buyback would be enacted or that many owners would comply with that law. Certainly, some would for fear of the consequences of being caught in violation of the law, but others would not in defiance of what they saw as a violation of their rights. Criminals might see an opportunity here to create a larger black market for firearms and make greater profits from weapons they have or could procure. They would certainly not willingly turn them in to any governmental authority. In short, we can make it more difficult for people to obtain guns, but we cannot make it impossible.

We can also quickly dispense with some of the more extreme arguments on both sides of the debate. No constitutional protection is absolute. The First Amendment does not protect all types of speech nor every type of religious expression. The Second Amendment does not allow every person to purchase or possess any firearm they choose at any time. Many gun regulations are permissible under the Constitution; most gun bans are not. On the other side, we hear the argument that we are morally obligated to enact laws if they will save even one life. Under that theory, we would enact the draconian traffic rules outlined above and ban swimming pools, as well as swimming in the ocean and many other recreational activities, including visiting amusement parks. All of those would, without question, save lives.

Rather than engage in polemics that have no real purpose other than to promote a specific position and obscure the issue, we should look at the reality we face in the world and country in which we live.

WHO OWNS GUNS?

Gun ownership in the United States is difficult to determine because there is no national registry for guns or gun owners. Therefore, public opinion surveys are the best method to establish gun ownership rates. Different polls have reached different conclusions regarding trends in gun ownership.[12] The percentage of households with a gun has been estimated at between 34 percent and 44 percent. The trend in gun ownership may be steady or declining.[13]

Changing household demographics may contribute to this trend as the percentage of single-person households and female-headed households have increased. The fact that many people are purchasing their first gun at any point in time does not mean that the rate of ownership is rising. Households are regularly created as couples marry or cohabitate, children move out on their own, and marriages or partnerships dissolve. At the same time, households disappear through death, or children moving back in with parents or vice versa. In short, households are constantly in flux.

A recently conducted longitudinal analysis provides insight into the demographics of gun ownership. Gallup[14] aggregated six national surveys that asked about gun ownership from 2007 to 2012, including interviews with more than 6,000 adult Americans to provide an in-depth view of who owns guns in America. Overall, they found that 30 percent of Americans personally own a firearm, while another 14 percent live in a household with someone who does. As expected, men (45%) are three times as likely to own a gun as compared to women (15%). Regionally, residents of the South (38%) were most likely to own a firearm, and those in the East (21%) were least likely. More than a third of married adults

(37%) own a firearm compared to only 22 percent of those who are not married, although having children was not an important difference. Non-Hispanic whites (33%) outnumber both blacks (21%) and Hispanics (18%) in terms of gun ownership, and older Americans are more likely to own a gun than younger residents.

Notably, while Republican Party identification is associated with higher rates of gun ownership—38% versus 22% for Democrats—the statistical model shows party is a weaker predictor of gun ownership, once other factors are taken into account. In other words, higher rates of Republican gun ownership likely result more from the fact that men, Southerners, and married people tend to identify as Republicans than from something about being a Republican drawing one to owning a gun.

[T]he highest rate of gun ownership Gallup found among subgroups is for married Southern males. The greater influence of marital status than race is evident from the fact that married Southern males have higher gun ownership than white Southern males, and married men (of all races) are more likely to own a gun than white men (of all marital statuses). Also, the strong effect of gender is apparent from the preponderance of male subgroups near the top of the list of gun ownership, and female groups near the bottom. The lowest-ranked group is non-Southern unmarried women.[15]

A 2014 survey in Virginia had similar findings with regard to gun ownership. The urban Northern Virginia region had the lowest rate of gun ownership, while residents of the more rural regions were nearly twice as likely to have a gun in the household. Men were significantly more likely to report a firearm in the home, and ownership rates rose with age. Whites were almost twice as likely as blacks to report a gun in the household. In terms of politics, conservatives were more than twice as likely to have a gun than were liberals, and Republicans were almost twice as likely as Democrats. Education was not related to the presence of a gun, and income also had little impact, although the lowest income group had the lowest rate of reporting a gun in the household.[16]

FIREARMS IN THE UNITED STATES

There is somewhat of a consensus on the number of firearms in the United States, although that number is also an estimate. Several sources estimated the number of guns in the United States in 1994 at 192 million, including 65 million handguns, increasing to 242 million firearms overall and 72 million handguns in 1996. By 2000, the estimates were 259 million and 92 million, respectively; and by 2007, those numbers were 294 million and 106 million.[17] According to BATF reports, there were more than 8.5 million guns manufactured in the United States in 2012. After subtracting those that were exported, there were still about 8.3 million firearms available for purchase in that year. That represents a significant increase from 2011 (6.541 million), 2010 (5.47 million), and 2009 (5.222 million).[18] The number of background checks has also increased, from about 9 million in 1999 (that number was relatively steady through 2005) to 10 million in 2006, 14 million in 2009, 16.5 million in 2011, 19.6 million in 2012, and over 21 million in 2013.[19] The number of firearms in circulation today is certainly larger than 300 million. While the actual number is not known, there is no doubt that the number of firearms in the United States continues to grow rapidly. Whether that number is 290 million or 320 million is practically irrelevant.

Simple extrapolation to 2014 suggests that we will have seen an increase of almost 70 percent in the number of firearms in the United States in a 20-year period, with the growth in handguns almost that large. There has also been a significant increase in the number of AR-type rifles, commonly referred to as "assault rifles" during this period. Most of the new firearms are semiautomatic. That is true of the large majority of pistols, and semiautos are also a larger share of the rifle market as well.

Even if public opinion supported the idea and the political will existed to attempt to implement it, there is no effective way to eliminate all, or even most, guns currently in circulation. Of course, opinion does not support gun bans, and the Supreme Court has ruled that at least some bans are unconstitutional.

Any regulations will be circumvented by some gun owners, although circumvention is a reality with all laws. Many of those who would ignore firearms restrictions are not criminals per se. They are law-abiding gun owners who distrust the government. An example of this is opposition to laws that would require citizens to report stolen firearms within 24 or 48 hours. Many people see this as an innocuous requirement, which would help law enforcement track guns that are now, by definition, in the hands of criminals. It may also help the theft victims to recover their stolen property. For some gun owners, though, this is an opportunity for the government to learn that they own firearms, which could lead to registration or even, in the worst-case scenario, confiscation of their weapons.[20] While we do not know what percentage of gun owners fit into this category, we know this view is not uncommon.

As the number of firearms in circulation has increased dramatically, so has the number of Americans with concealed-carry permits. Over a period of 20 years, the number of citizens lawfully carrying concealed firearms has grown from fewer than 1 million to more than 8 million. Are all those gun-toting people likely to cause a new crime wave? Or are they simply law-abiding citizens who seek the opportunity to defend themselves and others? Anecdotal evidence notwithstanding, the latter seems to be a more accurate description.

> "I don't argue that there are no problems with [concealed-carry permit holders], but when you look at the data it's pretty hard to find any other group in the population that's as law-abiding as permitted gun carriers," says John Lott Jr., an economist and gun-rights advocate and author of "More Guns, Less Crime."
>
> "The type of person who's going to go through the process of getting a concealed-carry permit is not the kind of person you have to worry about," he says. "They're law-abiding citizens who have a lot to lose if they make a mistake."
>
> Statistics support Mr. Lott's assertion. The number of incidents in which concealed-gun carriers kill innocent people is a fraction of 1 percent of all gun-related homicides. In North Carolina, one of only a handful of states that reveals the identities of permit holders, 200 of the 240,000 concealed carriers (.08 percent) committed felonies of all types, including eight shooting deaths, in the five-year period ending in 2011. This compares with about 2.5 percent of voting-age Americans who have a felony rap sheet, according to The Sentencing Project.[21]

Regardless of how one analyzes the numbers, there are a large number of firearms in the United States, and many Americans own guns. An increasing number of citizens have permits to carry concealed weapons. In short, American firepower is growing.

GUN-RELATED DEATHS

According to FBI statistics and the Department of Justice, homicide has been declining in the United States for more than a decade (Table 3.1). Current rates match those from the early 1960s. The homicide rate more than doubled between 1962, when it was 4.6 per 100,000 residents, and a peak in 1980 of 10.2 per 100,000. The rate declined somewhat in the 1980s, but it peaked again at 9.8 per 100,000 in 1991. The rate then fell sharply to 4.7 per 100,000 in 2011.[22] Other violent crime also declined

Table 3.1 Homicide in the United States Criminal Firearm Violence, 1993–2011

Year	Total Fatal and Nonfatal Firearm Violence	Firearm Homicides	Nonfatal Firearm Victimizations[a]	Nonfatal Firearm Incidents[b]	Rate of Nonfatal Firearm Victimization[c]	All Violence Involving Firearms (percent)	All Firearm Violence That Was Homicide (percent)
1993	1,548,000	18,253	1,529,700	1,222,700	7.3	9.2	1.2
1994	1,585,700	17,527	1,568,200	1,287,200	7.4	9.3	1.1
1995	1,208,800	15,551	1,193,200	1,028,900	5.5	7.9	1.3
1996	1,114,800	14,037	1,100,800	939,500	5.1	7.9	1.3
1997	1,037,300	13,252	1,024,100	882,900	4.7	7.7	1.3
1998	847,200	11,798	835,400	673,300	3.8	7.0	1.4
1999	651,700	10,828	640,900	523,600	2.9	6.1	1.7
2000	621,000	10,801	610,200	483,700	2.7	7.3	1.7
2001	574,500	11,348	563,100	507,000	2.5	7.7	2.0
2002	551,800	11,829	540,000	450,800	2.3	7.4	2.1
2003	479,300	11,920	467,300	385,000	2.0	6.2	2.5
2004	468,100	11,624	456,500	405,800	1.9	6.9	2.5
2005	515,900	12,352	503,500	446,400	2.1	7.4	2.4

Year							
2006	627,200	12,791	614,400	2.5	552,000	7.4	2.0
2007	567,400	12,632	554,800	2.2	448,400	8.3	2.2
2008	383,500	12,179	371,300	1.5	331,600	6.0	3.2
2009	421,600	11,493	410,100	1.6	383,400	7.4	2.7
2010	426,100	11,078	415,000	1.6	378,800	8.6	2.6
2011[d]	478,400	11,101	467,300	1.8	414,600	8.2	2.3

[a] A victimization refers to a single victim that experienced a criminal incident.

[b] An incident is a specific criminal act involving one or more victims or victimizations.

[c] Per 1,000 persons age 12 or older.

[d] Preliminary homicide estimates retrieved from D. L. Hoyert and J. Q. Xu, "Deaths: Preliminary Data for 2011," *National Vital Statistics Reports* 61, no. 6 (2012).

Sources: Bureau of Justice Statistics, *National Crime Victimization Survey, 1993–2011;* and Centers for Disease Control and Prevention, National Center for Injury Prevention and Control, Web-Based Injury Statistics Query and Reporting System (WISQARS), 1993–2010. Retrieved March 2013 from http://www.cdc.gov/ncipc/wisqars.

significantly during this time, including nonfatal gun-related assaults. So, this was not a simple case of medical technology improving and saving lives that would have otherwise been lost. There was a real decline in violent crime in the United States, both gun-related and non-gun-related. The causes of this decline in the face of an ailing economy have yet to be fully explained.

Despite understandable, but disproportionate coverage from the news media, the notion that mass shootings have increased to epidemic proportions is disputed.[23] According to a Department of Justice Statistics report, while the percentage of homicides involving two victims has increased from 2.7 percent in 1980 to 3.7 percent in 2008, the percentage of homicides in which there are three or more victims remains below 1 percent, although it has increased slightly.[24]

Using a different measure—active shooters—Blair and Martaindale found that there were 84 such events in the decade from 2000 to 2010, with 37 of the incidents occurring in 2009 and 2010.[25] An analysis conducted by Gregg Lee Carter, using data compiled by *Mother Jones*, found the number of spree shootings was between 5 and 10 for four 4-year periods (1984–1988, 1989–1993, 1994–1998, and 1999–2003) before increasing to 13 in 2004–2008 and then spiking to 20 in 2009–2013.[26]

About two-thirds of homicide victims are killed with a firearm, a rate that has been relatively stable. The percentage of homicides in which a handgun was the primary weapon has declined slightly, while the percentage in which other firearms were used has increased slightly. Still, twice as many homicides involve a handgun as compared to other guns, and this is true of mass shootings as well as more common homicides. Size of the area in which one lives also impacts homicide rates. In the 1990s, rates were significantly higher in cities with a population of 1 million or more. By 2008, rates for cities sized 500,000–999,999 and those with populations between 250,000 and 499,999 slightly exceeded that for the largest cities. Smaller cities (population 100,000–249,999) consistently had the lowest rate. Rural areas generally had a slightly higher homicide rate than the smallest cities, but a smaller percentage of homicides in rural areas involve a firearm (just under 60% compared to about 75% in larger cities), and about half of those involved a firearm other than a handgun.[27]

Like gun ownership, homicide is not evenly distributed across the United States or among demographic groups. As seen in Table 3.2, young adults, males, and blacks are disproportionately victims of homicide. Those same groups are disproportionately offenders as well. Most of the homicides are committed within group, except for males killing females. Most homicides are also intraracial; fully 93 percent of black victims are killed by black offenders, while 84 percent of white victims are killed by white offenders. Most offenders are somehow acquainted with their victims, although that percentage has been slowly declining.[28] Without belaboring the point, the groups most likely to own a firearm are not the groups most likely to be either victims or killers. The exception, of course, is simply being male.

For more than a decade, the number of firearms in circulation has increased significantly, while both the homicide and crime rates have declined. These numbers make it difficult to make the case that more guns equals more homicides. One can argue that the decreases in homicides would have been greater if stronger gun regulations had been adopted, but it is barely plausible to argue that more guns in circulation cause more people to be murdered. The statistics simply do not support the argument. Even if gun ownership rates were steady or even declined slightly, that decline does not come close to matching the decline in homicides. Other factors such as demographic changes can come into play here, of course, but the basic facts remain.

Table 3.2   Victims and Offenders, by Demographic Group, 1980–2008

	Percent of Victims	Percent of Offenders	Percent of Population	Rate per 100,000 Victims	Rate per 100,000 Offenders
Total	100%	100%	100%	7.4	8.3
Age					
Under 14	4.8%	0.5%	20.0%	1.8	0.2
14–17	5.2%	10.6%	5.8%	6.6	15.0
18–24	24.4%	37.5%	10.6%	17.1	29.3
25–34	28.7%	28.0%	15.6%	13.7	14.9
35–49	22.8%	17.1%	21.1%	8.0	6.7
50–64	8.9%	4.9%	14.7%	4.5	2.7
65 or older	5.1%	1.6%	12.3%	3.1	1.1
Sex					
Male	76.8%	89.5%	48.9%	11.6	15.1
Female	23.2%	10.5%	51.1%	3.4	1.7
Race					
White	50.3%	45.3%	82.9%	4.5	4.5
Black	47.4%	52.5%	12.6%	27.8	34.4
Other*	2.3%	2.2%	4.4%	3.8	4.1

*Other race includes American Indians, Native Alaskans, Asians, Native Hawaiians, and other Pacific Islanders.
Source: Alexia Cooper and Erica L. Smith, "Homicide Trends in the United States, 1980–2008," Bureau of Justice Statistics, November 2011, http://www.bjs.gov/content/pub/pdf/htus8008.pdf.

There are competing philosophical arguments related to the possible impact of gun control on suicide. Because such a high percentage of suicides in the United States are the result of gunshots, one side argues that reducing the number of firearms would almost inevitably result in fewer suicides even if some of those who intended to use a firearm, but could not find one, would then use another means of suicide. The other camp suggests that method substitution would negate any reduction in firearm-related suicides.

There were 36,364 suicides in the United States in 2010, making it the tenth-leading cause of death nationwide among people 10 years or older. Firearms accounted for 19,392, or about 53 percent of that total. While the firearm homicide rate had declined from 7.0 per 100,000 in 1993 to 3.8 per 100,000 in 2000, and 3.6 per 100,000 in 2010, the suicide firearm rate declined from 7.3 to 5.9 per 100,000 between 1993 and 2000, but it had risen to 6.3 per 100,000 by 2010.[29] In short, both the number and rate of firearm deaths by suicide is larger than that of firearm-related homicides. Significant differences related to gender are evident in suicides, with males significantly more likely to use a firearm to take their own life.[30]

INTERNATIONAL COMPARISONS

Comparisons are frequently drawn between the United States and other developed nations. It is more valid to compare the United States to other developed nations rather than to all other countries. In any such comparison, one must attempt to compare countries that are more similar than dissimilar. Determining which nations are most like one another is difficult. Should we examine the types of governments in the nations, their economic systems and various economic measures, or their populations, specifically with regard to cultural and ethnic heterogeneity? Which of those factors are most important? How legitimate is the idea of American exceptionalism, and does it apply in the area of gun control?

Regardless of how one answers those queries, most people would agree that comparisons to other developed democracies are probably the most valid, while comparisons with developing nations have significantly less value. Certainly the history of firearms in the United States and their reference in the Constitution sets the United States apart from most, if not all, developed nations.

International comparisons are more often made by supporters of gun control, who point out that the United States has both a significantly higher homicide rate and higher rates of gun ownership and homicides with firearms than most of the peer nations.[31] "America has long reigned supreme in levels of violence among the developed nations of the world."[32] Gun-rights supporters occasionally cite the examples of Israel and Switzerland, which have higher rates of gun ownership than most other developed nations, but also have relatively low homicide rates. They also point to higher overall crime rates in other nations as evidence that guns help reduce crime.[33] The reader is free to place the appropriate value on Table 3.3 and to look at those nations most comparable to the United States.

As Table 3.3 clearly suggests, the homicide rate in the United States is more than twice that of any of the other countries in this list (except for Russia, whose rate is double that of the United States). Depending upon the source, the United States also has the highest or one of the highest percentages of households that have at least one firearm.

The correlation between private ownership of firearms and homicides (as well as suicides) using firearms is clear, indisputable, and in no

Table 3.3   Homicide Rate per 100,000 Population by Country and Percent Committed with Firearm

Country	2005 rate/ percentage	2010 rate/ percentage	2011 rate/ percentage	2012 rate/ percentage
Australia	1.3/13%	1.0/17%	1.1/17%	1.1
Austria	0.7/8%	0.6/9%	0.8/10%	0.9
Canada	1.8/36%	1.4/34%	1.5/29%	1.6
Denmark	1.0/21%	0.8/26%	0.8/34%	0.8
Finland	2.2/25%	2.2/12%	2.1/14%	1.6
France	1.6	1.1	1.2	1.0
Germany	1.0/24%	0.8	0.8	—
Israel	2.5	2.0	2.0	1.8
Italy	1.0	0.9	0.9	0.9
Japan	0.5	0.4	0.3	—
New Zealand	1.5/15%	1.0/16%	0.9/8%	0.9
Norway	0.7	0.6	2.2	—
Russia	—	10.1	9.6	9.2
Spain	1.2	0.8	0.8	0.8
Sweden	0.9	1.0/16%	0.9	0.7
Switzerland	1.0	0.7/25%	0.6/48%	—
United Kingdom	1.5	1.2/10%*	1.0/7%*	—
United States	5.6/61%	4.7/60%	4.7/59%	4.7

*Percent with firearms for England and Wales only; Scotland—2005 (37%), 2010 (54%), 2011 (58%)
Source: United Nations Office on Drugs and Crime, *Global Study on Homicide, 2013*.

way surprising. Causation is not as obvious. The non-gun-related homicide rate in the United States is higher than the overall rate in these other nations (again, except Russia). In other words, Americans kill Americans with means other than guns more often than residents of the other nations kill one another by all means—including guns. In short, the United States is a violent nation. It is virtually impossible to reach any other conclusion. Are we violent because we have too many guns? Do we have guns because we are violent? Are the two mostly unrelated, even if firearms help facilitate lethal violence? Once again, different people will offer very different answers to those very complex questions.

Would the homicide rate in the United States decline if we somehow removed most of the guns currently owned by civilians, both law-abiding and criminal? Of course. Would it be higher than the current non-gun-related rate? Yes, because without question, there would be some method substitution, and some homicides that are now prevented by the defensive use of guns would not be prevented. With the current number of firearms in circulation and constitutional protections, however, these are moot points. As stated elsewhere, it is neither politically feasible, logistically possible, nor constitutionally permissible to remove most guns from American homes. Whether one thinks that would be a wise or foolish policy is irrelevant.[34]

It is, of course, true that virtually all of those countries in Table 3.3 regulate firearms much more stringently than the United States. Most have owner-licensing and safe-storage requirements. Some feature training requirements prior to purchase of a gun and/or prohibit handgun ownership purely for protection. At the same time, the U.S. ranks no more than in the middle of these countries in suicide rate, although, again the gun-related suicide rate is much higher.[35] This statistic is rarely mentioned by gun-control supporters because it clearly suggests that method substitution is prevalent in suicides and that more guns do not necessarily lead to a higher suicide rate.

In addition, there should be little doubt that culture plays a role in both violence against others and in taking one's own life.[36] Those cultural patterns of behavior may be related to a group with which an individual identifies, or they may be part of a subculture. Like the individual psychology or psychopathy at work in some cases, the cultural norms and mores that impact violence are beyond the scope of this book. The intent here is not to assign "blame" for violent behaviors, but rather to argue that there are numerous factors beyond the presence or absence of firearms that impact violence.

THE POTENTIAL IMPACT OF STRICTER GUN LAWS

Whether stricter gun laws can reduce gun violence is, of course, the central question to be addressed. There are several important components to the response. While we know the number of lives taken with firearms, we do not know how many lives are saved. There is considerable debate regarding the latter. There is also the matter of the recreational uses of firearms and how they would be impacted by stricter laws. In addition, many shooting victims do not die, but there are costs associated with their treatment and potential disabilities. Policy makers should consider both the positive and negative impacts of any proposed policy and perform some type of calculation of the costs and benefits of the regulation as well as those associated with the activity itself.[37]

One big question is if criminals will obey gun laws. Gun-rights advocates often argue that criminals, by their very nature, are not rule-followers. Therefore, gun laws are irrelevant to them. Gun-control supporters suggest they might obey the law because not everything is black and white. Most people do not obey every law, nor do they disobey every law. This may better describe reality than a statement that criminals will not obey any law. Clearly, there are nuances here.

More savvy criminals will certainly obey some laws. For example, anyone who is smuggling contraband in a motor vehicle—liquor, drugs, humans, guns, etc.—will obey all traffic laws fastidiously in order to avoid being pulled over by police for a minor offense that would lead to an arrest for a much more serious charge. There is, however, less reason to expect that violent criminals would obey any law regarding firearms. Drug dealers and gang members need those guns as a part of their trade, and they will do what is necessary to procure them. That includes stealing the guns themselves or purchasing them on the black market. There should be little doubt that serious restrictions on guns would create an even larger black market than currently exists. While average- or low-income individuals may balk at those prices or not even know how to make the contacts, experienced criminals will have no problem locating weapons.

There is a disconnect on the part of both liberals and conservatives on the issue of black markets and circumvention of the law. For example, liberals argue that restrictions on abortion or drugs create a black market and force people underground without a significant impact on the number of abortions or illegal drugs, but they argue that restrictions on firearms would actually decrease the number of guns in circulation and make people safer. Conservatives, for their part, argue the opposite on all three. The argument advanced here is that a restriction on any of those activities does decrease the incidence to some extent, but it forces others underground, and those who want the item or service will find it. In the case of firearms, we need to ask who will locate them illegally, and who will obey the law and be disarmed. If only law-abiding citizens obey the laws and they are disarmed, or they are forced to jump numerous hurdles to obtain firearms, then what have we accomplished?[38]

There are also questions regarding compliance of law-abiding citizens with laws they may feel are unjust. For example, in 2013, Connecticut adopted laws requiring the registration of most semiautomatic rifles and large-capacity magazines. The estimated rate of compliance by the deadline was extremely low—possibly as low as 15 percent for rifles. The rate for magazine registration was thought to be even less. While some of the failure to comply may have been related to ignorance of the requirement, there seemed little doubt that some was due to intentional noncompliance. One state legislator said, "I honestly thought from my own standpoint that the vast majority would register. If you pass laws that people have no respect for and they don't follow them, then you have a real problem." The legislator was told by a constituent that many of the constituent's friends were not complying. "He made the analogy to Prohibition. I said, 'You're talking about civil disobedience,' and he said 'Yes.' "[39]

CONCEALED CARRY

"More guns, less crime" is not only the title of a book, it is also a rallying cry for gun-rights supporters. John Lott made the first attempt to conduct an academic study of the impact of concealed-carry laws.[40] He used complex statistical techniques and examined a large amount of data, concluding that more lenient concealed-carry laws have a deterrent effect, reducing most types of violent crime. Lott's work was immediately attacked by pro-control groups.[41]

Early academic challenges to Lott were numerous and varied.[42] They focused on methodological points and potential coding errors that could have affected the results. Lott responded to these charges with varying degrees of success in the second edition of his book.[43] Later substantive criticisms of Lott were more serious.[44] These responses also focused on the methodology employed by Lott, and they extended his analysis to include other variables and additional data. They corrected some coding errors and demonstrated that the inclusion or exclusion of a single variable, one that may seem to be unrelated to the crime rate, can affect the results. In a humble, uncommon, and welcome recognition of the limits of quantitative analysis, Donohue, one of Lott's most serious academic critics, concludes that it is not possible, at present, to determine if shall-issue laws increase, decrease, or have no effect on crime rates.[45]

With a relatively small percentage of the populace having a permit to carry concealed weapons in any state, the deterrent effect of such legislation is probably minimal. There is little doubt that those who have concealed-carry permits are a very law-abiding group of citizens. The increasing number of citizens who obtain permits may increase whatever deterrent effect currently exists.

Gun-rights supporters also argue for a general deterrence effect of gun owning. Theoretically, this benefit should accrue to all members of society, assuming that (1) criminals have some fear of confronting an armed victim and may avoid a situation in which they believe the potential victim is armed, and (2) criminals know that they cannot accurately predict which potential victim may be armed. As anecdotal evidence, we may point to the relatively low rates of "hot burglaries," that is, a burglary in which someone is in the house, in rural areas and other places where gun ownership is relatively high.[46] Hot-burglary rates are also lower in the United States than in many other developed nations with lower rates of gun ownership.

Perhaps the best evidence for deterrence comes from the Wright and Rossi survey of convicted felons. Among the felons who reported committing a violent crime or a burglary, 42 percent said they had encountered an armed victim, 38 percent claimed they had been scared off, shot at, wounded, or captured by an armed victim, and 43 percent reported not committing a crime they had planned because they knew or thought the victim was carrying a gun.[47] More recent research suggests that while some criminals say they would be deterred by a victim who may be carrying a weapon, others think that they would simply be forced to increase their own firepower in order to accomplish their task. This could, then, increase violence.[48] Still, even pro-gun scholar Gary Kleck can find little direct evidence of a deterrent effect.[49] He does, however, suggest that anecdotal evidence of deterrence does exist and that studies have not disproved the hypothesis.

Much of the political debate regarding concealed carry in the past decade has focused on where those with permits should be allowed to carry their firearms. Restaurants/bars, public buildings, schools, and churches are most commonly off limits for those carrying concealed firearms. College campuses have also been in the discussion. The thrust of the gun-rights argument is twofold. First, those with permits should be allowed to carry anywhere because the threat of attack is everywhere. No one suggests drinking and shooting, so those who carry should abstain from alcohol, but they should be allowed to carry. Second, most of the mass shootings in the past decade have taken place in so-called "gun-free zones." By designating such areas, it is essentially advertising an area where one can open fire on large numbers of people with no fear of armed resistance. Of course, those opposed to concealed carry argue that those places should be free of firearms so that people can dine, socialize, worship, or learn without fear of being shot. Allowing concealed carry would only increase the risk of someone being injured or killed.

One of the lynchpins in the discussion of the utility of various gun-control strategies is the question of defensive gun use. While it is well established that guns are used in the commission of various crimes, the question of how frequently an individual uses a firearm to prevent a crime and the general deterrent value of firearms is less well known. This question will be discussed as part of the review of the public health literature.

THE PUBLIC HEALTH APPROACH TO FIREARMS

Much of the research on gun control has been conducted by social scientists—criminologists, sociologists, and political scientists, as well as a few economists and law professors. As can be seen throughout this book, there is significant disagreement among social scientists regarding the potential impact and policy wisdom of stricter forms of gun control. Regardless of their views, the vast majority of the researchers in this area share the social scientific approach to the study of firearms. While their findings and conclusions are often very different, they share a research paradigm.

Another group of researchers is also involved in the study of the impact of guns and gun control. Most of these researchers are in the medical field, and their perspective, typically referred to as the public health approach, is similar to that taken with regard to diseases and other health hazards. They tend to view guns as an unsafe product and firearm-related deaths as a public health problem, not a criminological problem.[50] Much of their research was funded by the Centers for Disease Control (CDC) until 1996 when Congress cut CDC funding by $2.6 million, arguing that the money was being used primarily to promote a gun-control agenda. This is not surprising insofar as the vast majority of the research funded by the CDC concluded that guns were a health hazard and should be significantly restricted. Most of the public health research concludes that guns in the home are quite dangerous and that stricter gun control would lead to fewer accidental shootings, homicides, and suicides. While the flow of money for research was not completely shut off in 1996, the focus and the process were shifted.

While the CDC financing for research on gun violence has not actually stopped completely, it is currently limited to research where firearms are treated only as a component of a broader problem. The CDC asks researchers it funds to give it a heads-up whenever they publish studies related to firearms and, as a courtesy, typically relays this information to the NRA. As a result of the CDC's sensitivity to controversy, the number of public health researchers who study gun-related issues has fallen off dramatically, a circumstance that disturbs this research community.[51]

One of the major contributions of the field is the discussion of suicide, which is somewhat lacking in the social scientific literature. At the same time, there has been and continues to be much criticism of the public health approach and the research it has produced. One of the leading scholars in this field has described the public health approach as follows:

> Since the mid-1980s, it has become increasingly recognized that the most promising approach to reduce firearm injury is to emphasize prevention, focus on the community, use a broad array of policies, and bring together diverse interest groups. This approach is proactive rather than reactive, is pragmatic rather than doctrinaire, and has a distinguished history of success in addressing problems that affect the public's health ... [T]he public health community recognizes that advocacy, based on sound scientific evidence, is essential for securing gains in social justice as well as health, well-being, and the quality of life.[52]

In 1992, Surgeon General Antonia Novello wrote an editorial in the *Journal of the American Medical Association*, referring to violence as a public health emergency and urging doctors to take a leading role in an antiviolence movement. Some physicians and others in the health care field heeded the call. As a result, the public health literature is much more of a blend of research and advocacy than the social scientific research.[53]

Some of the basic premises of the public health approach are quite logical. Firearms are clearly more lethal than most other weapons. They facilitate the killing of self or others, and they provide a surer means of accomplishing that than most other weapons. They allow killing from a distance. There is no question that firearms are inherently dangerous.

Gun safety is stressed on shooting ranges and while hunting, and should be paramount within the household.

The public health literature fails to see much benefit of gun ownership. Their studies consistently find that firearms in the household are much more likely to be used intentionally to harm another person or in a suicide attempt, or to be involved in an accidental shooting, than they are to be used in self-defense. They tend to cite other public health studies and pay little attention to research that may contradict their findings. These studies generally treat all deaths related to firearms in similar fashion in the sense that they are all preventable deaths.

With regard to guns in the household, the findings are almost unanimously negative. For example, a recent article written by one of the leading experts in the field summarized the "scientific literature" on the subject and provided one example when a firearm in the household might be useful. This would occur in a scenario similar to the one in the film *Mad Max*, when it was necessary for survivors of the apocalypse to defend against "predominantly psychopathic male bikers." Hemenway concluded:

> However, for most contemporary Americans, the scientific studies suggest that the health risk of a gun in the home is greater than the benefit. There are no credible studies that indicate otherwise. The evidence is overwhelming that a gun in the home is a risk factor for completed suicide and that gun accidents are most likely to occur in homes with guns. There is compelling evidence that a gun in the home is a risk factor for intimidation and for killing women in their homes, and it appears that a gun in the home may more likely be used to threaten intimates than to protect against intruders. On the potential benefit side, there is no good evidence of a deterrent effect of firearms or that a gun in the home reduces the likelihood or severity of injury during an altercation or break-in.[54]

The field was in its infancy when in 1975, four Cleveland physicians published an article concluding that guns kept in the household were "more dangerous than useful" and that owning a gun was an ineffective way to protect against crime.[55] They found there were six times as many fatal gun accidents in the homes that had a gun than criminals killed with those guns. One of the important researchers in this field, and perhaps the most frequently cited, concluded that for every time a gun kept in the home was effectively used in self-defense, there were slightly more accidental deaths, nearly five times as many criminal homicides, and 37 gun-related suicides.[56] A subsequent study found that guns in the home were four times more likely to be involved in an accident, seven times more likely to be used in a criminal assault or homicide, and 11 times more likely to be used in an attempted or completed suicide than to be used to injure or kill in self-defense.[57]

The major problem with these studies is how defensive gun use (DGU) is measured. For Kellermann, the only effective defensive use of a gun is if the intruder is shot and killed. If the potential assailant is scared away by a firearm or merely wounded, then that does not count. With that measuring stick, it is not surprising that he found that guns in the home were so dangerous. While measuring defensive gun use is very difficult, most would agree that it is not necessary to kill someone to prevent a crime with a firearm.[58] These studies and others have been roundly criticized for their methodology as well as for their unwillingness to always share their data, a hallmark of sound academic research. In addition, Kellermann has been criticized for misrepresenting the work of others.[59]

Following the publication of the early studies in public health, the debate expanded to the criminology literature and focused on the annual number of defensive gun uses—that is, the number of crimes prevented by firearms. The estimated annual DGUs ranges from a low of 65,000[60] to a high of 2.5 million.[61] The tremendous disparity in the estimates results from the method used to calculate the estimate.

For McDowall and Wiersema as well as for many other pro-control scholars, including Cook and Ludwig,[62] the estimates are based on the National Crime Victimization Survey (NCVS), a U.S. Bureau of Justice Statistics survey that interviews between 40,000 and 60,000 households every six months over a three-year period. Respondents who report being the victim of a crime are asked if they "did anything" with the idea of protecting themselves while the crime was occurring. Those who do not report being a victim are not asked if they prevented a crime from happening. The NCVS data undoubtedly underestimate the number of defensive gun uses. Anyone who prevented a crime from occurring would not report a crime and, therefore, would not be asked if they did anything to protect themselves. Others, such as criminals who fought off an attack by a fellow criminal, might have an incentive to lie.[63]

The highest estimates of DGUs were obtained by Kleck and Gertz in a 1993 survey of 4,977 adults that was specifically designed to determine the number of defensive gun uses. They asked if anyone in the household had used a gun, even if it was not fired, for self-protection or to protect property at home, work, or elsewhere.[64] They estimated between 1 million and 2.5 million annual DGUs, but they suggest the higher estimate is more accurate because several factors at work might cause underreporting of a defensive gun use.

Smith suggests that the true number of DGUs lies between the high estimate of Kleck and Gertz and the low estimate of Hemenway.[65] He agrees with Kleck and Gertz that the NCVS estimates are low because that survey only includes DGUs as a victim's response to specific crimes. Second, it does not ask directly about DGUs, a survey technique that almost certainly results in underreporting of a behavior. He agrees with Hemenway that the Kleck and Gertz survey overestimates DGUs and that sampling error may be an issue in their work. Smith asserts that making adjustments to both estimates would bring them closer together and yield an estimate somewhere around 1 million annual DGUs.

In a logical, cogent, and reasonable analysis of this work, informed by decades of personal experience in law enforcement, Vizzard, like Smith, states that the actual number of DGUs is most likely somewhere between the low and high estimates.[66] The National Institute of Justice (NIJ) sponsored a survey in 1994 with a questionnaire designed by Kleck, Cook, and Hemenway.[67] The methodology employed in this survey was slightly different than that used by Kleck and Gertz, and it produced a lower figure. This NIJ survey suggested that the annual number of DGUs is approximately 1.3 million.

Following the reasoning of avoiding the danger of having a gun in the household for self-defense, another leading researcher in the public health field counsels readers that baseball bats, clubs, and knives are also useful weapons. "A household without a firearm is not an unarmed household or one incapable of defending itself."[68]

In addition to the dangers of a gun in the household, children should never be taught gun safety. "Rather than trying to teach all children about gun safety (which may just increase their curiosity and interest in guns), many pediatricians and public health and child advocates believe we should target parents, teaching them how to prevent firearms injuries."[69] It is interesting that teaching children about gun safety "may just increase their curiosity and interest in guns," which is inherently a bad idea. Yet, many if not most medical professionals argue that providing children with appropriate sex education will not lead them to experiment with sex at a younger age. It is not illogical to think that what holds for one should also hold for the other.[70] Of course, the idea here is to keep children away from firearms; hence convincing the parents of the potential risks of gun ownership is a sound policy from the public health perspective.

Similarly, the public health literature encourages physicians to ask their patients if they have firearms at home and to counsel them regarding the dangers to them and their children. For many gun-rights advocates, this practice goes beyond the proper role of a physician and treads on their personal rights. Safe-storage laws are also strongly advocated.[71] Another idea that has become more popular in some areas is to have parents ask other parents if there are any guns in the household to help in determining if they think it safe for their children to be in the neighbor's home. That is certainly the prerogative of any parent in the same fashion as a parent may choose not to allow their children to visit a neighbor who has a swimming pool or a pet they consider to be dangerous.

The policy prescriptions that emerge from the public health literature are mostly predictable. Firearms should be regulated as consumer products in order to be made safer. The government entity in charge of firearm regulation—either a very beefed-up ATF or a new agency—should be given the power to require "safety and crime-fighting characteristics" on all firearms manufactured or sold in the United States, the power to "ban from regular civilian use certain products that are not needed for protection and endanger the public," and the authority to also regulate ammunition.[72] In addition, there should be a system of universal background checks, and all sales should be made at licensed retail premises, thus eliminating gun shows and any purely private sales. Recognizing that many crime guns are purchased on the secondary market, Hemenway concludes "The problem lies not only with scofflaw dealers but with the entire secondary market, including gun shows and other private transfers."[73] A major problem not recognized here is that many, if not most, of those private transfers of *crime guns* are conducted on the black market with stolen weapons or from straw purchasers who could pass any background check.[74]

Further, the public health literature argues, there should be a one-gun-per-month national restriction to cut down on gun-running. All crime guns should be traced. All violent misdemeanants as well as felons should be prevented from purchasing a firearm. All gun owners should be licensed by the government, and there should be a national gun registry. A waiting period of unspecified length should be required for any gun purchase. Gun owners should be held legally liable if a juvenile accesses an improperly stored gun. Taxes on firearms and ammunition should be increased to help defray the costs associated with gun violence. "Gun carrying laws should give police discretion to prohibit gun carrying by persons they believe to be dangerous to the community."[75]

Others would like to see an expansion of the types of people who are disqualified from legally purchasing a firearm. For example, those individuals with two or more convictions for drug- or alcohol-related offenses in any three-year period should be disqualified from gun ownership for 10 years, the age for handgun purchase or possession should be raised to

21, and those with one or more serious juvenile offenses (records that are typically sealed) should be prevented from purchasing until they reach the age of 30.[76] These "reasonable" gun regulations go far beyond those proposed by the most ardent supporters of gun control in Congress and in the vast majority of states as well.

SUICIDES AND MENTAL ILLNESS

While the Newtown and other recent mass shootings have focused a great deal of attention on mental illness and gun violence, both mental illness and suicide remain understudied topics. Reporting of mental illness to the National Instant Criminal Background System (NICS) system has been sporadic, at best, with many states reporting no records at all. There is little agreement regarding exactly who should be disqualified from purchasing a firearm, and any reporting of mental illness raises issues of privacy and possible discouragement of those who need treatment from seeking it.

A recent study in Connecticut examined those who had been deemed to have a serious mental illness, records reported to NICS, and their incidences of violence. This included over 23,000 people who had a serious mental illness—diagnosis of schizophrenia, bipolar disorder, or major depressive disorder and hospitalization in a state psychiatric hospital—and who was in the state's mental health or criminal justice databases. A violent crime conviction was used as a proxy for gun violence.[77]

About 40 percent of the sample was disqualified from a firearm purchase at some point during the study, most for a criminal violation (only 7% for mental health issue alone). The large majority (94%) of those who were convicted of a violent crime were never involuntarily committed to an institution or disqualified for a mental health record. During the eight years of the study, fully 39 percent of the group was convicted of a violent crime. Having a gun-disqualifying record actually increased the chances of that person committing a violent offense in the future (of course, that offense may not have been gun-related). "[V]iolent crime was associated with having a substance abuse disorder, being younger, male, of African-American or Hispanic background, and having bipolar disorder versus depression. These tend to be factors associated with crime in the population without mental disorders."[78] They found little evidence that background checks reduced violent crime, largely because there are many other sources of guns in addition to Federal Firearms Licensees (FFLs).

Regarding suicide, they found that a majority of the subjects had identified mental health problems and a history of some treatment. " 'How did

they get a gun?' is an important question to answer. 'Where was the treatment, and why did it fail?' may be even more important."[79] Depression is
the mental illness most strongly associated with suicide, but that diagnosis
is not sufficient to have one involuntarily committed to a mental health
facility or disqualified from purchasing a firearm.

Certainly not everyone who is depressed is suicidal, and reporting all suicide threats may lead to fewer people seeking treatment. "Arguably, though,
better access to evidence-based treatment for depression . . . might prevent
more firearm fatalities than would relying solely on improved NICS reporting to keep guns out of the hands of dangerous people."[80]

Most other studies of suicide and firearms in the public health literature
have, not surprisingly, found very strong links between access to firearms
and suicide. They acknowledge that it is difficult to identify those who are
likely to attempt suicide, but several studies found links between a gun in
the household and suicide, and they found higher suicide rates in states
with higher levels of gun ownership.[81] For example, one study found that
individuals with a family history of a handgun purchase were more likely
than a control group to commit suicide. Even though the study had limitations, "it did seem to show that the higher risk for gun purchasers could
not be fully explained by victims buying guns to commit suicide." This
risk for suicide remained higher after five years and held even if it was
another family member who purchased the firearm.[82] Even when noting
that the U.S. suicide rate is about average among developed nations,
Hemenway suggests that firearm availability may explain higher suicide
rates among American youth.

THE CONSEQUENCES OF RESTORING CDC FUNDING
FOR GUN RESEARCH

Most gun-control researchers would like to see increased funding for
gun research and better tracking of gun homicides and injuries as well as
tracing of guns used in crimes. Regardless of one's perspective, if you
truly believe that your approach and conclusions are correct, then they
will only be borne out by more objective and thorough research. Research
funding must be distributed in an evenhanded fashion, though, so that all
sides of the question can be investigated.

The public health approach to gun research would certainly flourish
under renewed and unfettered CDC funding. That was true in the past,
and there is little doubt it would be true in the future. When President
Obama issued the executive order in January 2013 directing various agencies, including the CDC, to investigate the causes, impact, and possible

prevention of gun violence, the wheel was set in motion. How far Congress will allow that wheel to turn remains in doubt. Funding the CDC is still within the purview of Congress, and now the agency has mixed directives, so the research may proceed slowly.[83]

At the request of the CDC, the Institutes of Medicine formed a committee to outline a research agenda. The group identified 13 priorities under five major topics: (1) characteristics of firearms violence; (2) risk and protective factors; (3) firearms violence prevention and other interventions; (4) impact of gun safety technology; and (5) video games and other media.[84] How these priorities might influence the type of research conducted or its conclusions is not certain. It is clear, though, that there is a certain amount of skepticism attached to CDC-sponsored research. Everyone should agree that it is unfortunate, because more objective research on firearms and gun violence is needed.

POLICY MAKING AND GUN CONTROL

Several distinct theories and models may be used to describe and explain public policy and policy making. The "garbage can model," which was developed by Cohen, March, and Olson and adapted by Kingdon into "streams" theory, best fits gun-control policy.[85] He describes three distinct streams of issues, politics, and actors. Kingdon first identifies problem streams as issue definition and policy proposals. Issues are typically framed by the media and interest groups, and policy proposals emerge from those particular frames. Second, the political stream consists of numerous actors—elected officials, bureaucrats, congressional and presidential staff, academics, interest groups, and researchers—who help set the governmental agenda. Third are the policy streams, which are defined by actors who help shape specific policy proposals. These include preferences expressed by citizens, interest groups, and governmental officials in forms such as the general national mood, more specific public opinion, elections, partisan politics in Washington, and interest group lobbying.

The primordial policy soup contains both problems and solutions, although it can be difficult to know which comes first. There are problems in need of a solution, and there are solutions (and individuals and groups advocating those solutions) in search of a problem. When the problem, political, and policy streams converge, we can see new policies adopted or existing policies modified.

This merging typically results in the opening of a policy window. Windows can open predictably, such as with newly elected officials taking office and possible changes in political party control following an election. Others causes, such as budgeting, occur cyclically. Still others happen in response to a significant event or a crisis. It is also possible that a policy window can be opened by a person with disproportionate influence in the policy-making process, such as a president or a governor.[86]

Restrictions on firearms are typically adopted when a policy window has been opened due to a crisis or a trigger event. Virtually all of the major pieces of gun-control legislation that have been passed by Congress were adopted in response to a crime wave or a trigger event such as a political assassination or a mass shooting. Gun control is less likely to change on a regular schedule, although the change in administrations from Bill Clinton to George W. Bush to Barack Obama had clear implications for gun policy. During more quiescent times, it is difficult to pass stricter laws. During those periods, we typically see few gun laws at all, or we may see incremental advances by gun-rights supporters. For example, the decade leading up to the Newtown shootings was characterized by slow but steady movement in the direction of gun rights in most states and nationally.

TYPES OF FIREARMS REGULATIONS

Regulations regarding firearms come in several different forms. They can be categorized as follows: (1) laws preventing certain categories of people from purchasing or owning firearms; (2) laws restricting the types of firearms that may be legally sold; (3) gun safety and carry regulations; (4) market regulations; and (5) criminal justice system responses.

Restrictions on Who May Purchase/Own Guns

Some of the earliest gun laws in the United States prohibited African Americans from possessing firearms.[87] By the twentieth century, many states had abandoned race as a means of classification and adopted individual status. For example, many states made it illegal for convicted felons to carry concealed weapons.[88] Eventually, most states and the federal government adopted laws that established a minimum age for purchasing a firearm and prohibited possession by convicted felons, those with a history of drug abuse, and those with certain types of mental disabilities.

The primary method of enforcement of these laws is the background check, which must be conducted prior to the sale of a firearm by someone who holds a federal firearms license. This background check was mandated nationally with the passage of the Brady Bill in 1993, but many states already had such requirements in place at that time.

At the national level, these laws only restrict transfers from a FFL. Private citizens, although they may not legally sell a firearm to someone in a restricted class, are not required to process a background check whether they sell from their home or at a gun show. This is often referred to as the "gun-show loophole." Some states require more comprehensive background checks.

Expanded background checks have become the cause célèbre for gun control advocates in recent years. There were numerous calls for closing the "gun-show loophole" following the Virginia Tech shootings, and those calls were intensified after the tragedy at Newtown. The push after Newtown was to extend background checks to all firearms transactions, not just at gun shows.[89] The argument in favor of universal background checks is that they will prevent those who should not have guns from obtaining them. Anyone who is legally permitted to possess a firearm would pass the check and be able to make the purchase.

In theory, it is difficult to oppose this regulation, as is evidenced by the strong support it received in public opinion polls. The arguments against these regulations are: (1) they would not prohibit anyone not on a restricted list from purchasing a firearm, and few of the perpetrators of mass shootings were on any such list; (2) they create significant obstacles to private transactions among people who do not have ready access to a FFL who can perform the check and will increase the costs of a firearms purchase; (3) they will lead to other restrictions such as permits, licensing, or a national gun registry; and (4) criminals will not obey the laws but will illegally purchase firearms on the black market.

The efficacy argument against checks is strong. Adam Lanza and Sung Hui Cho, the Newtown and Virginia Tech shooters, would not have been prevented from obtaining guns. Cho, in fact, twice passed background checks and abided by the one-handgun-per-month law in effect in Virginia at the time. Lanza took the guns from his mother, who had passed background checks and had them registered in Connecticut, a state with comparatively strict gun laws. Expanded checks would add to the cost of a purchase, though that cost is often about the same as sales tax paid on guns purchased at gun shops. They would be a significant obstacle for people who live in rural areas with few FFLs to conduct checks. Any firearms sold on the black market, whether stolen (about 1.4 million firearms were stolen between 2005 and 2010[90]) or purchased for resale by "straw purchasers" would avoid such checks. Whether or not they would lead to other restrictions is a point of great contention. No one can say for certain.

Restrictions on Types of Firearms That May be Sold or Possessed

Legislatures may pass laws that prohibit anyone from possessing or selling a certain type of firearm. An example of this type of regulation is the 1994 Assault Weapons Ban, which prohibited the sale of new weapons and the manufacture of a large number of semiautomatic firearms. Restrictions on the capacity of magazines for semiautomatic weapons are also included in this category.

The greatest difficulties with such laws lie in defining firearms that are covered and the number of firearms already in the marketplace. The terms that are commonly used, such as assault weapons, do not correspond to a particular weapon. They describe broad categories such as "military style" semiautomatic rifles. These somewhat vague descriptions make it difficult to effectively implement the law because it is not obvious which weapons are included in the ban. For example, the Assault Weapons Ban prohibited the sale of firearms that had certain physical characteristics, but other guns that functioned almost identically but looked slightly different were still legal.[91] In order for a law to be effective, it must be more specific than that. With regard to magazines, size does matter, but a person who is proficient with a rifle would "lose" only a second or two changing three 10-round magazines as opposed to having a 30-round magazine. Smaller magazines are also slightly less likely to jam.

The number of firearms already in the marketplace may also reduce the potential positive impact of gun restrictions. Again, the Assault Weapons Ban did not touch existing stock, and increased sales between passage of the law and its implementation date meant that there were plenty of such firearms available to those who wanted one, although the price did increase. The number of firearms that can be purchased at one time may also be restricted. For example, Virginia legislators voted in 1993 to permit citizens to purchase only one handgun per month in response to charges that the state was a haven for gun runners to Washington, D.C., and New York City, but the law was repealed in 2012.

Gun Safety and Carry Regulations

This category includes a large number of regulatory schemes, such as laws that specify safety features that a gun must have. This could be a trigger lock, a light indicator when the firearm is loaded, and fingerprint recognition so the gun could be fired only by its owner. Safe storage of firearms can also be mandated. Requiring that guns be kept unloaded and locked in a gun cabinet or safe and that access by children be restricted are examples of this type of law.

Laws regarding carrying concealed weapons also fall under this heading. The laws of individual states vary—from allowing anyone to carry concealed; to requiring a permit, which may be relatively easy or difficult to obtain; to outright prohibition. Similarly, gun possession on school property or in public buildings is commonly prohibited.

The largest issues surrounding safety regulations are their effectiveness, whether those who own a gun for personal protection can still gain quick access to the firearm, and the added cost to the purchase price. Many gun owners, however, support the addition of such safety devices and willingly pay the additional cost. Gun-safety measures primarily target accidental shootings, which are relatively uncommon.

Described as "a dream for gun control advocates for decades," smart gun technology was introduced to the market in early 2013. The Armatrix iP1 is a .22 caliber pistol that includes electronic chips located in a handgun and a watch that the user must wear. When the watch is within a certain range of the gun, then the gun will fire. When the watch is out of that range, the gun will not function. The system is designed to prevent unauthorized access to the gun by children or thieves. The gun would clearly appeal to some consumers, but not to others.[92]

While many were enthusiastic about the possibilities, there were, of course fears from others—on both sides. Some gun-control advocates worried that people would be led to think that guns were now "safe," and that might increase the number of gun owners. Some gun-rights advocates were concerned about potential failures in the technology that would make the gun inoperable, and possible access by others who may need the gun for protection but might not have access to the watch. There was also concern that this could lead to the government banning all firearms that did not have the technology.[93] Simply offering the technology to consumers did not seem to be a problem, so long as it was not mandatory.

The response from some quarters, however, was swift and negative. The California gun shop and shooting range that offered the gun received such negative comments on social networks and online forums that it completely backed away from the gun, going so far as to deny that it was ever involved and removing any trace of the firearms from the premises.[94]

When introduced, the gun retailed for $1,399, and the watch cost an additional $399. A comparable pistol without the technology would cost about $300–$400. Certainly, the cost would be prohibitive to most consumers, but the cost would probably decrease as is typical when a technology becomes more developed. How many gun owners would prefer such a firearm was not immediately clear, with conflicting surveys suggesting it might be as low as 14 percent or as high as 59 percent.

Registration, Licensing, and Other Market Regulations

Another strategy to reduce gun ownership and facilitate criminal investigations is to require that all firearms be registered with the state. Under a registration policy, the state would maintain a list of all legal owners of firearms sold in the state. A crime gun that is recovered could then be traced back to its legal owner.

Some control advocates have suggested that owners be licensed, similar to the system we use to certify automobile drivers. Applicants would have to pass a test and would probably have to renew their license and be tested in the future. Advocates argue this would increase gun safety. Opponents fear that this could lead to gun confiscation, since the government would know who owns firearms.

Other ways to regulate the market include taxes on firearms or ammunition, licensing of firearm dealers, and waiting periods. If taxes are sufficiently high, then they might drive some potential customers out of the market. Licensing of dealers may be strict or lax in terms of defining exactly what constitutes a dealer versus a private seller. Like taxes, high fees can keep some from registering as dealers or renewing their license. Waiting periods are designed to prevent spur-of-the moment shootings and suicide attempts or decrease the number of firearms sold by increasing the inconvenience to purchasers.

"Ballistic fingerprinting" was once thought to be the future in gun control and crime solving. It is based on the premise that each firearm leaves a unique set of marks on bullets after it has been fired. This technology is used to compare bullets from different crime scenes to see if the crimes are linked. Anyone who has watched a few crime programs on television is generally familiar with this technique. It is argued that if the government had a bullet from every gun, then the bullets could be traced back to the gun from which they were fired. A National Academy of Sciences report found that the method was not sufficiently accurate and recommended against establishing a federal ballistic database.[95] All of the strategies mentioned to this point are strongly favored by gun-control groups and are almost universally opposed by gun-rights groups.

Criminal Justice System Responses

There are three primary methods of using the criminal justice system to try to reduce gun violence. The most common is a sentence enhancement for gun-related crimes. A specific amount of time, usually two or three years, is added to the sentence of any felon who used a firearm in the commission of the crime. The second method is to use the police to crack down on illegal gun carrying or to increase patrols in high-crime areas. The first tactic increases patrols and also instructs police to be extra vigilant with regard to someone who might be carrying a firearm. The second simply increases the number of patrols in high-crime areas, most often during peak hours for crime. Third, those people who are prevented from purchasing a gun through background checks are, in some cases, prosecuted for that illegal act. As we shall see, such prosecutions are very rare.

Criminal justice responses, particularly enhanced sentences, are strongly favored by gun-rights groups such as the NRA. They see this as a way of preventing gun crime by punishing those who commit crimes while protecting the rights of law-abiding citizens.

STATE GUN CONTROL LAWS

The United States is a federal system of government in which the states and the national government share power. The origins of this system date to the founding of the nation. The Federalists argued for a stronger central government, while the Anti-Federalists were concerned about the ability of a strong government to tyrannize its citizens. They preferred a weaker national government and stronger state governments.

We generally think that the Federalists won the debate in that the national government is supreme, because federal law trumps state law if or when there is a conflict. Similarly, states may not enact legislation that violates the U.S. Constitution. Yet, the Anti-Federalists were instrumental in the adoption of the Bill of Rights, which explicitly limits the power of the national government over both individual citizens and over the state governments.

There are several advantages to a federal system of government. First, it keeps government closer to the people, because state governments can better reflect the wishes of their citizens than can the national government. It allows local differences to be reflected in different laws and policies in different states, thereby reducing conflict at the national level. Independent subnational governments allow for flexibility and experimentation. Supreme Court Justice Louis Brandeis referred to the states as "laboratories of democracy." Policy innovations that are successful in one state may be adopted by other states or even the federal government, while those that are not successful will not create problems for the entire country.[96]

There are also some disadvantages to federalism. Fifty-one sets of laws and regulations can be confusing and complex, both for individuals and for businesses. It can increase conflict, both between the states and between a state and the federal government. It makes national efforts more difficult to coordinate and can make national goals more difficult to achieve while creating inequalities in policies and in services.[97]

In the case of gun laws, all of the advantages and disadvantages are evident. The Constitution and national policy set broad parameters within which the states have significant leeway. This has allowed states to adopt policies generally favored by their residents, and states have adopted what they perceive to be successful policies first enacted elsewhere. In some ways, it has also reduced pressure on the federal government to adopt gun laws. At the same time, different regulations in different states have created problems for gun sellers who have to navigate various laws in purchasing or selling guns and for owners who are transporting firearms or when traveling with concealed firearms. Those who argue that lax laws in state A create crime problems in state B are also unhappy with different state laws.

In the absence of a national consensus on firearms and gun policy, a system that allows states to set their own policies appears to be quite logical. There are instances in which this system creates problems for people on both sides of the issue, but the advantages outweigh the disadvantages. Even within states, some people will be displeased with the course that has been set, but it is generally easier to change state policy than national policy. Regardless of where you stand on the issue of guns, ask yourself this question: Would you be happier with some states having policies you think are reasonable and effective and create the opportunity there to demonstrate the logic and effectiveness of those regulations, or would you prefer a national policy that may well be contradictory to your view with no chance to demonstrate the efficacy of the policies you espouse?

States can and do impose very different regulations on owners and on firearms themselves. Concealed-carry regulations vary significantly between states, ranging from allowing any law-abiding citizen to carry concealed with no restrictions, to much more stringent "may issue" permits that can be extremely difficult to obtain. A few states have bans on particular weapons—mostly AR-type semiautomatic rifles. Some states limit the number of guns that may be purchased simultaneously, particularly handguns. Others require permits to purchase or own a gun, while some have a registration requirement. Waiting periods (usually for handgun purchases), child access laws, and age restrictions are more common among the states. The most restrictive states feature several of the above, while the least stringent states have none of those.[98]

Laws regarding how and when a person may use force to defend themselves or others have been both popular and controversial in the past several years. Self-defense has long been recognized as a legal defense, but some states required a person to retreat as much as possible prior to using force in defense in public. This requirement began to change with the adoption of "Castle Doctrine" laws in many states. These laws do not require a person to retreat in the face of danger, but rather allow them to respond with lethal force if a person reasonably fears the imminent possibility of death or serious bodily injury to themselves or another person. More than 40 states have adopted some form of the Castle Doctrine, with some limiting it to the home only, while others have expanded the idea to include vehicles or other areas that the person legally inhabits.

So-called "Stand Your Ground" laws have been enacted in almost 20 states in the past few years. These laws completely remove a person's obligation to retreat in the face of physical danger. Citizens are permitted to use force to defend themselves so long as they are in a place they are legally allowed to occupy, thus extending the reach of Castle Doctrine laws. About 20 other states legally require a person to retreat when confronted. Stand Your Ground became very controversial in the wake of the shooting of Trayvon Martin by George Zimmerman in Florida in 2012. Although the Trayvon Martin case sparked protests and debate both about race and the wisdom of Stand Your Ground laws, Florida's self-defense statute was not considered in the legal proceedings.

On February 26, 2012, 17-year-old Trayvon Martin was shot by George Zimmerman, a neighborhood watch captain in Sanford, Florida. The African American youth was visiting his father, who lived in Sanford. That evening, Zimmerman called 911 and reported a "suspicious person" in the neighborhood. Zimmerman was instructed to stay in his vehicle and wait for police to arrive. Zimmerman pursued and caught Martin, a struggle ensued, and Zimmerman sustained wounds on his head and face. He then shot Martin, who was unarmed.[99]

Sanford police investigated the shooting and declined to charge Zimmerman, saying that there was no evidence to dispute his account of the events—that he had acted in self-defense. The case was then turned over to the Florida State Attorney's office. A petition on Change.org demanding that Zimmerman be arrested gathered more than 1.3 million signatures. Governor Rick Scott then appointed Judge Angela B. Corey as the state attorney to investigate the case. President Obama spoke out on the case, saying that the nation should do some "soul searching" and "If I had a son, he'd look like Trayvon."

On April 11, 2012, Zimmerman was formally charged with second-degree murder. On March 5, 2013, Zimmerman's attorney decided against seeking a Stand Your Ground immunity hearing, citing a lack of time for preparation. On April 30, 2013, Zimmerman formally waived his right to the hearing, and his attorneys decided to mount a self-defense case instead. At a Stand Your Ground hearing, a judge would have ruled if Zimmerman's actions were protected by the law. If the judge had then ruled in Zimmerman's favor, he would have been shielded from both criminal and civil charges.

On July 13, 2013, a six-woman jury found Zimmerman not guilty. They could have found him guilty of second-degree murder or the lesser charge of manslaughter, but after more than 16 hours of deliberation, they found him not guilty. Two representative, but very different accounts of the outcome appear below.

> He [Zimmerman] can drive around Sanford, Florida until he spots an asshole or a f—king punk . . . the one who is in the wrong neighborhood, or who is dressed inappropriately . . . If the [person] turns around and objects to being stalked—or, worse . . . decides physically to confront the person stalking him—then George Zimmerman can . . . shoot the [person], dead right there on the spot . . . it's open season . . . because that is what American society has told George Zimmerman, and all the rest of us, is the just outcome of what happened on one dark and rainy night in February of 2012.[100]

> The United States has had its fair share of travesties, but the Florida verdict is not one of them . . . Taking the evidence as a whole, it is not clear who approached whom first or who initiated the use of force . . . An imperfect eye-witness account pointed to Trayvon being on top of Zimmerman, beating his head into the concrete, which would account for the bloody scrapes on the back of Zimmerman's head. If Martin had lived and Zimmerman died, charges of homicide—perhaps of second-degree murder—might have been brought against Martin.[101]

Despite the absence of the legal defense of Stand Your Ground, the policy came under much scrutiny, including moving congressional testimony from Martin's mother, Sybrina Fulton. "I just wanted to come here to . . . let you know how important it is that we amend this Stand Your Ground, because it certainly did not work in my case . . . The person that shot and killed my son is walking the streets today. This law does not work."[102]

Both racial bias and the appropriateness of the Stand Your Ground laws came into question. An analysis of 192 cases involving the defense found that black defendants and white defendants were equally likely to be set free following a Stand Your Ground hearing. There was a difference, however, if the victim was white (59% of defendants were freed) or black (73% were released). Black victims, however, were more likely to be carrying a weapon or committing a crime when they were killed. More disturbing, perhaps, was the finding that the defense was being successfully used in cases such as a man who stepped out of his home and shot his ex-wife's boyfriend as he sat in a car; a burglary suspect who was shot while running away from the house; and a man who shot two other men who were pounding on his truck and shouting racial slurs.[103] Both Castle Doctrine laws and Stand Your Ground statutes are strongly supported by gun rights groups.

A LOOK AT SOME STATES

Several interest groups provide rankings or issue "grades" to individual states. It is not surprising that a recent Brady Campaign "report card" did not issue a single A and only five states received an A- (California, Connecticut, Maryland, New Jersey, and New York). Half of the states—25 in all—earned a grade of F.[104] The NRA provides links to Web sites that compile the laws of each state, but the group does not issue rankings or report cards on the states. Below are brief summaries of regulations from several states, many of which were passed in 2013 in the aftermath of the Newtown shootings.

Colorado has adopted some of the more restrictive gun policies among the states. Although the state is located in a region that is more generally known for lax gun laws, Colorado is more urban than most of its neighbors. The shootings at Columbine and Aurora did little to increase support for stronger gun measures in a state that boasts relatively low crime and homicide rates. However, the Newtown shooting seemed to be a tipping point for the governor and many in the state legislature.[105] As a result, the state passed several regulations in 2013. Colorado now requires background checks for all firearms sales as well as a ban on magazines with a capacity greater than 15 rounds. It failed to pass an assault weapons ban.

The legislative battle in Colorado drew national attention. As a result of the passage of the new regulations, two state senators, including the Senate president, were defeated in recall elections, and a third senator resigned just prior to a recall election. In the general election of 2013, five rural counties voted to secede from the state while six voted to remain in what was a symbolic vote. This vote does, however, exemplify the divide within the state of Colorado and the broader differences in the views of urban dwellers and those who live in rural areas.

Connecticut had very strict gun laws prior to the Newtown shootings, but that state also strengthened its laws in 2013. Connecticut now requires universal background checks for all sales of guns, ammunition, and magazines. Any magazines with a capacity greater than 10 are prohibited, and there is an assault weapons ban as well (which now bans AR-style rifles). A permit is required for any firearm or ammunition purchase. Assault rifles purchased prior to the ban may be used only at a firing range and must be registered with the state. These laws are among the strongest in the nation. We have previously noted that these laws prompted civil disobedience from some gun owners who refused to register their firearms.

The state of New York also adopted stricter laws following the Newtown shootings. As described by the NRA, "On January 15, 2013, Governor Cuomo *seized your gun rights overnight*! *S.2230* was signed into law only 24 hours after it was introduced. The law went into effect immediately upon signature [emphasis in original]."[106] New York adopted universal background checks and a ban on assault weapons and large-capacity magazines. Any assault weapons already owned must be registered with the state. A permit is required to purchase a handgun, and there is a handgun registry. In addition, New York residents are required to report lost or stolen firearms. Some of these laws have been modified and have been challenged in court.

New Jersey also considered new laws in 2013, but several were vetoed by Governor Chris Christie. Universal background checks and proof of safety training prior to purchase were among the regulations that were rejected. Still, the state has a restrictive assault weapons ban in place, and it requires a permit or state-issued ID card for any firearms purchase.

California has the most restrictive laws in the country, including universal background checks, a 10-day waiting period for any firearm purchase, proof of safety training prior to purchase, a stringent assault weapons ban, a ban on magazines larger than 10 rounds, and a first-in-the-country ban on lead ammunition. The combination of these laws is sufficient that many dealers will not sell firearms in the state.

In contrast, Alaska and Arizona are among the most lenient states with regard to gun laws. Both allow open and concealed carry of firearms and have no additional firearms bans, licensing, or background checks other than those required by federal law. The loosening of concealed-carry laws has been the focus of gun rights groups and legislators for the past decade or more. In many states, the restrictions regarding where one may carry a concealed firearm and regulations regarding how those licenses are obtained have been modified in favor of gun rights. Virginia is an example of such a state, as each successive legislative session has seen a loosening of those laws for several years, even when Democrats were in power in the governor's mansion.[107]

FEDERAL GUN CONTROL LAWS

Most federal laws have regulated the classes of people who may purchase or possess firearms. The sale of certain types of weapons is prohibited at the national level, and there are enhanced sentences for those convicted of certain gun-related crimes. Most federal legislation has been passed in response to a specific event, set of events, or a recurring crime problem. Using the terminology of Kingdon, the federal policy window has typically been opened by a focusing event.

The first federal legislation was passed in 1927, when Congress voted to prohibit the transfer of handguns via the Postal Service.[108] Given that other common carriers were not included under this legislation, it is not surprising that it was thought to be ineffective, although it might have made both legislators and citizens feel better because criminals could no longer obtain these weapons through the mail.[109]

National Firearms Act of 1934 (NFA)

Gangster violence, carried out by organized crime groups during the early 1930s, was the major impetus behind the National Firearms Act. The NFA was an attempt to regulate the marketplace through taxes that made certain types of firearms, including sawed-off shotguns and machine guns, quite expensive. Each weapon transfer carried a $200 tax (a hefty sum in 1934), and importers, manufacturers, and dealers were taxed in addition to the transfer tax. All such weapons had to be registered with the national government.[110] The NFA was upheld by the U.S. Supreme Court in 1937 in *Sonzinsky v. United States*.[111]

Due to opposition from various sporting groups and the NRA, handguns were excluded from the legislation despite support for their inclusion by the Justice Department. In addition, the definition of a machine gun did not include semiautomatic weapons with a 10-round magazine, a definition that would have included today's AR-style weapons.[112]

A formal evaluation of the NFA has never been undertaken, and it is difficult to ascertain the effectiveness of the law. Although use of these weapons declined, it is not clear if that was a consequence of the NFA or a shift in the weapons of choice and the decline of the organized crime groups. Nonetheless, the law did establish that there was some limitation on the weapons that could legitimately be possessed by average citizens. Most important, Congress gained, or at least assumed, the power to regulate firearms.

Federal Firearms Act of 1938

By 1937, the Justice Department unsuccessfully renewed its efforts to include handguns in the National Firearms Act. The bill known as the Federal Firearms Act (FFA) was a compromise act written largely by the NRA.[113] It applied to all firearms, but the controls it mandated were relatively modest. It required interstate dealers to be licensed (the cost was $1), and there were some additional restrictions on the interstate shipment of firearms. Manufacturers and importers were required to purchase licenses. Selling to a restricted class of persons was criminalized, but the enforcement mechanism was weak. Dealers were required to keep records of sales, but penalties for violation of this law were minimal. Dealers were defined as "any person engaged in the business of selling firearms or ammunition . . . at wholesale or retail" as well as gunsmiths and manufacturers. Thus, obtaining a license was neither difficult nor expensive. Over the years, many average citizens became dealers to facilitate purchasing firearms for themselves.

Successful prosecution under the law required proof that sales were made in knowing violation of the law, a standard of proof that is very difficult to meet. Until the 1960s, fewer than 100 persons per year were arrested under the act.[114] Perhaps the most important impacts of the law were the establishment of the dealer licensing system and the emergence of the NRA as an important player in the legislative arena. Interestingly, while working on the FFA, the NRA developed a model handgun act for states that included a waiting period.[115]

Much of the impetus for gun control had dissipated by the time the FFA was adopted, probably as a result of the declining murder and crime rates. The policy window that had been opened due to concern with organized crime in the early 1930s had closed. The desire for further gun control would not be manifest again until the assassination of President John F. Kennedy in 1963 increased interest in firearms regulation.

Considering the dearth of prosecutions, gun-control advocates might point to the FFA as a policy failure. Still, it created new types of regulations for firearms and dealers. The regulations went beyond the taxes imposed by the NFA and created a system of firearms transfers in which the rules were established by the government. That was a very important step.

The Gun Control Act of 1968

While the push for stricter gun laws began prior to President Kennedy's assassination, final passage of the Gun Control Act (GCA) did not come until 1968.[116] Senator Thomas Dodd (D-CT) had proposed further restrictions on mail-order handguns prior to Kennedy's assassination by a man armed with a mail-order surplus military rifle. The Dodd bill died in the Senate Commerce Committee in 1964, but he reintroduced a more restrictive bill in 1965 at the request of the Johnson administration, and the legislative battle was joined. By 1965, Dodd had added long guns to the bill.

The 1965 bill received some support from the NRA, which led to an important split in its membership. A strongly negative response from many of the rank-and-file members of the organization resulted in a change of position by the leadership and stronger opposition to any further controls on firearms. This was a pivotal shift in the position of the NRA.

There was significant political wrangling in 1965 and the following years between the Johnson administration and members of Congress. The logjam broke following the assassinations of Martin Luther King Jr. and Robert Kennedy in 1968. These murders increased support for gun control in Congress and also served to make the often silent voices of gun-control supporters much more audible while the cries of control opponents were largely muted.[117] The gun-control policy window had opened again.

During debate over the GCA, the Johnson administration backed provisions that provided for registration of all firearms and the licensing of all gun owners. These requirements were deleted from the bill, largely due to the efforts of the NRA and other gun control opponents.

As enacted, the law prohibited interstate firearms sales, added to the categories of persons who could not purchase firearms, and prohibited importing inexpensive handguns often referred to as Saturday Night Specials. The GCA also created the Bureau of Alcohol, Tobacco and Firearms within the Treasury Department, and made this agency responsible for the administration of all federal firearms laws.[118]

The definition of a dealer was modified to read someone "dealing in firearms as a regular course of trade or business," and there was a requirement that an FFL maintain a business premises. This provision of the bill was rarely enforced, and the number of private citizens who sought and were granted licenses increased to 284,000 by 1992.[119] Perhaps the most effective restrictions of the legislation were those that dealt with interstate commerce. The purchase of out-of-state firearms decreased, although this was probably never a large proportion of firearm sales.

The GCA did not presage the passage of more gun-control legislation, and, in fact, the push for further restrictions declined. In the political arena, the forces that opposed gun control were stronger than the forces that supported it. They could be defeated if those who favored control took advantage of a policy window that was open due to a tragic event or concern with increasing crime. In more normal times, however, gun-control legislation was unlikely to pass.

Armed Career Criminal Act of 1984

The policy preferences of the Reagan administration were very clear in the legislation that was approved in the 1980s, which reflected Reagan's "get tough with criminals" positions. The major piece of gun-related legislation of the first Reagan administration was the Armed Career Criminal Act of 1984. The signature provision of this legislation was a 15-year mandatory prison term for any convicted felon who had three previous convictions for robbery or burglary and who was involved in a firearm transfer.

The Federal Sentencing Guidelines, passed in 1986, also provided a sentence enhancement for anyone possessing a firearm while committing a crime. Finally, the Drug Abuse Amendments Act of 1988 made it a crime to transfer a firearm to an individual knowing that the gun would be used in criminal activity. While this may reflect a popular wish to punish those who knowingly transfer firearms to criminals, the standard of proof required for conviction is high. All of these bills targeted criminals rather than law-abiding citizens and were passed easily.[120]

Firearms Owners' Protection Act (1986) (McClure-Volkmer)

Nearly two decades of complaints by the NRA and other gun-rights groups about ATF enforcement of the GCA resulted in the passage of the Firearms Owners' Protection Act (FOPA), often referred to as the McClure-Volkmer Bill. As amended and passed, the bill permitted long-gun interstate purchases that complied with the laws of both states. Record keeping for ammunition dealers was eliminated. It reduced FFL record-keeping violations from a felony to a misdemeanor and limited the ATF to one unannounced inspection per FFL per year. It prohibited the federal government from centralizing the records of firearms dealers or creating or maintaining any type of registration system. Another provision of the bill redefined the business location of FFLs to include gun shows, which increased the number of gun shows. On the pro-control side, the FOPA prohibited the manufacture or transfer of machine guns (except for those who hold a Class 3 Firearms License), prohibited the importation of barrels for Saturday Night Specials, and added to the list of those who are ineligible to purchase firearms.

The bill's passage was seen as both the high point of the NRA's political influence as well as the beginning of political trouble for the group.[121] While the NRA exerted significant influence in the writing of FOPA and worked tirelessly for its passage, the legislation exacerbated a growing rift between the NRA and various police organizations, which had opposed the bill. This split was quickly capitalized upon by the newly energized Handgun Control Inc. (HCI) and its new leader, Sarah Brady.

The effects of FOPA were more symbolic than substantive. Still, there was a substantive component in that gun shows and the number of dealers at gun shows increased. At the same time, a machine gun market that was in its infancy never developed.[122] Because they were never indexed to inflation or increased, the taxes on those weapons imposed by the NFA were no longer as onerous as they were in the 1930s, and it is reasonable to assume that a market for machine guns would have developed along with the market for assault weapons.

Cop Killer Bullets and Plastic Guns

Two pieces of gun control legislation passed in the late 1980s represent the NRA's temporary fall from power and a lack of political savvy on the part of the NRA.

The Law Enforcement Officers Protection Act, passed in 1986, banned the importation, manufacture or sale of armor piercing or so-called "cop killer bullets."[123] Promoted by HCI and supported by police and law enforcement organizations, the original bill banned bullets that were made from certain hard metals and then coated with Teflon. In some situations, these bullets were capable of penetrating the Kevlar bulletproof vests worn by police officers. The NRA argued that the ammunition had been available for years and that there were no documented cases of bullets penetrating police body armor. The NRA was successful at amending the bill because many types of bullets, including some hunting ammunition, could penetrate soft body armor at close range.

While the NRA may have been technically correct on these points, it was clearly on the losing side of the public relations battle. Lining up against what was portrayed as reasonable gun control designed solely to save the lives of police officers was a risky strategy. HCI had created an issue that put the NRA in the position in which it had to choose between supporting a piece of gun-control legislation or appear to oppose police safety. The NRA took the bait rather than remain silent, and there was a political price to pay. The bill was passed, and, once again, the NRA was on the opposite side from law enforcement groups.

The Undetectable Firearms Act of 1988 (UFA) banned a type of firearm that did not exist. These "plastic guns" were allegedly invisible to metal detectors and x-ray devices. The guns at issue were not made of plastic and were detectable, although not as easily visible as firearms constructed of metal.[124] Still, the prospect of guns being smuggled onto airplanes was a frightening thought even prior to September 11, 2001. The NRA opposed the original bill, but eventually supported the legislation after it was amended.

By 2013, technology had, in some respects, caught up with the fear of "plastic guns." It appeared to be possible to produce such a firearm, although its safety and accuracy were questionable. The cost of producing a 3-D gun was less controversial. A 3-D printer cost about $10,000, which would buy a small arsenal of conventional firearms and ammo as well.[125] Nonetheless, the ban was renewed by strong majorities in both houses of Congress and was signed by President Obama. All of this occurred with little fanfare this time, and with silence on the part of the NRA and virtually all other gun-rights groups.[126]

The Brady Bill

The emergence of Handgun Control Inc. (HCI) and the Bradys as national figures continued after the legislative activity of the late 1980s. White House press secretary James Brady was wounded and partially disabled in the assassination attempt on President Ronald Reagan in 1981. His wife Sarah became active in the years after the shooting and was the preeminent spokesperson for gun control. As president of HCI, Sarah Brady increased the visibility, the political clout, and the size of the organization.

In the late 1980s, HCI began to lobby Congress to enact a national waiting period for handgun purchases and a background check for firearms purchases. Many states already had some form of background check in place, and it was the waiting period that proved to be the major stumbling block in getting the bill passed. First introduced in 1987, the Brady Bill was finally signed into law in November 1993.

For reasons related to political expediency, the waiting period applied only to handguns, and the background checks would be required only for purchases from FFLs. The secondary market of private sales would remain unregulated. This would reduce the number of purchasers and sellers who would be impacted, a political tactic designed to reduce opposition to the bill. Also, handguns are used in the large majority of homicides, so they logically would be targeted.

Those who favored passage argued that a background check would help prevent criminals and others who could not legally purchase a firearm from obtaining a gun. The waiting period would serve as a cooling-off period for those who would buy a gun in a fit of homicidal passion or rage or during a period of suicidal thoughts.

Those opposed to the legislation were concerned primarily with the background check as a potential first step to gun registration. As introduced, sales reports would be sent to local authorities, not to the federal government, and these reports would have to be destroyed relatively soon after the transaction was completed. This would, in effect, prevent the establishment of gun registration.

The waiting period presented a nuisance of varying degrees to law-abiding citizens who simply wished to purchase a legal product depending in part on how easy it is for a purchaser to access an FFL in their area. If they had to travel a great distance, then it added another obstacle of having to make the trip twice. The waiting period also presented a larger obstacle to a buyer who was purchasing the firearm to protect themselves or a loved one from an immediate threat and believed they needed a firearm immediately. In reality, the number of people who purchase a gun and use it *immediately* in the commission of a crime is relatively small, as is the number who needs to purchase a gun *today* for self-defense. There is anecdotal evidence of both types of events, but they constitute a very small percentage of homicides and defensive gun uses.

The bill was defeated in the House of Representatives in 1988 with the passage of an amendment that mandated a study of an instant background check. Again, the waiting period was the larger political problem. In 1990, both the House and the Senate passed the bill, but the version that made it out of the conference committee was defeated by a Republican-led filibuster in the Senate.[127]

While the election of President Clinton in 1992 meant that the White House now supported the bill, the bill's prospects in Congress were not greatly improved. The bill passed the House again and, after much debate, hand-wringing, arm-twisting, and public posturing in the Senate, finally resulted in a compromise that was passed in November 1993.

The law created a five-day waiting period for handgun purchases from FFLs. The dealer also was required to submit information about the buyer to local authorities to check if the buyer was indeed eligible to purchase the handgun. Authorities could not retain the purchase records.[128] Within five years, the Brady Bill mandated that a National Instant Criminal Background System (NICS) be created to replace the local authorities' check and the waiting period. Those states that already had background checks or handgun licensing were exempted.

It is difficult to assess the impact of the Brady Bill. There is no doubt that many potential purchasers have been denied firearms by the background checks. Between 1994 and 2012, nearly 1 million, or about 1.3 percent, of background check applicants were rejected.[129] About two-thirds of those rejected were felons or had a domestic violence conviction or a restraining order. The system is still weak with regard to identifying those who are ineligible due to mental illness, drug use, or alien status.[130]

On the other hand, we do not know what happened to these individuals after their purchase was denied. Some may have decided not to purchase, but certainly many others turned to straw purchasers or other means of obtaining a gun. Few were prosecuted as a result of the denied purchase. A *Washington Post* investigation found that in 2010, about 4 percent of the denials were overturned, while 90 percent were deemed not worthy of further investigation. Of the more than 73,000 denials in that year, only 62 cases were referred for prosecution, resulting in 13 guilty pleas.[131]

In a more rigorous study of the impact of the Brady Bill, Ludwig and Cook examined homicide and suicide rates in states in which the Brady Act resulted in a change of policy and those in which it did not:

> We find no statistically discernible difference in homicide trends between the Brady (treatment) and non-Brady (control) states among people aged 21 and older. While our point estimates are negative, they are even more negative for non-gun homicide than for gun homicide (and in every case statistically insignificant). In this pattern of results we see no case for a causal effect of Brady ... [O]ur analysis of suicide rates found some evidence that Brady may have reduced gun suicide rates among people aged 55 and older. However, these gains were at least partially offset by an increase in non-gun suicides (perhaps due to weapon substitution), so whether waiting periods reduced overall suicides among this age group is unclear.[132]

They acknowledge an apparent disconnect between their findings of no impact of the Brady Act and the fact that about 2.4 percent of potential handgun buyers were denied the right to purchase a gun during their period of study. One possible explanation they offer is that individuals who are legally disqualified from buying a gun but who shop at a FFL-licensed gun shop anyway may be at low risk of misusing a gun. This theory is supported by research from the 1990s that found that only about 20 percent of criminals purchased their guns at a gun shop even before FFLs were required to conduct background checks. Most of the crime guns were obtained from acquaintances and family members in private transactions.[133]

Many on both sides of the debate viewed the Brady Bill as a first step toward greater gun control. Those expecting a second step would not have to wait very long.

The Assault Weapons Ban (1994)

The impetus for the proposed Assault Weapons Ban was the January 1989 school shooting in Stockton, California, in which five children were killed and 29 wounded by a mentally disturbed drifter using a legally imported Chinese 7.62 mm AKM-56S.[134] Led by California, several states subsequently acted to ban certain types of semiautomatic firearms.[135]

The market for these firearms greatly expanded in the late 1970s and early 1980s with the influx of inexpensive Chinese copies of the AK-47 rifle. The relatively high cost of domestically produced versions of the rifle, such as the Colt AR-15, had previously reduced demand for the weapons.

At the national level, President George H. W. Bush reversed his previously stated position and supported federal action. He directed ATF to implement a "suitable for sporting purposes" test to imported rifles as a way of reducing the number of these weapons in the marketplace. The ATF standards, however, focused on appearance rather than function. As a result, manufacturers changed the appearance of their rifles to comply with the standards. In addition, these actions stimulated demand for the rifles amid fears that they would soon be banned.[136]

The 1992 election of President Bill Clinton meant that gun-control advocates now had a very strong ally in the White House. Once again, the legislation faced an uphill battle in both houses of Congress, but a compromise bill was passed. Political pressure was exerted by President Clinton, and Republicans were concerned with appearing to be obstructionist. Thus, an intense lobbying effort by the NRA was overcome.[137]

The final version of the bill banned the manufacture or importation of dozens of specific rifles, pistols, and shotguns, but it left untouched weapons that were nearly identical to those banned. It prohibited magazines with a capacity greater than 10 rounds. All currently owned assault rifles and magazines were grandfathered in as legal. Guns were also banned if they possessed two or more of a list of specific physical characteristics that made them appear menacing. A key component was that the law had a sunset provision. If not renewed, it would expire in 10 years, which it did in 2004.

The biggest problem with the Assault Weapons Ban was its lack of definition of the term "assault weapon." The choice to use cosmetic appearance to determine which firearms, beyond those specifically listed, would be banned left many copycats on the market as well as many guns that function identically but are cosmetically slightly different from a banned gun. The vague definition was the result of the bill's proponents choosing the path of least political resistance and, perhaps, indicative of their general lack of knowledge regarding how firearms function.[138] A more specific definition would have included all semiautomatic guns, which would have greatly increased the number of gun owners who were impacted by the law and would likely have doomed it to failure.[139]

The impact of the Assault Weapons Ban was probably minimal. Although Koper and Roth found a small decline in homicides that might be attributable to the ban, they also acknowledged that the number of banned weapons sold in the months prior to implementation date increased by 120 percent.[140] Kleck argues that the ban could have prevented no more than two homicides annually.[141] According to Jacobs, "[L]aws like this reflect and fan the flames of the symbolic conflict between gun owners and gun controllers, with little, if any, relevance to the crime problem."[142] The most extensive research, conducted by Ludwig and Cook, found that the effects of the ban were minimal.[143]

The battle over renewal of the ban began in 2003, but it did not come to the forefront of the political debate until the spring of 2004, when it was amended to legislation that would have granted gun manufacturers immunity from some lawsuits. The Senate defeated the bill, and the ban expired in 2004.

This is a reasonable place to discuss what has come to be known as the AR-platform.

Back in the 1950s, Eugene Stoner of the Fairchild ArmaLite Corporation developed the AR. (The AR designation comes from ArmaLite, not, as is commonly believed, "assault rifle.") The gun was originally to be chambered in 7.62 mm (essentially a .308) for use in Southeast Asia.

Many believed that combat in the Asian Rim would be in close quarters, creating a specific need for a lightweight, accurate, small caliber rifle. The military favored the .222 Special, later to become the .223 or 5.56 NATO because it offered soldiers more ammo carrying capacity. An AR weighed about six pounds and offered far less recoil than the NATO round, the 7.62 or the .308.[144]

Although the AR began as purely a military rifle, by the late twentieth century, it had morphed into many other applications. It is now available in many calibers that are associated with hunting "varmints" such as groundhogs or even large game animals. Available in calibers ranging from .17 to .458, the AR is suitable for anything from shooting prairie dogs at 500 yards to bears, moose, or elk at 300 yards or even longer distances. It is also a favorite of target shooters.

In addition, the AR can be accessorized in numerous ways. Most of the accessories are cosmetic, but they are not inexpensive. Some of those accessories are designed to make the gun look more like a military weapon, although they may or may not have any impact on function. Of course, they may not be legally converted to fully automatic rifles. It is not uncommon for the cost of ARs to run into the thousands of dollars. ARs are simply semiautomatic rifles, like any other semiautos, that can be used as the operator chooses. They are no more inherently dangerous or deadly than any other semiautomatic rifle, whether that rifle was manufactured in the 1940s or the 2010s.[145]

LAWSUITS AGAINST GUN MANUFACTURERS AND GUN DEALERS

It is common in American politics for those who fail in the legislative arena to take the battle into the legal system. In recent history this has been a favored tactic of the political left, primarily on the issues of civil rights, abortion, and gay rights, while in the past it was the more conservative groups that sought relief from economic regulation in the courts.

In the early 2000s, lawsuits were filed against gun manufacturers under several different theories of liability. The abnormally dangerous theory of liability can be used against a party that carries on "an abnormally dangerous activity" even if the party has exercised "the utmost care to prevent the harm."[146] This tactic was unsuccessful insofar as it is difficult to demonstrate that firing a gun is an abnormally dangerous activity. While there is no question that firearms are inherently dangerous, the large majority of owners use them safely.

A second legal approach is strict liability, such as an unreasonably dangerous or defective product. This approach was also unsuccessful in the courts. The standard applied is that the product must function in a way that is more dangerous than an ordinary consumer would expect. Consumers expect firearms to be dangerous, so this avenue also tended to fail.[147]

A third tactic was to charge the gun manufacturer with negligent distribution and marketing. A finding of liability for negligence requires that the seller did not use reasonable means to prevent the sale of the product to someone who is likely to cause harm to the public or if the product is marketed in such a way as to induce its purchase by someone who will foreseeably misuse the product.[148] These suits were somewhat more successful.

The most difficult hurdle for all of these suits was that the harm resulted from the criminal conduct of a third party, except in cases of some accidental shootings. Most juries and judges were reluctant to hold a firearms dealer or manufacturer responsible for the actions of a criminal unless they knew the buyer's criminal record and intent.

The earliest municipal suits were filed by New Orleans and Chicago in 1998. By late 2001, more than 30 municipalities had filed similar suits.[149] These suits, in addition to pressure from the Clinton administration, led Smith & Wesson, the largest firearms manufacturer in the country, to settle with 15 of the 30 plaintiffs.[150] This settlement received a great deal of media attention, but its actual impact on how firearms are sold was negligible. The company generally agreed to reexamine its marketing practices and to include certain safety devices with its firearms as they became practical.[151] This led to a temporary ostracism of Smith & Wesson from the firearms community.

Virtually all of the lawsuits failed, but the cost to the gun manufacturers was significant. Some have suggested that the suits may have contributed to the bankruptcy of several smaller manufacturers.[152] Even if manufacturers were not driven out of business, the cost of firearms would inevitably rise to cover the costs of the litigation. These suits clearly presented a threat to the gun industry, both economically and perceptually. The next step in this dance, then, was for gun manufacturers, the National Shooting Sports Foundation, and their ally, the National Rifle Association, to turn to the legislatures to try to preempt the suits.

In 1999, Georgia became the first state to pass legislation preventing any local government from bringing suit against gun manufacturers, dealers, ammunition manufacturers, or trade associations. By 2005, more than 30 states had passed legislation granting immunity to gun manufacturers.[153] These bills were frequently sponsored and strongly supported by the NRA and other trade and shooting organizations. While the NRA enjoyed some measure of success at the state level, it also pursued federal legislation.

Protection of Lawful Commerce in Arms Act of 2005

The Protection of Lawful Commerce in Arms Act (H.R. 1036) passed in the House of Representatives in April 2003 by better than a 2–1 margin. The bill had 250 cosponsors in the House, and it passed with relatively little fanfare. All parties understood that the real political test would be in the Senate.

S. 1806 was introduced by Senator Larry Craig (R-ID), a NRA board member, on October 31, 2003. By early 2004, the bill had 59 cosponsors, one less than the 60 votes need to defeat a filibuster. The bill was supported by the Bush administration, which opposed any amendments to the legislation.[154] Two critical amendments were offered by Senators John McCain (R-AZ) and Dianne Feinstein (D-CA) including the requirement of background checks on all firearm sales at gun shows and a 10-year extension of the Assault Weapons Ban, respectively. McCain's amendment passed on a 53–46 vote, and Feinstein's amendment passed by a 52–47 margin.

These amendments were "poison pills," which were unacceptable to the NRA and supporters of S. 1806. There was a great deal of pressure from other gun-rights groups who suggested that the NRA might be willing to compromise on these items to get the immunity bill passed. The NRA Web site reassured readers that there would be no accommodation of the other side, and it subsequently asked its supporters in the Senate to vote against the measure.[155] As a result, the bill was overwhelmingly defeated on a 90–8 vote by a strange coalition of pro-gun-control and pro-gun-rights senators. Neither side was willing to accept the compromise.

As a result, gun control and the Assault Weapons Ban became issues in the presidential election of 2004. Democratic presidential nominee and Massachusetts senator John F. Kerry voted in favor of both amendments and against the overall bill. The NRA's Wayne LaPierre predicted the votes would come back to haunt those senators who backed the amendments, including former majority leader Tom Daschle.[156] LaPierre's statement proved prophetic when Daschle was defeated in November.

With the outcome of the 2004 elections seemingly favoring the gun-rights side, the immunity bill was reintroduced as S. 397 and H.R. 800 in 2005. It was essentially the same legislation as that introduced in 2004. It prohibited lawsuits against third parties unless those parties have violated criminal law in the transfer of the firearm. In addition, all handguns transferred by a FFL must be accompanied with a trigger lock.

S. 397 passed on a 65–31 vote on July 29, 2005. The bill was carefully managed by Senator Craig and the Republican leadership, which limited amendments. The bill garnered the support of 50 Republicans, 14 Democrats, and the Senate's lone Independent. It was opposed by 29 Democrats and two Republicans. It would be easy to characterize the vote as partisan, but it was more complex than that. Bear in mind that the partisan split in the Senate to a large extent reflects that of the country as a whole—the red states and blue states. None of the Democrats who voted for the bill represented states in the Northeast or the Midwest, and no Southern Democrat voted against it. The only Republicans voting against S. 397 were DeWine of Ohio and Chafee of Rhode Island. The House of Representatives substituted S. 397 as its bill, and it passed by a 283–144 margin on October 20, 2005. Although only four Republicans voted against the legislation, 59 Democrats voted for it.[157] President Bush then signed it into law.

The rhetoric of the interest groups notwithstanding, final passage of the bill can only be interpreted as a major victory for gun-rights groups in general and the NRA in particular. The NRA fought for the legislation for several years and turned down the opportunity to have it pass in 2004 in exchange for extending the Assault Weapons Ban. Their success in the 2004 elections ensured passage without any "poison pill" amendments in 2005. The Protection of Lawful Commerce in Arms Act clearly indicated that gun-control supporters were losing the legislative battle among many Democrats as well as the strong majority of Republicans.

The impact of this legislation was felt more in terms of what did not happen. If some of the lawsuits had been successful, then the ripple effects could have been felt by average gun owners through higher prices and, perhaps, reduced availability of firearms. This victory was also symbolic insofar as the NRA reestablished itself as the major force in gun-related legislation.

Lack of Federal Gun Legislation since 2005

It is not surprising that the only significant piece of legislation passed between 2000 and 2005 protected gun rights. The Bush administration was sympathetic to gun rights, and Republicans controlled Congress as well. Even the April 2007 Virginia Tech shootings did not spur Congress into significant action. Some major bills were introduced, but they were never given much of a chance of passage.

Congress did pass the NICS Improvement Amendments Act of 2007, which provided grants to states to incentivize the reporting of mental health records to the NICS system. This was a rare instance of the two opposing sides agreeing on legislation. The bill included some key components for both sides, with the NRA supporting the reporting of mental health records and extracting requirements to purge certain records, provide a process to have gun rights restored, and permanently prohibiting the FBI from charging a fee for a background check.[158] While the bill resulted in many states increasing the number of records reported, and particularly mental health records (from 126,000 in 2004 to 1.2 million in 2011), there were still more than 20 states with fewer than 100 mental health records added to the system during that period.[159]

It is more surprising that no significant gun legislation was advanced in the first Obama administration. President Obama favored stronger gun regulations, and the Democrats took control of both houses of Congress in the 2008 election. There are several possible explanations for this lack of legislation. First, Obama was focused on other issues, including health care, immigration, and the economy. There was little political capital left to spend on gun control. Second, the administration was reluctant to raise an issue it would almost certainly lose. Republicans could mount a filibuster in the Senate, and many, though certainly not all, Democrats were reluctant to take on the issue given the conventional wisdom that it had cost them elections in the past. Third, while there were mass shootings during that time period, none of them received significant media attention, and thus none captured the attention of the country.

The Newtown shootings occurred even before Obama's second term began. It clearly ignited the flames of passion for gun control across the country, but, as was discussed in the Introduction of this book, it did not result in legislation being passed by Congress.

CONCLUSION

Much of the national gun-control legislation that has been passed has, not surprisingly, had little effect on gun owning or crime. It can generally be described as tinkering at the edges. Few weapons have been banned, and most of those were neither popular crime guns nor firearms commonly owned by law-abiding citizens. The legislation passed because relatively few gun owners were directly impacted. Much of the legislation was designed by the sponsoring legislators and interest groups with that in mind. They understood that regulations that affect large numbers of gun owners are likely to engender strong and deep opposition that cannot be overcome.

Most of the gun-control legislation has passed because of a focusing event, a crime wave, political assassination, or a school shooting. In more typical times, gun control is not high on the list of priorities for the public, and therefore, it is not a priority for elected officials. For example, the Assault Weapons Ban was passed following a tragic school shooting, but there was relatively little fanfare when it expired in the absence of such an event.

The convergence of the three policy streams—the problems stream, political stream, and policy stream—is a rare event that opens a policy window for a brief period of time. If legislative action is not taken within that limited time frame, then significant changes to existing law are unlikely to pass. Incremental changes, which often expand gun rights, are likely to be adopted when the streams do not converge. Keeping the streams moving in unison is a difficult task for those who favor stronger gun regulations.

Gun-control legislation has often focused on restricting the types of people who can own or possess firearms, primarily criminals, the mentally unstable, and children. These bills tend to be popular with a wide cross-section of the population, including gun owners. At other times, certain types of guns have been targeted, such as machine guns, assault weapons, and small, inexpensive handguns. Attempts have been made to enact more comprehensive regulations, such as gun registration and owner licensing, but those policies have failed to come even close to passage at the national level.

Although often overlooked, the state legislatures have been the scene of some of the strongest debates as well as the most activity. The states continue to move in different policy directions, with some favoring stricter gun-control laws and others having fewer restrictions on firearms. This leaves the country with a patchwork set of laws with little national uniformity. Both sides of the gun-control debate view that as a problem. Gun-control advocates cite the lax laws in some states as fueling gun violence in the states with stricter laws, while gun-rights supporters worry that law-abiding citizens can unknowingly become criminals when they cross the border into a state with tougher laws.

While the political stakes are very high on issues such as background checks, assault weapons bans, concealed carry laws, and gun-safety mandates, the reality is that these regulations have relatively little effect on most law-abiding gun owners or the average criminal gun owner.[160] Limiting the liability of gun manufacturers and dealers defeated a tactic that had the potential to take a serious toll on the gun industry. At its core, gun control is a truly substantive issue, but as it has been addressed in legislatures in the United States, it has been more symbolic.

With regard to the most important question, perhaps, "Does anything work?" the honest answer is, "We don't know." Even governmental agencies are skeptical, however. An internal memo from the National Institute of Justice suggests that gun laws would have to be very stringent in order to have an impact on crime.[161] It begins by noting that mass shootings are uncommon and strategies designed to address "the larger firearm homicide issue" will be much more effective. Gun buybacks are judged to be ineffective. They are too small; the guns that are turned in are at low risk of being used in a crime; and they can easily be replaced. Restrictions on the size of magazines could be effective, but only if future sales were banned and current stock was confiscated.

Citing a 2000 ATF study, which found that only 20 percent of crime guns were purchased from a private seller and few are carried across state lines, the memo states, "These figures indicate informal transfers dominate the crime gun market. A *perfect* universal background check system can address the gun shows and might deter many unregulated private sellers. However, this does not address the largest sources (straw purchasers and theft), which would most likely become larger if background checks at gun shows and private sellers were addressed [emphasis in original]."

The memo recommends that all gun transactions occur at an FFL. "Such a process can discourage a normally law-abiding citizen to spend the time and money to properly transfer his or her firearm to another. To be effective, requiring all transfers to occur at an FFL needs to be coupled with all the necessary incentives (or at least no disincentives) for unlicensed sellers to follow the law. Sanctions and threats of penalties are insufficient." However, even universal background checks are insufficient for ensuring that gun owners remain eligible to possess a firearm. The solutions are gun registration and continuous checks for eligibility. "The challenge to implementing this more broadly is that most states do not have a registry of firearm ownership."[162]

A two-year study conducted by the National Academy of Sciences and supported by the National Institute of Justice, the CDC, and several private foundations, which examined the actual impact of gun laws, concluded that the research on firearms and violence was conflicting and was not of sufficient persuasion to permit any conclusions.[163] The committee found that answers to some of the most pressing questions cannot be addressed with existing data and research methods, however well designed. Drawing causal inferences is always complicated and, in the behavioral and social sciences, fraught with uncertainty. Some of the problems that the committee identified are common to all social science research. In the case of firearms research, however, the committee found that even in areas in which the data are potentially useful, the complex methodological problems inherent in unraveling causal relationships between firearms policy and violence have not been fully considered or adequately addressed.

Nevertheless, many of the shortcomings described in this report stem from the lack of reliable data itself rather than the weakness of methods. In some instances—firearms violence prevention, for example—there are no data at all. Even the best methods cannot overcome inadequate data and, because the lack of relevant data influences much of the literature in this field, it also colors the committee's assessment of that literature.

The existing data on gun ownership, so necessary in the committee's view to answering policy questions about firearms and violence, are limited primarily to a few questions in various national public opinion polls. There are virtually no ongoing, systematic data series on firearms markets. Aggregate data on injury and ownership can only demonstrate associations of varying strength between firearms and adverse outcomes of interest. Without improvements in this situation, the substantive questions in the field about the role of guns in suicide, homicide, and other crimes, and accidental injury are likely to continue to be debated on the basis of conflicting empirical findings.[164]

In terms of research, little has changed in the decade since the committee's report. Results are still conflicting, and the battle that continues among academics, interest groups, and average citizens is manifest in the apparent policy gridlock at the national level and the states, which continue to move in different directions.

NOTES

1. James B. Jacobs, *Can Gun Control Work?* (New York: Oxford University Press, 2002), 214.

2. Franklin E. Zimring and Gordon Hawkins, "Concealed Handguns: The Counterfeit Deterrent," *Responsive Community* 7 (1997): 199–201.

3. Zimring and Hawkins, "Concealed Handguns," 1.

4. Zimring and Hawkins, "Concealed Handguns," 2.

5. Adam Winkler, *Gunfight: The Battle over the Right to Bear Arms in America* (New York: W. W. Norton & Company, 2013), xiii–xiv.

6. Suicides as a percentage of gun-related deaths has been increasing as homicides have declined while suicides have not, or not to the same degree. In 2010, there were 31,672 gun-related deaths—19,392 suicides (61%), 11,078 homicides (35%), 606 accidental deaths (2%), 344 justifiable killings (1%), and 252 deaths (1%) were not classified. See, CDC, WISQARS, "Fatal Injury Reports, 1999–2010, for National, Regional, and States," http://webappa.cdc.gov/cgi-bin/broker.exe. This link is updated periodically. Users should locate Fatal Injury Reports for National, Regional, and State, then use the interactive site to located up-to-date statistics.

7. Some of the research in the public health field comes close to suggesting this, but merely possessing a firearm is no more a *cause* of violence than is possession of an automobile a *cause* of reckless driving. Both objects, of course, facilitate the behavior, but they do not cause it.

8. Min Yang, Stephen C. P. Wong, and Jeremy Coid, "The Efficacy of Violence Prediction: A Meta-Analytic Comparison of Nine Risk Assessment Tools," *Psychological Bulletin* 136, no. 5 (September 2010): 740–67; Richard Van Dorn, Jan Volovka, and Norman Johnson, "Mental Disorder and Violence: Is There a Relationship beyond Substance Use," *Social Psychiatry and Psychiatric Epidemiology* 47, no. 3 (March 2012): 487–503; Christopher R. Engelhardt et al., "This Is Your Brain on Violent Video Games: Neutral Desensitization to Violence Predicts Increased Aggression Following Violent Video Game Exposure," *Journal of Experimental Social Psychology* 47, no. 5 (September 2011): 1033–36.

9. Leslie Roos, Jitender Sareen, and James M. Bolton, "Suicide Risk Assessment Tools, Predictive Validity Findings and Utility Today: Time for a Revamp?" *Summary Neuropsychiatry* 3, no. 5 (October 2013): 483–95.

10. It is equally obvious that other means can be substituted for firearms, although most of them would not enable the perpetrator to kill or injure as many people.

11. There is, however, disagreement regarding including violent misdemeanors as a disqualifier for gun purchasing.

12. This is discussed more fully in Chapter 4.

13. Pew Research Center for the People and the Press, "Why Own a Gun? Protection Is Now the Top Reason," March 12, 2013, http://www.people-press.org/2013/03/12/section-3-gun-ownership-trends-and-demographics/.

14. Jeffrey M. Jones, "Men, Married, Southerners Most Likely to Be Gun Owners," Gallup Politics, February 1, 2013, http://www.gallup.com/poll/160223/men-married-southerners-likely-gun-owners.aspx.

15. Ibid.

16. Harry Wilson, "RC Poll: Virginians' Views on Ethics, Mental Health Reforms, and Medicaid Expansion Plus Warner vs. Gillespie for US Senate," Roanoke College, January 21, 2014, http://roanoke.edu/News_and_Events/News_Archive/RC_Poll_Jan_2014.htm.

17. William J. Krouse, *Gun Control Legislation* (Congressional Research Service, November 14, 2012), 8, http://www.fas.org/sgp/crs/misc/RL32842.pdf.

18. Bureau of Alcohol, Tobacco, Firearms and Explosives, Department of the Treasury, "Annual Firearms Manufacturing and Export Report 2012," January 17, 2014, https://www.atf.gov/sites/default/files/assets/pdf-files/afmer_2012_final_web_report_17jan2014.pdf; Bureau of Alcohol, Tobacco, Firearms and Explosives, Department of the Treasury, "Annual Firearms Manufacturing and Export Report 2011," January 7, 2013, https://www.atf.gov/files/statistics/download/afmer/2011-final-firearms-manufacturing-export-report.pdf; Bureau of Alcohol, Tobacco, Firearms and Explosives, Department of the Treasury,

"Annual Firearms Manufacturing and Export Report 2010," January 30, 2012, https://www.atf.gov/files/statistics/download/afmer/2010-final-firearms-manufacturing-export-report.pdf; Bureau of Alcohol, Tobacco, Firearms and Explosives, Department of the Treasury, "Annual Firearms Manufacturing and Export Report 2009," January 20, 2011, http://www.atf.gov/files/statistics/download/afmer/2009-firearms-manufacturers-export-report.pdf.

19. The number of background checks does not represent all gun sales or only sales of newly manufactured firearms. It counts those transactions that were processed through an FFL. All private sales are excluded in most states, but the vast majority of private sales are of used firearms. Federal Bureau of Investigation, "Total NICS Background Checks: November 30, 1998–January 30, 2014," http://www.fbi.gov/about-us/cjis/nics/reports/1998_2014_monthly_yearly_totals-013114.pdf. This site is often updated. Users should search for "Total NICS Background Checks."

20. Benjamin Hayes, "Stolen Guns: Why You Should Worry," *Crime Report*, September 10, 2013, http://www.thecrimereport.org/viewpoints/2013-09-stolen-guns-why-you-should-worry.

21. Patrick Jonsson, "Gun Debate: Is Price of an Armed America a More Dangerous America?" *Christian Science Monitor*, February 2, 2014, http://www.csmonitor.com/USA/2014/0202/Gun-debate-Is-price-of-an-armed-America-a-more-dangerous-America-video.

22. Alexia Cooper and Erica L. Smith, "Homicide Trends in the United States, 1980–2008," Bureau of Justice Statistics, November 2011, http://www.bjs.gov/content/pub/pdf/htus8008.pdf; Erica L. Smith and Alexia Cooper, "Homicide in the U.S. Known to Law Enforcement, 2011," Bureau of Justice Statistics, November 2011, http://www.bjs.gov/content/pub/pdf/hus11.pdf.

23. A well-balanced, brief, and not optimistic view of mass shootings and mass shooters may be found in James Alan Fox, "Top 10 Myths about Mass Shootings," Boston.com, December 19, 2012, http://www.boston.com/community/blogs/crime_punishment/2012/12/top_10_myths_about_mass_shooti.html.

24. Cooper and Smith, "Homicide Trends, 1980–2010."

25. Active shooters were defined as one or more shooters engaged in killing or attempting to kill multiple people in an area occupied by multiple unrelated individuals. One of the victims must be unrelated to the shooter(s), and the apparent motive is mass murder. See, J. Pete Blair and M. Hunter Martaindale, "United States Active Shooter Events from 2000 to 2010: Training and Equipment Implications" (Advanced Law Enforcement Rapid Response Training, Texas State University, 2013), http://alerrt.org/files/research/ActiveShooterEvents.pdf.

26. Gregg Lee Carter, table from public speech shared with author; original data taken from Mark Follman, Gavin Aronsen, Deanna Pan, and Maggie Caldwell, "US Mass Shootings 1992–2012: Data from Mother Jones' Investigation," *Mother Jones*, December 28, 2012, http://www.motherjones.com/politics/2012/12/mass-shootings-mother-jones-full-data.

27. Cooper and Smith, "Homicide Trends, 1980–2010."

28. It should be noted that offender characteristics are not known in every homicide, either because they were not reported or because the crime was not cleared, but these data are based on all homicides for which there are data.

29. Drew DeSilver, "Suicides Account for Most Gun Deaths," Pew Research Center, May 24, 2013, http://www.pewresearch.org/fact-tank/2013/05/24/suicides-account-for-most-gun-deaths/.

30. Centers for Disease Control and Prevention, "FastStats, 2013," http://www.cdc.gov/nchs/fastats/homicide.htm.

31. These data are most frequently cited by those in the public health field, but they may also be found in texts on gun control. See, for example, David Hemenway, *Private Guns, Public Health* (Ann Arbor: University of Michigan Press, 2004), 197–205; Daniel W. Webster and Jon S. Vernick, *Reducing Gun Violence in America: Informing Policy with Evidence and Analysis* (Baltimore: Johns Hopkins University Press, 2013), part IV; and Robert J. Spitzer, *The Politics of Gun Control*, 5th ed. (Chatham, NJ: Chatham House Publishers, 2004), 50–56.

32. Spitzer, *Politics of Gun Control*, 50.

33. Gun Facts, "Guns in Other Countries," http://www.gunfacts.info/gun-control-myths/guns-in-other-countries/.

34. Drunk driving deaths would plummet if we reinstituted Prohibition. Other automobile accidents, resulting in injury or death, would decrease if we lowered speed limits, greatly curtailed purely recreational driving, and prohibited any form of distracted driving—talking on a cell phone, eating, changing radio stations, etc. Banning swimming pools would greatly decrease incidents of accidental drowning. They are all about as likely as taking most guns out of circulation.

35. "Suicide Rates by Country," *Washington Post*, 2014, http://www.washingtonpost.com/wp-srv/world/suiciderate.html.

36. Matthew R. Lee, "Reconsidering Culture and Homicide," *Homicide Studies* 15, no. 4 (2011): 319–40; Hari D. Maharajh and Petal S. Abdool, "Cultural Aspects of Suicide," *Scientific World Journal* 5 (2005): 736–46.

37. An extended discussion of the costs of gun violence, including the costs of those victims who are wounded but not killed, may be found in Philip Cook and Jens Ludwig, *Gun Violence: The Real Costs* (New York: Oxford University Press, 2000). For a more complete discussion of the costs and benefits of firearms, see Harry Wilson, *Guns, Gun Control, and Election* (Lanham, MD: Rowman & Littlefield Publishers, 2007), 56–69. The decision to adopt a policy should not necessarily be a strict cost-benefit analysis, but that has to be considered. In addition, policies generally have unintended consequences, which should also be considered, if it is possible to anticipate them.

38. If guns are viewed as increasing the chances of an accidental shooting or suicide, with negligible benefits, then, perhaps, disarming anyone, including law-abiding citizens, is inherently good.

39. Dan Haar, "Dan Haar: Untold Thousands Flout Gun Registration Law," *Hartford Courant*, February 10, 2014, http://touch.courant.com/#section/-1/article/p2p-79243214/.

40. John R. Lott Jr., *More Guns, Less Crime* (Chicago: University of Chicago Press, 1998); John R. Lott Jr. and David Mustard, "Crime Deterrence and Right-to-Carry Concealed Handguns," *Journal of Legal Studies* 26, no. 1 (January 1997): 1–68.

41. The primary charge was that his work was influenced by the fact that he held the John M. Olin fellowship at the University of Chicago Law School. The fellowship is funded by the Olin Foundation. The Olin Corporation's Winchester division manufactures ammunition. These charges were without merit.

42. Dan Black and Daniel Nagin, "Do 'Right to Carry' Laws Deter Violent Crime?" *Journal of Legal Studies* 27, no. 1 (January 1998): 209–19; Jens Ludwig, "Concealed-Gun-Carrying Laws and Violent Crime: Evidence from State Panel Data," *International Review of Law and Economics* 18 (1998): 239–54; Zimring and Hawkins, "Concealed Handguns," 46–60.

43. John R. Lott Jr., *More Guns, Less Crime: Understanding Crime and Gun Control Laws*, 2nd ed. (Chicago: University of Chicago Press, 2000).

44. Ian Ayres and John Donohue, "Nondiscretionary Concealed Weapons Law: A Case Study of Statistics, Standards of Proof, and Public Policy," *American Law and Economics Review* 1 (1999): 436–70; Ian Ayres and John J. Donohue III, "Shooting Down the More Guns, Less Crime Hypothesis," *Journal of Political Economy* 109 (October 2001): 1086–114.

45. John J. Donohue, "The Impact of Concealed-Carry Laws," in *Evaluating Gun Policy*, ed. Jens Ludwig and Philip J. Cook (Washington, DC: Brookings Institute Press, 2003), 287–325.

46. The author's grandmother lived alone in rural Pennsylvania. There were numerous loaded firearms in the house in which she lived for over 50 years, more than 20 years by herself after her husband died. There were no burglary attempts during those years. After suffering a stroke in her late 70s, she was forced to leave the homestead. Within two months, the home was broken into and ransacked, and all valuables were stolen.

47. James D. Wright and Peter H. Rossi, *Armed and Considered Dangerous: A Survey of Felons and Their Firearms* (New York: Aldine de Gruyter, 1986), chap. 7.

48. Mark R. Pogrebin, Paul B. Stretesky and N. Prabha Unnithan, *Guns, Violence and Criminal Behavior: The Offender's Perspective* (Boulder, CO: Lynne Rienner Publishers, 2009), 117–19.

49. Gary Kleck, "The Nature and Effectiveness of Owning, Carrying, and Using Guns for Self-Protection," in Gary Kleck and Don B. Kates, *Armed: New Perspectives on Gun Control* (Amherst, NY: Prometheus Books, 2001), 285–342.

50. For a discussion of the different methods and conclusions of criminologists and those in the public health field, see Don B. Kates, Henry E. Schaffer, and William B. Waters, "Public Health Pot Shots," *Reason*, April 1997.

51. Larry Bell, "Why the Centers for Disease Control Should Not Receive Gun Research Funding," *Forbes*, February 12, 2012, http://www.forbes.com/sites/larrybell/2013/02/12/why-the-centers-for-disease-control-should-not-receive-gun-research-funding/.

52. Hemenway, *Private Guns*, 8, 10.

53. It should be noted here that social scientists in the gun-control field may lean slightly more toward advocacy than those in other fields. Many tend to produce research that consistently favors one side or the other in the gun-control debate. That said, there have been instances of collaboration between social scientists on opposite sides of the issue, and, with only a few exceptions, the debate has been civil.

54. David Hemenway, "Risks and Benefits of a Gun in the Home," *American Journal of Lifestyle Medicine* (2011): 7, http://www.iansa.org/system/files/Risks +and+Benefits+of+a+Gun+in+the+Home+2011.pdf.

55. Norman Rushforth et al., "Accidental Firearms Deaths in a Metropolitan County (1958–1975)," *American Journal of Epidemiology* 100 (1975): 499–505.

56. Arthur L. Kellermann and Donald T. Reay, "Protection or Peril? An Analysis of Firearm Related Deaths in the Home," *New England Journal of Medicine* 314 (1986): 1557–60.

57. Arthur L. Kellermann et al., "Injuries and Deaths Due to Firearms in the Home," *Journal of Trauma* 45 (1998): 263–67.

58. For example, Hemenway, *Private Guns,* chap. 4, strongly criticizes the methodology of several studies that have found a very large number of defensive gun uses, but he fails to acknowledge that his preferred method of measurement has been criticized for significantly underreporting defensive gun uses. He also does not reference other studies that have found higher numbers of defensive gun uses.

59. Kates, Schaffer, and Waters, "Pot Shots."

60. David McDowall and Brian Wiersema, "The Incidence of Defensive Firearm Use by U.S. Crime Victims, 1987 through 1990," *American Journal of Public Health* 84 (1994): 1982–84.

61. Gary Kleck and Marc Gertz, "Armed Resistance to Crime: The Prevalence and Nature of Self-Defense with a Gun," *Journal of Criminal Law and Criminology* 86, no. 1 (Fall 1995): 150–87.

62. Philip J. Cook and Jens Ludwig, *Guns in America: Results of a Comprehensive National Survey on Firearms Ownership and Use* (Washington, DC: Police Foundation, 1996).

63. One might argue that one criminal using a firearm to defend against an attack from another criminal should not count as a DGU. At the same time, one criminal shooting another counts as a homicide or an assault. Parsing who "counts" as a victim or a perpetrator would be counterproductive and potentially misleading.

64. Follow-up questions determined the number of incidents, if they had occurred in the past year, and excluded cases in which the gun was used to defend against an animal or cases in which the respondent was employed by the police, military, or private security.

65. Tom W. Smith, "A Call for a Truce in the DGU War," *Journal of Criminal Law and Criminology* 87, no. 4 (1997): 1462–69. See also Jens Ludwig, "Gun Self-Defense and Deterrence," *Crime and Justice* 27 (2000): 363–417.

66. William J. Vizzard, *Shots in the Dark: The Policy, Politics, and Symbolism of Gun Control* (Lanham, MD: Rowman & Littlefield Publishers, 2000), 15–19.

67. Philip J. Cook and Jens Ludwig, "Defensive Gun Uses: New Evidence from a National Survey," *Journal of Quantitative Criminology* 14, no. 2 (1998): 111–31.

68. Hemenway, *Private Guns,* 81. Others may counter that with advice similar to an observation made by the character played by Sean Connery in *The Untouchables* when he used a gun to frighten off a knife-wielding gangster in his apartment. "Isn't that just like a [slur]? Brings a knife to a gunfight."

69. Hemenway, *Private Guns,* 87.

70. The opposing side often makes the opposite analogies with the same reasoning. We should teach children about firearms, but not about sex.

71. Of course, individuals with children in the household are wise to balance the potential threats of home invasion and the need for a gun for protection with the possibility of an accidental shooting or other inappropriate use of the firearm by the children.

72. Hemenway, *Private Guns,* 214–15.

73. Ibid., 149–50.

74. Garen J. Wintemute, "Comprehensive Background Checks for Firearms Sales: Evidence from Gun Shows," in *Reducing Gun Violence in America*, ed. Daniel W. Webster and Jon S. Vernick (Baltimore: Johns Hopkins University Press, 2013), 95. Wintemute has written about private sellers at gun shows selling firearms to purchasers who admit they may not be able to pass a background check. This author does not dispute those findings. One can find individuals willing to circumvent the law in any walk of life. From his personal experience at numerous gun shows in Southwest Virginia, this author has observed very few young attendees (the primary crime group). There are many private sellers at gun shows (though few have signs advertising that fact), and some buyers prefer them, perhaps for convenience, perhaps because they do not think anyone has the right to know if they purchase a firearm even though they could pass a background check. There is no doubt that some purchasers prefer private dealers and no background check because they could not otherwise purchase a gun. There are obviously many firearms at these events and even private individuals with guns over their shoulders for sale, but they are very peaceful events. While the author has never witnessed a situation such as that described by Wintemute, he has not searched for them. He has, however, spent many, many hours at gun shows and in conversation with vendors and customers.

75. Hemenway, *Private Guns,* 227.

76. Katherine A. Vittes, Daniel W. Webster, and Jon S. Vernick, "Reconsidering the Adequacy of Current Conditions on Legal Firearm Ownership," in *Reducing Gun Violence in America*, ed. Daniel W. Webster and Jon S. Vernick (Baltimore: Johns Hopkins University Press, 2013), 65; Garen J. Wintemute, "Broadening Denial Criteria for the Purchase and Possession of Firearms: Need,

Feasibility, and Effectiveness," in *Reducing Gun Violence in America*, ed. Daniel W. Webster and Jon S. Vernick (Baltimore: Johns Hopkins University Press, 2013), 77.

77. The problems with the measurements in this study and its limits are readily acknowledged by the authors. Unfortunately, this is not characteristic of most of the public health literature. In defense of their measure, the authors state, "Violent crime is an important public health and safety outcome—arguably the distal goal of reducing the illegal use of guns—and the two variables are correlated." Jeffrey W. Swanson et al., "Preventing Gun Violence Involving People with Serious Mental Illness," in *Reducing Gun Violence in America*, ed. Daniel W. Webster and Jon S. Vernick (Baltimore: Johns Hopkins University Press, 2013), 38.

78. Swanson et al., "Preventing Gun Violence," 44.

79. Ibid., 49.

80. Ibid., 50.

81. Hemenway, *Private Guns*, 35–45.

82. Ibid. If this is true, then it appears that the mere presence of a gun prompts some people to commit suicide, a truly remarkable finding.

83. Brad Plumer, "Here Are the Questions about Gun Violence the CDC Would Study—if It Could," *Washington Post*, June 8, 2013, http://www.washingtonpost.com/blogs/wonkblog/wp/2013/06/08/here-are-the-questions-about-gun-violence-the-cdc-would-study-if-it-could/.

84. Institute of Medicine of the National Academies, "Priorities for Research to Reduce the Threat of Firearm-Related Violence," June 2013, http://www.iom.edu/~/media/Files/Report%20Files/2013/Firearm-Violence/FirearmViolence_Insert.pdf.

85. Michael Cohen, James March, and John Olsen, "A Garbage Can Model of Organizational Choice," *Administrative Science Quarterly* 17 (March 1972): 1–25; John W. Kingdon, *Agendas, Alternatives, and Public Policies*, 2nd ed. (New York: Longman, 2003), 83–89.

86. Kingdon, *Agendas,* chap. 8.

87. Robert J. Cottroll and Raymond T. Diamond, "The Second Amendment: Toward an Afro-Americanist Reconsideration," *Georgetown Law Journal* 80 (1991): 309–61.

88. Vizzard, *Shots in the Dark*, 87–88.

89. Many have also called for background checks for Internet sales. This term may be misleading in that one could think that firearms laws at present do not apply to sales conducted via the Internet. That is not accurate; all laws do apply. As with any law, individuals will circumvent it, but they can be, and many would say they should be, prosecuted for such violations. In addition, the term "Internet sale" may be applied to any medium which has a presence on the internet. So, running an ad in the local newspaper, if they accepted ads for firearms, that was available online would constitute an Internet sale even though it could be two individuals who live only blocks apart. In addition, a private citizen may

not legally ship modern firearms to anyone who is not a licensed dealer. For example, the author wanted to ship a hunting rifle in advance of an out-of-state hunting trip. The rifle had to be sent to an FFL and picked up at that business. Similarly, on the return trip, he could not send the rifle to himself, but had to ship it to an FFL and pick it up there when it arrived.

90. "About 1.4 Million Guns Stolen during Household Burglaries and Other Property Crimes from 2005 through 2010," Bureau of Justice Statistics, November 8, 2012, http://www.bjs.gov/content/pub/press/fshbopc0510pr.cfm.

91. Within a year of the passage of an assault weapons ban in New York state, there were modified AR-type rifles that were compliant with the law and available for purchase. They had different cosmetic features, but functioned in the same fashion as a banned rifle.

92. Michael S. Rosenwald, " 'We Need the iPhone of Guns': Will Smart Guns Transform the Gun Industry?" *Washington Post*, February 17, 2013, http://www.washingtonpost.com/local/we-need-the-iphone-of-guns-will-smart-guns-transform-the-gun-industry/2014/02/17/6ebe76da-8f58-11e3-b227-12a45d109e03_story.html.

93. For example, New Jersey law requires that all guns sold there must be "smart guns" one year after the technology was commercially available.

94. Michael S. Rosenwald, "Calif. Store Backs Away from Smart Guns after Outcry from 2nd Amendment Activists," *Washington Post*, March 6, 2013, http://www.washingtonpost.com/local/california-smart-gun-store-prompts-furious-backlash/2014/03/06/43432058-a544-11e3-a5fa-55f0c77bf39c_story.html.

95. Daniel L. Cork et al., eds., *Ballistic Imaging* (Washington, DC: National Academies Press, 2008).

96. Kevin B. Smith and Alan Greenblatt, *Governing States and Localities*, 4th ed. (Washington, DC: CQ Press, 2014), 32–33.

97. Ibid., 33–34.

98. For a compendium of state gun laws, see the NRA at http://www.nraila.org/gun-laws/state-laws.aspx or the Brady Campaign at http://bradycampaign.org/?q=programs/million-mom-march/state-gun-laws/. Other Web sites contain similar information.

99. "Trayvon Martin Shooting Fast Facts," CNN Library, August 29, 2013, http://www.cnn.com/2013/06/05/us/trayvon-martin-shooting-fast-facts/.

100. Charles P. Pierce, "What George Zimmerman Can Do Now," *Esquire: The Politics Blog*, July 14, 2013, http://www.esquire.com/blogs/politics/The_End_Of_The_Daily_Trayvon.

101. Richard A. Epstein, "Justice for Trayvon Martin?" *Hoover Institution Journal*, July 22, 2013, http://www.hoover.org/research/justice-Trayvon-Martin.

102. Laurie Kellman, "Trayvon Martin's Mother Testifies at Senate Hearing on 'Stand Your Ground' Laws," *Washington Post*, October 29, 2013, http://www.washingtonpost.com/politics/trayvon-martins-mother-testifies-at-senate-hearing-on-stand-your-ground-laws/2013/10/29/94285480-40c6-11e3-a624-41d661b0bb78_story.html.

103. Susan Taylor Martin, Kris Hundley, and Connie Humburg, "Race Plays Complex Role in Florida's 'Stand Your Ground' Law," *Tampa Bay Times*, June 2, 2012, http://www.tampabay.com/news/courts/criminal/race-plays-complex-role-in-floridas-stand-your-ground-law/1233152.

104. Brady Campaign to Prevent Gun Violence, "2013 State Scorecard," December 9, 2013, http://bradycampaign.org/?q=2013-state-scorecard.

105. Matt Ferner, "Gun Violence in Colorado: From Columbine to Aurora, Mass Shootings Reignite Gun Control Debate," *Huffington Post*, December 17, 2012, http://www.huffingtonpost.com/2012/12/17/gun-violence-in-colorado-_n_2316633.html.

106. NRA–Institute for Legislative Action, "Gun Laws, State Gun Laws, New York," http://www.nraila.org/gun-laws/state-laws/new-york.aspx.

107. For a slightly dated, but mostly still accurate discussion of Virginia gun politics, see Wilson, *Guns, Gun Control*, chap. 7.

108. Franklin E. Zimring and Gordon Hawkins, *The Citizen's Guide to Gun Control* (New York: Macmillan, 1987).

109. Jacobs, *Can Gun Control Work?*, 20; Spitzer, *Politics of Gun Control*, 131.

110. Jacobs, *Can Gun Control Work?*, 20–21.

111. *Sonzinsky v. United States*, 300 U.S. 506 (1937).

112. Vizzard, *Shots in the Dark*, 89–90.

113. Vizzard, *Shots in the Dark*, 90–91; Spitzer, *Politics of Gun Control*, 131.

114. Spitzer, *Politics of Gun Control*, 132.

115. Vizzard, *Shots in the Dark*, 90.

116. An excellent and more detailed discussion of the Gun Control Act of 1968 may be found in Vizzard, *Shots in the Dark*, chap. 7.

117. Vizzard, *Shots in the Dark*, 95–97.

118. Jacobs, *Can Gun Control Work?*, 24.

119. Bureau of Alcohol, Tobacco, and Firearms, Department of the Treasury, "Commerce in Firearms in the United States," February 2000.

120. Jacobs, *Can Gun Control Work?*, 26–27.

121. Spitzer, *Politics of Gun Control*, 140; Vizzard, *Shots in the Dark*, 131–32.

122. Vizzard, *Shots in the Dark*, 130.

123. A brief, but thorough, discussion of the details of how bullets can penetrate body armor can be found in Vizzard, *Shots in the Dark*, 129–30.

124. Jacobs, *Can Gun Control Work?*, 29; Osha Gray Davidson, *Under Fire: The NRA and the Battle for Gun Control* (Iowa City: University of Iowa Press, 1998), 98–99.

125. Paul M. Barrett, "Are 3D Plastic Guns Really a Threat? Four Blunt Points," *Bloomberg Businessweek*, November 21, 2013, http://www.businessweek.com/articles/2013-11-21/are-3d-plastic-guns-really-a-threat-four-blunt-points.

126. Ed O'Keefe, "Congress Reauthorizes Ban on Plastic Guns," *Washington Post: Post Politics*, December 9, 2013, http://www.washingtonpost.com/blogs/post-politics/wp/2013/12/09/plasticguns/. Gun Owners of America was

opposed to the ban renewal and expressed their opinions in a national newspaper but with little effect. Erich Pratt, "A Truly Plastic Gun Ban: Opposing View," *USA Today*, December 3, 2013, http://www.usatoday.com/story/opinion/2013/12/03/plastic-guns-gun-owners-of-america-editorials-debates/3863917/.

127. While Republicans led the filibuster, political party affiliation was not the only factor that influenced an elected official's vote. This is true of all gun-control legislation. The strongest support for gun control comes from urban legislators, while those from the South, the West, and those who represent rural areas constitute the strongest opponents. This is also true within states.

128. Although there is no gun registry in the United States, the records of FFLs who retire or otherwise relinquish their license are sent to the BATF. These records are in paper form, and it would take a Herculean effort to make sense of them, digitize them, and create a registry of sorts, but it is possible to do so. This registry would not be up to date, and it would not be complete, but it would be a starting point if one wished to create a list of gun owners. This is a fear of some gun owners. Similarly, when legislators tried to reassure gun owners that universal background checks would not lead to a registry and even inserted that into the failed Manchin-Toomey bill, some gun owners shrugged it off, arguing that a simple act of Congress could do away with that "promise."

129. Federal Bureau of Investigation, "National Instant Criminal Background Check System (NICS) Operations 2012," http://www.fbi.gov/about-us/cjis/nics/reports/2012-operations-report.

130. Jacobs, *Can Gun Control Work?*, 95–96. The problems with regard to mental disqualifications are varied. It is difficult to identify those whom we wish not to purchase a firearm, that is, which illnesses make one ineligible—any psychological treatment, confinement in a facility, voluntary or involuntary, etc. It is also difficult to determine if or when that person's rights should be restored. Finally, those records are almost always confidential and are not available to the public and, many argue, should not be.

131. Glenn Kessler, "The Fact Checker: The Claim That the Brady Law Prevented 1.5 Million People from Buying a Firearm," *Washington Post,* January 24, 2013, http://www.washingtonpost.com/blogs/fact-checker/post/the-claim-that-the-brady-law-prevented-15-million-people-from-buying-a-firearm/2013/01/23/77a8c1d4-65b4-11e2-9e1b-07db1d2ccd5b_blog.html.

132. Philip Cook and Jens Ludwig, "The Limited Impact of the Brady Act," in *Reducing Gun Violence in America,* ed. Daniel W. Webster and Jon S. Vernick (Baltimore: Johns Hopkins University Press, 2013), 26.

133. Wright and Rossi, *Armed and Considered Dangerous.*

134. As explained by Vizzard, *Shots in the Dark*, 138, this semiautomatic rifle externally looks virtually identical to the automatic AK-47. Spitzer, *Politics of Gun Control*, 141–42, identifies the Stockton weapons as an AK-47. Spitzer also mentions the Killeen, Texas, restaurant shooting in 1991 as another event that spurred interest in the Assault Weapons Ban. Interestingly, the Killeen shooting is often used by gun-rights groups to argue in favor of liberal concealed-carry

laws, because one of the patrons argued she would have shot the gunmen if she had been allowed to carry the handgun she left in her car into the restaurant.

135. Vizzard, *Shots in the Dark*, 139.

136. Ibid., 140.

137. For a more detailed discussion, see Vizzard, *Shots in the Dark*, 140–42.

138. A quick glance at the 2013 Assault Weapons Ban that failed to pass the Senate demonstrates that the authors had significantly improved understanding of how firearms function. Assault Weapons Ban of 2013, S. 150, 113th Cong. (2013), https://www.govtrack.us/congress/bills/113/s150/text.

139. Vizzard, *Shots in the Dark*, 142.

140. Christopher S. Koper and Jeffrey A. Roth, "The Impact of the 1994 Assault Weapons Ban on Gun Violence Outcomes: An Assessment of Multiple Outcome Measures and Some Lessons for Policy Evaluation," *Journal of Quantitative Criminology* 17, no. 1 (March 2001): 33–74.

141. Gary Kleck, "Impossible Policy Evaluations and Impossible Conclusions: A Comment on Koper and Roth," *Journal of Quantitative Criminology* 17, no. 1 (March 2001): 75–80.

142. Jacobs, *Can Gun Control Work?*, 32.

143. Cook and Ludwig, "Limited Impact."

144. Peter B. Mathiesen, "Calibers That Hunt," Military.com Outdoor Guide, http://www.military.com/entertainment/outdoor-guide/ar-hunting/calibers-that-hunt.html.

145. The author collects military surplus rifles or "milsurps," some of which are semiautomatic rifles, designed for use in World War II. Many of those are still functional, and some are relatively accurate. Some of those weapons are banned by states that have assault weapons bans, although they are almost never used in violent crimes.

146. Scott R. Preston, "Targeting the Gun Industry: Municipalities Aim to Hold Manufacturers Liable for Their Products and Actions," *Southern Illinois Law Journal* 24 (Spring 2000): 596.

147. Ibid., 598.

148. Ibid., 601.

149. For a detailed discussion of these cases, see Dennis A. Henigan, "Lawsuits again Gun Manufacturers," in *Guns in American Society*, edited by Gregg Lee Carter, 2nd ed., vol. 2 (Santa Barbara, CA: ABC-CLIO, 2011), 491–500.

150. An excellent summary of the contents of the Smith & Wesson settlement may be found in Andrew J. McClurg, David B. Kopel, and Brannon P. Denning, *Gun Control and Gun Rights* (New York: New York University Press, 2002): 347–52.

151. Jacobs, *Can Gun Control Work?*, 182–83. Only the Boston case settlement was filed in court, and none ever went into legal effect.

152. Jacobs, *Can Gun Control Work?*, 184.

153. As is so often the case, the exact number here depends upon how you count. According to the NRA Fact Sheet "Courts Reject Lawsuits against Gun

Makers" (http://www.nraila.org/news-issues/fact-sheets/2003/courts-reject
-lawsuits-against-gun-make.aspx), 33 states "have enacted NRA-backed legislation that does just that [prohibiting localities from filing these suits]." The Brady
Campaign, in "Special Protection for the Gun Industry: State Bill" (http://www
.bradycampaign.org/facts/issues/?page=immun_state), claims that 21 states "do
not grant special immunity to the gun industry," 12 states prohibit localities
from filing suits, and 17 states prohibit municipal lawsuits and some individual
suits as well.

154. Helen Dewar, "Bush Opposes Additions to Gun Bill," *Washington Post*,
February 26, 2004, A4.

155. NRA statement on S. 1805, http://www.nraila.org/news-issues/news
-from-nra-ila/2004/nra-statement-on-S1805.aspx.

156. Sheryl Gay Stolberg, "Looking Back and Ahead after Senate's Votes on
Guns," *New York Times,* March 4, 2004, http://www.nytimes.com/2004/03/04/
politics/04GUNS.html.

157. United States House of Representatives, http://clerk.house.gov/evs/
2005/roll534.xml.

158. NRA-ILA, "Senate Passes NICS Improvement Act, House Concurs,"
December 19, 2007, http://www.nraila.org/news-issues/news-from-nra-ila/2007/
senate-passes-nics-improvement-act,-hou.aspx.

159. Congressional Research Service, "Submission of Mental health Records
to NICS and the HIPAA Privacy Rule," April 15, 2013, http://www.fas.org/sgp/
crs/misc/R43040.pdf

160. The increasing popularity of the AR platform suggests that any future
assault weapons bans would impact a larger number of gun owners.

161. Greg Ridgeway, "Summary of Select Firearm Violence Prevention
Strategies," National Institute of Justice memo, January 4, 2013. http://www
.nraila.org/media/10883516/nij-gun-policy-memo.pdf.

162. Ibid.

163. The committee's charge was described as follows: "Given the importance of this issue and the continued controversy surrounding the debate on firearms, the need was clear for an unbiased assessment of the existing portfolio of
data and research. Accordingly, the National Academies were asked by a consor-
tium of both federal agencies—the National Institute of Justice and the Centers
for Disease Control and Prevention—and private foundations—the David and
Lucile Packard Foundation, the Annie E. Casey Foundation, and the Joyce
Foundation—to assess the data and research on firearms.

The Committee to Improve Research and Data on Firearms was charged with
providing an assessment of the strengths and limitations of the existing research
and data on gun violence and identifying important gaps in knowledge; describing new methods to put research findings and data together to support the design
and implementation of improved prevention, intervention, and control strategies
for reducing gun-related crime, suicide, and accidental fatalities; and utilizing
existing data and research on firearms and firearm violence to develop models

of illegal firearms markets. The charge also called for examining the complex ways in which firearm violence may become embedded in community life and whether firearm-related homicide and suicide become accepted as ways of resolving problems, especially among youth; however, there is a lack of empirical research to address these two issues." Charles F. Wellford, John V. Pepper, and Carol V. Petrie, eds., *Firearms and Violence: A Critical Review* (Washington, DC: National Academies Press, 2004), 13. While some of the sponsoring agencies may have a bias in favor of gun control, the committee and its findings were not biased in either direction.

164. Wellford, Pepper, and Petrie, *Firearms and Violence*, 2–3.

FOUR

Public Opinion, Gun Control, and Elections

As is true for many issues in the public domain, public opinion polling is the source for much of what we know about the public's view of firearms and gun control. While many constituents contact elected officials through phone calls, letters, or e-mails, using those individuals to represent the opinion of everyone can be very misleading. Those people who take the time to contact elected officials are often the most interested and engaged, and they are often not representative of the general population. Winning candidates in elections often claim a mandate from the people to enact certain policies, but elections rarely turn on a single issue. It is even rarer that a candidate will have staked out a specific, clear, and unequivocal position on an issue and that voters were aware of it and used that issue as the deciding factor in their voting decision.

Polling is both an art and a science. Wording a question in a way that is simple, is easily understood, and accurately reflects the intended idea is the art component. The science of polling is reflected in several ways. First is to utilize proper sampling techniques to ensure that those who respond to the questions are representative of the population. The data must be compiled accurately and summarized, and typically are statistically weighted.[1] Finally, the results are interpreted by placing them in an appropriate context.[2] Elections are another way of measuring the public's views on issues. While less precise than a survey question on a specific issue, elections serve as a somewhat blunt instrument for measuring voter preferences.

This chapter examines public opinion regarding firearms and gun control and the importance of gun control as an electoral issue. The focus is primarily on the national level, but some state examples are used as well.

WHY IS OPINION IMPORTANT? SHOULD POLICY ALWAYS FOLLOW OPINION?

Governments in the United States—federal, state, and local—are republican forms of government in which citizens choose their leaders. They are not true democracies in the sense that most policy decisions are made by elected officials (or appointed judges in some cases). We elect our leaders who then vote on policy. To some extent, this insulates elected officials from the vagaries of the masses and allows them to make more considered, reasoned decisions. Of course, this also allows other individuals and groups to influence the decision-making process. While we value the opinions of citizens, we recognize that those views can be shortsighted and can be based on incomplete or inaccurate information. Reserving policy making for elected officials does not guarantee that only wise decisions will be rendered. We hope and believe that it makes wise decisions more likely.

Elected officials must decide if they will follow a delegate or trustee model of representation. A delegate will represent constituent sentiment as accurately and as frequently as possible. Of course, the wishes of the citizens will not always be obvious, but when they are, they direct delegates' votes. A trustee, conversely, acts in what they perceive to be the best interest of their constituents or in the interest of the greater good. Citizens put their faith in a trustee. They were chosen for their wisdom and knowledge, and they are expected to exercise their best judgment when rendering decisions.

In reality, most elected officials act as delegates at some times and as trustees at others. They reference public opinion when it agrees with their policy preferences, and they tend to ignore it when that suits their needs. This is true of members of both major political parties as well as people with differing political ideologies.[3] In practice, elected officials will follow the will of their constituents on issues that are of great salience to the citizens. If the people care about an issue and have a strong preference, then elected officials ignore that preference at their electoral peril. The opposition party or even another wing of their own party may produce a challenger at the next election who will remind the citizens that their representative ignored their will. On many issues, however, the will of the people is either not clear or it is not strongly held, thus giving the legislator greater leeway in how they will vote.

Why, then, do we care about what citizens think? Clearly, while we agree with the Founding Fathers that our representative democracy is preferable to simple majoritarian rule, we also think that elected officials should act in the best interest of the citizens and that they should consider the wishes of their constituents as they make policy.[4]

Even though we generally think that majorities should have their way, we recognize the limitations of such a position. Minority rights can be trampled in that situation. Therefore, we may wish to make allowance for the possibility that a minority position should direct policy if that minority cares intensely about a policy while the majority disagrees in terms of what course should be followed, but it does not care as much about the issue. For example, the reintroduction of the gray wolf in Yellowstone National Park in the past two decades has generated significant controversy. Multiple surveys conducted in the surrounding states prior to the wolf reintroduction showed that a majority of residents favored the policy, but those who lived closest to the park, and would thus be most impacted, were more opposed. At the same time, less than half of the respondents were able to answer factual questions about wolves correctly.[5]

In this situation, how could policy makers best represent the wishes of citizens? Should they weigh the views of those more likely to be impacted more heavily than others? Should they consider only the views of those who are most knowledgeable? Should they simply look at the wishes of the majority? An argument can be made for any of the above positions.

Similar conundrums are faced by decision makers regarding gun policy. While public opinion has generally favored numerous gun regulations, gun bans have been less popular, and the trend had been in the direction of gun rights prior to and some months following the Newtown shootings. The salience of the issue is also important, and we may also wish to consider the level of knowledge of the public, although these are debatable.

MEASURING GUN OWNERSHIP

As described in Chapter 3, because there is no gun registry in the United States, gun ownership rates have to be estimated. Although they are not the only method of measuring gun ownership, public opinion surveys are arguably the best method. According to Gallup, respondents reporting a firearm in the household have varied between 34 percent and 51 percent in the past two decades, although there is no clear trend.[6] Other polls have found declining gun ownership. Both the General Social Survey and the Pew Center found about a 10 percent drop—from the mid-40s percent to the mid-30s percent—in respondents stating there was a firearm in the household between 1993 and 2013.

Single-person households climbed from 13 percent in 1960 to 23 percent in 1980 and 27 percent by 2010.[7] Certainly, an increase in the percentage of households in which a female lives alone or as a single parent will drive down the percentage of households with a firearm. Research has shown some underreporting of gun ownership, especially by females, but the rate of underreporting has been disputed.[8] Still, questions asked consistently by the same polling firm using the same methodology should be useful for measuring the stability of opinion and for trend analysis.

Those trends may be impacted by the underreporting of firearm ownership. Gun owners tend be less trustful of the government and other institutions.[9] This lack of trust could translate into reluctance to tell a stranger, even with promised confidentiality, that one is a gun owner.[10] Pollsters generally assume that nonresponse is evenly distributed and thus does not impact the results. Nonresponse that is disproportionate, however, can lead to inaccurate measures. If gun owners are more likely to fail to respond to the question, then we may underreport gun ownership.

The number of hunters in the United States steadily declined throughout the 1990s, but has largely stabilized since then. According to the U.S. Fish and Wildlife Service, 14.6 million hunting licenses were sold nationwide in 2013.[11] Given that not all hunters are required to purchase licenses, this would somewhat underestimate the total number of hunters. For more than a decade, sales of handguns have greatly outpaced long guns, more commonly used for hunting, and the reasons for owning a firearm have changed as well. In short, measuring gun ownership is not as simple as we might think.

MULTIFACETED ISSUE, OFTEN SIMPLE QUESTIONS

An inherent problem in public opinion polling is difficulty in capturing complex issues in simple questions. Questions should be as brief and simple as possible, especially in the case of telephone surveys. On the phone it is nearly impossible for most people to follow lengthy or complex questions or to recall response options when the number of possible responses exceeds five or six. These problems are process-related; they are not the result of intentional bias.

For questions such as election choices—whether you would vote for candidate A or candidate B—this is not a problem. The question is simple, and the choices are limited. Probing views on issues, however, is more difficult. Issues can be multifaceted, and simple questions elicit simple responses that lose much of the nuance that is a part of many people's opinions. For example, if one were measuring opinion related to abortion policy, a simple question such as "In general, do you consider yourself to be pro-choice or pro-life?" would yield very general orientations, but it could incorrectly categorize respondents whose position is not absolute. A better method might be to ask if respondents think abortions should be permitted under a variety of specific conditions, i.e., the pregnancy is the result of rape or incest, a child is likely to be born with multiple birth defects, economic hardship, choosing the child's gender, etc.

In the same way, a simple question on gun control such as "In general, do you think that current gun control laws are too strict, about right, or not strict enough?" will provide general orientations, but it teaches us little about what people really think. It also assumes that people are familiar with current law, which we know is not true for most Americans. Providing response categories can also bias the results. For example, wording such as "Do you think stricter gun laws would reduce crime or make no difference in crime?" ignores the possibility that stricter laws may increase crime (or that a respondent would believe that).

The Pew Center has tracked support for gun rights for over 20 years, beginning in 1993.[12] The baseline data showed that 57 percent favored controlling ownership and only 35 percent favored protecting gun rights. That split was at its greatest in March 2000 (67%–29%), but it began to narrow after that time. In 2011 and early 2012, the percentage favoring gun rights was equal to or greater than that favoring gun control. In December 2012, following Newtown, opinion shifted back in favor of control (49%–42%); but by May 2013, it had rebounded to a nearly even split (50%–48%).[13] By early 2014, gun rights again came out on top (49%–48%).[14]

Earlier research by Pew found that much of the longitudinal change in opinion regarding gun control was due to several groups moving toward the gun-rights position. Among them were men, people who identified as partisan Independents, and those who lived in the Midwest, the South, and the West. In other words, those groups that were already more likely to favor gun rights moved more solidly in that direction. Women, Democrats, and those who lived in the East saw little or no change in their opinions, while Republicans saw only a small trend toward increased support for gun rights.[15]

Similarly, Gallup found a high-water mark for support for gun control in September 1990, with 78 percent of respondents favoring stricter gun laws.[16] That support steadily declined until October 2011, when 44 percent preferred to keep existing laws and 43 percent wanted stricter laws. In December 2012, support for stricter laws increased to 58 percent, but it almost certainly declined again as more time passed after Newtown.[17]

Support for several measures, including universal background checks, was strong in most polls in early 2013, typically over 80 percent. Yet, the Pew Center found that while 47 percent of respondents were angry or disappointed that the Manchin-Toomey bill was defeated in the Senate in 2013, 39 percent were very happy or relieved it did not pass, again suggesting that opinion is not easily measured.[18]

Gun bans are almost always less appealing to citizens than more simple restrictions on firearms or gun owners. Support for a handgun ban declined in the Gallup polls from 42 percent in 1993 to 24 percent in December 2012. At the same time, support for a ban on assault rifles usually garners more support, although support had declined somewhat from 50 percent in 2004 to 44 percent in 2012 according to Gallup.[19]

In early 2014, an ABC News/*Washington Post* poll asked respondents which of the political parties was closer to their views on a series of social issues. Democrats led on the issues of abortion (Democrats, 46%; Republicans, 37%), gay marriage (Democrats, 45%; Republicans, 33%), and raising the minimum wage (Democrats, 49%; Republicans, 35%), but Republicans were favored on the issue of gun control by a 48%–37% margin.[20]

Some of the fluctuation in support for gun control, both generally and in specific measures, is due to whether gun control is in the news. Some of that depends upon mass shootings, which always receive blanket coverage from the news media. Support also depends upon which measure is being touted by gun-control proponents at any point in time. If there is a push for an assault weapons ban, then we would expect support for that measure to spike. Likewise, if the regulation being sought is "closing the gun-show loophole," then we would expect to see increased support for background checks at gun shows. We do not have longitudinal data for universal background checks because they were generally not pushed very strongly until they were proposed as a response to the Newtown shootings.

Results from two polls taken in Virginia in early 2013 reached similar conclusions to those of the national surveys. Strong majorities supported requiring background checks for all firearms purchases at gun shows (86%) and universal background checks for firearms purchase, including private transactions (75%). Smaller majorities favored government registration of all firearms (61%) and requiring all gun owners to be licensed by the government (59%). A majority (58%) favored banning "assault rifles" and marginally opposed banning semiautomatic handguns

Table 4.1   Comparison of Those with Gun in Home, No Gun in Home, and Gun Owners: Support for Various Gun-Control Measures

Regulation	Overall	Gun in Home	No Gun in Home	Gun Owner
Favor background checks at gun shows	85%	79%	92%	74%
Favor universal background checks	75%	62%	87%	56%
Favor ban of semiautomatic rifles	47%	31%	60%	28%
Favor ban of semiautomatic shotguns	45%	29%	57%	25%
Favor ban of assault rifles	55%	44%	64%	44%
Favor ban of semiautomatic handguns	43%	31%	51%	27%
Favor ban of all guns	26%	19%	31%	13%
Favor ban on magazines > 10 rounds	49%	39%	58%	36%

Source: "RC Poll: Virginians' Views on Ethics, Mental Health Reforms, Medicaid Expansion Plus *Warner vs. Gillespie for US Senate*," Roanoke College, January 21, 2014.

(42% favored, 50% opposed) and semiautomatic shotguns (41% favored, 50% opposed). Only 16 percent of those interviewed favored banning all guns. A ban on magazines that can hold more than 10 rounds was favored by 53 percent.[21] Results from a poll taken less than three months later yielded virtually identical results. A more recent survey in three states— New Jersey, New York, and Virginia—found a majority of respondents in each state (74%, 68%, and 63%, respectively) said they would vote in favor of a national gun registry if they were a U.S. senator.[22]

Not surprisingly, virtually all polls find significant differences in opinion between those who own a gun (or are familiar with them) and those who do not. Logically, we would expect those who own a firearm to be less likely to favor gun regulations and background checks and to be less positive about the impact of stricter laws. Comparisons from one such poll can be found in Table 4.1. These results are typical of what we see in all surveys. The differences in attitudes when comparing gun owners and those who live in a household without firearms is stark, but probably not shocking. More surprising is that 13 percent of gun owners favor banning all guns. If a person holds that belief, one has to wonder why they would own a firearm.

The Pew Center has found evidence of a gap between those with or without a gun in the household and a gender gap. When asked if it was more important to protect the right to own a firearm or to control gun ownership, more than twice as many of those with a gun in the home chose protecting gun rights, while those without a gun preferred controlling gun ownership by a 2–1 margin. There was a significant gender gap in each group as well, with males being more likely to choose protecting gun ownership. It is possible that some of these differences were related to gun ownership and not to gender, although it was also present in those who did not have a gun in the household.[23]

It is not surprising that gun owners have different views on firearms-related issues from those who do not own guns. Gun owners would predictably think that firearms make them safer in their homes, can be handled safely, and can be used to prevent crime. Non-owners may have little or no experience with firearms, and lack of familiarity with any object can cause a sense of unease and worry. Familiarity with any item typically reduces discomfort, and eventually one accepts the object as part of the scenery. Familiarity is almost always a part of ownership, but it may extend to other family members as well or to those who are exposed to the object. Many would say it is simply a part of human nature to fear that which we do not know.

For many who are not familiar with guns, they are dangerous objects to be avoided. Needless to say, children and adolescents should never be near them. For those who are familiar with firearms, they are objects—dangerous objects, to be sure, but objects. They can be used in various ways, for good or for evil, but if they are handled correctly, then they are no more to be feared than other things that are dangerous. That is a large chasm to be bridged to facilitate rational debate.

Support for specific gun-control policies is not a recent phenomenon. A longitudinal analysis found support for many different types of gun regulations over decades. A majority of respondents supported 16 of the 19 gun-control measures included in several surveys conducted by the National Opinion Research Center (NORC) between 1972 and 1999. To varying degrees, a majority of those interviewed supported universal background checks, waiting periods, mandatory gun registration, and requiring a permit to purchase a firearm. Gun-safety measures such as trigger locks, safe-storage laws, and requiring anyone purchasing a gun to take a safety course received even stronger support. In all, 14 of 16 gun-safety measures garnered majority support.[24] At the same time, other national surveys have found strong public support for the idea that the Second Amendment confers an individual right to possess firearms, although almost half believe that right must be balanced against other rights when determining policy.[25]

As summarized by Vizzard, "there can be little question that a large majority of the American public gives at least tacit support to more comprehensive gun control. But opinion-poll results do not reflect the depth of commitment, degree of interest, or depth of knowledge regarding a policy area."[26] In further discussion, Vizzard notes that for more than half of the population that does not own a firearm, additional regulation imposes no burden on them at all. It is a no-cost policy from their perspective. While some would argue they would be hurt by decreased deterrence, if they do not perceive themselves as currently receiving that benefit, then they do not perceive a cost to regulations that will hamper gun ownership.

In summary, if we had a direct democracy regarding gun laws, there would be more laws, and they would be stricter. But, is opinion really that simple? Is it reasonable to allow a majority to impose costs on a minority that will not be borne by the majority? Do people think that the laws they favor would really make a difference? Do they understand guns, the market for firearms, and the behaviors of the perpetrators of gun violence?

HOW WE VIEW GUN OWNERS

It is rare that we ask how people view gun owners. A glimpse into the minds of Americans may be found in a 2014 poll by the Pew Center. Focused on political polarization, the study asked 10,000 adults about a variety of issues. Included was a series of questions regarding what their response would be if a family member married a person with various characteristics.

The results, shown in Table 4.2, are both fascinating and instructive. It is clear that conservatives and liberals would be unhappy with a family member marrying certain types of people, and with the exception of atheists, conservatives are generally not less tolerant than liberals. For consistent liberals (as measured by responses to a series of 10 questions), a marriage to a gun owner would cause more people to be unhappy than a marriage to a born-again Christian, an atheist, or a Republican. Gun owners also rank second only to atheists as unhappiness-generators among those who are mostly liberal and those who have mixed views. Nearly half of consistent conservatives (49%) and one-third (30%) of mostly conservatives would be happy to have a gun owner join the family.

The study did not probe deeper into these sentiments, so we cannot speculate on the reasons for these feelings or the attributes ascribed to gun owners. Nonetheless, it is clear that gun owners are not welcome in many households, and these findings provide fairly strong evidence of an anti-gun culture and an inherent bias against those who own firearms.

Table 4.2   Percent of People in Various Groups Unhappy or Happy if a Family Member Married Different Types of People: Percentage Unhappy/Happy

Group	Consistently Conservative	Mostly Conservative	Mixed	Mostly Liberal	Consistently Liberal	Total
Someone of a different race	23%/6%	19%/6%	11%/10%	4%/8%	1%/14%	11%/9%
Someone born and raised outside the United States	11%/7%	13%/8%	8%/10%	4%/8%	1%/15%	7%/10%
Someone who did not go to college	8%/6%	11%/7%	14%/6%	15%/5%	17%/7%	14%/6%
Someone who does not believe in God	73%/2%	58%/3%	51%/3%	41%/5%	24%/10%	49%/4%
A "born-again" Christian	3%/57%	6%/42%	6%/31%	9%/26%	27%/16%	9%/32%
A Republican	1%/40%	3%/23%	9%/9%	8%/5%	23%/5%	9%/13%
A Democrat	30%/4%	15%/5%	5%/14%	1%/18%	1%/35%	8%/15%
A gun owner	1%/49%	7%/30%	22%/14%	25%/7%	31%/5%	19%/17%

Source: Pew Research Center for the People and the Press, "Political Polarization in the American Public," June 12, 2014. http://www.people-press.org/2014/06/12/political-polarization-in-the-american-public/.

MEDIA INFLUENCE ON OPINION

Attention to the news is one of the most important ways in which we learn about current events and their meaning. One significant consequence of news coverage is agenda setting. Often unintentional, the media help to define important issues and policies for both citizens and elected officials. A single event or a reported trend influence the news media to give more attention to those events, and the news consumer thus learns what is "important to know."[27]

Agenda setting is important; it helps establish the relative importance of issues and determines which policies will be debated by the public and by elected officials. It can narrow or enlarge the number of different policies that will be considered. Agenda setting is generally not thought to be the result of any media "conspiracy" of the political left or right. Rather, it is a product of the conventions of news gathering and reporting, as well as the market forces that are exerted on journalists and news organizations.

How the news is covered is crucial in helping to shape opinions regarding those issues. In traditional journalism, the news is covered "objectively." That is, reporters present facts and different interpretations of those facts (being careful to exclude their opinion), thus allowing the viewer/reader to determine for themselves which interpretation is correct. If the event is explained in similar ways by several media, that can influence how the news consumer perceives the issue. How an event is interpreted or explained is referred to as issue framing.

Research suggests that issue framing impacts citizens' opinions regarding gun policy. Haider-Markel and Joslyn[28] examined framing of a concealed handgun law and the Columbine High School shootings, concluding that issue frames did influence opinion, although the impact was mitigated by the individual's preexisting beliefs and their ability to be influenced by the frame. In other words, how the issue was framed did matter, but frames that comport with what people already believe to be true are more readily adopted than frames that contradict those preconceptions.

Callaghan and Schnell examined news coverage of the Brady Bill and the Assault Weapons Ban, assessing the influence of interest groups, elected officials, and the news media in framing the gun-control issue. The final news product may reflect the view of one side of the debate, some combination of views from two or more actors, or a "purely media-generated version" of the issue.[29]

The NRA promoted two separate frames—"feel-good laws" and "constitutional rights"—arguing that the laws would not reduce violent crime and would infringe on the rights of gun owners. Proponents of the laws argued that it was "sensible legislation" and discussed the "culture of violence." Politicians generally picked up on the themes promoted by the groups with which they agreed. Nearly half of the news stories emphasized the "culture of violence" theme. Although "feel-good laws" was slightly more common than "sensible legislation," they were mentioned less than 20 percent of the time in news coverage. The media also used their own themes of "political contest" and "court challenges." While the resulting news frames may not have been the result of ideological bias, but rather adopted to boost ratings, they clearly favored the pro-control side of the debate.

With regard to the public's knowledge of crime, polls have also shown that the public is often unaware of the trends in criminal activity. Most of the time, the public overestimates the rate of all crimes and their chances of being a victim of a crime. This is true even after two decades of mostly declining crime rates.

Despite the attention to gun violence in recent months, most Americans are unaware that gun crime is markedly lower than it was two decades ago. A new Pew Research Center survey (March 14–17) found that 56% of Americans believe the number of crimes involving a gun is higher than it was 20 years ago; only 12% say it is lower and 26% say it stayed the same. (An additional 6% did not know or did not answer.) ... Asked about trends in the number of gun crimes 'in recent years,' a plurality of 45% believe the number has gone up, 39% say it is about the same and 10% say it has gone down. (An additional 5% did not know or did not answer.)[30]

Women, ethnic and racial minorities, and older respondents were most likely to think that the crime rate was rising. Logically, the public's familiarity with existing gun laws is also somewhat lacking. Some have suggested that this phenomenon is related to television viewership. Those who watch more television, both news and entertainment, are more likely to overstate the crime rate and their chances of being a victim. Crime, particularly violent crime, is both overemphasized by the news media and more closely watched by viewers than other types of news.[31]

Certainly, the media are obligated to report violent crime, particularly homicides. The public also pays a great deal of attention to stories of crime, especially mass shootings. Two of the top five news stories in 2012 were the Aurora, Colorado, theater shooting (#5) and the Sandy Hook school shooting (#2) according to the Pew Center's news index. Only the presidential election topped Newtown in that measure.[32]

The coverage of guns, however, is both somewhat biased and disproportionate. In an analysis of coverage of gun control by the *CBS Evening News* and the *New York Times*, Wilson found that the bulk of the coverage was neutral, but that the pro-control position was presented much more frequently than the pro-gun-rights position, particularly on CBS. In addition, mass shootings garnered a disproportionate amount of news coverage as did shootings involving children. Conversely, mentions of defensive gun uses were almost absent.[33]

While it is impossible to draw a direct connection between news media coverage of the issues of crime and guns to public opinion and then to public policies, it is logical to suggest there is some impact on how people view the issues based on media usage. The Newtown shootings were qualitatively different because of the age of the victims. This fact was not lost on the media or the public.

As mentioned above, mass shootings receive significant and often disproportionate media attention. These shootings often involve a semiautomatic rifle or handgun—an "assault weapon"—and they have led to movements to ban certain firearms. The following quote is taken from a *Mother Jones* article that chronicles mass shootings in the United States over three decades. While the information is accurate, the impression is that these events are common and, perhaps, that they account for a large percentage of homicides in the United States.

It is perhaps too easy to forget how many times this has happened. The horrific mass murder at a movie theater in Colorado last July, another at a Sikh temple in Wisconsin in August, another at a manufacturer in Minneapolis in September—and then the unthinkable nightmare at a Connecticut elementary school in December—are the latest in an epidemic of such gun violence over the last three decades. Since 1982, there have been at least 62 mass shootings across the country, with the killings unfolding in 30 states from Massachusetts to Hawaii. Twenty-five of these mass shootings have occurred since 2006, and seven of them took place in 2012.[34]

Mass shootings are a matter of great importance to the public, and they receive a great deal of attention from legislators as well. Yet, they comprise a relatively small proportion of overall shootings. "[H]omicides that claimed at least three lives accounted for less than 1% of all homicide deaths from 1980 to 2008 ... A Congressional Research Service report, using a definition of four deaths or more, counted 547 deaths from mass shootings in the U.S. from 1983 to 2012."[35] Shootings involving children are also relatively uncommon, although they are covered extensively in the news.

All of this can easily lead to the public's misunderstanding of both crime and guns. That is not to say that thousands of firearm-related homicides are somehow acceptable (they are not) or that hundreds of children murdered by guns is not a problem (it is). Rather, it suggests that emphasis is not being placed where the problem is the greatest. The emotion of mass shootings and child shootings is inescapable. The logic of focusing on semiautomatic rifles when they are used in such a small percentage of shootings is not direct. In other words, policy response does not always focus on the problem.

THE PERCEIVED EFFICACY OF GUN LAWS

Surveys typically do not ask about the perceived effectiveness of gun laws. Polls that have asked those questions have generally found the public to be split, with gun ownership and familiarity with firearms to be important variables in determining one's opinion. Smith found a majority of those interviewed (66%) said that stricter laws would be at least somewhat helpful in reducing violent crime.[36] Those in households without a gun were nearly twice as likely to say stricter laws would be very helpful. Likewise, those who thought that guns in the household increased safety were only half as likely to say stricter laws would be helpful in reducing violent crime when compared to those who thought a gun in the household make a home less safe.[37]

Surveys conducted in Virginia over the past decade found similar results. Although Virginians were overall less positive about the possible impact of stricter gun laws on homicides, suicides, and accidental shootings, the significant differences between those who owned firearms or were familiar with them and those who were not were similar to the national results.[38]

In Virginia polls conducted in early 2013, residents were asked their thoughts regarding the causes of mass shootings such as those in Newtown, Connecticut, and Virginia Tech. The most common response was poor policies to deal with mental illness (56%); followed by an inability to stop those who want to kill others (38%); violence in the media, such as video games, TV, and movies (28%); poor enforcement of gun laws (26%); and weak gun laws (21%). Not surprisingly, respondents were more likely to think that better enforcement of existing gun laws (53%) was more likely to reduce gun violence than tougher gun laws (38%). Fully half (50%) of those interviewed said that stricter gun-control laws

Table 4.3   Three-State Survey—Gun Policy Efficacy

Policy	New Jersey	New York	Virginia
Support a national gun registry	74%	68%	63%
Stricter gun laws would make you			
More safe	44%	45%	35%
No difference	40%	43%	47%
Less safe	13%	12%	16%
Most responsible for mass shootings			
Weak gun laws	16%	15%	10%
Poor enforcement of gun laws	11%	11%	7%
Violent media	12%	17%	15%
Poor mental illness policies	36%	36%	44%
Can't stop those who want to kill	20%	18%	21%

Source: Harry Wilson, "RC Poll: The Opinions of Virginians on Guns, Gun Policy, and Gun Violence," January 28, 2013, http://roanoke.edu/News_and_Events/News_Archive/RC_Poll_Jan_2013_Guns.htm.

would make no difference to their personal safety, while one-third (34%) said stricter laws would make them more safe, and 12 percent said they would make them less safe.[39]

A poll conducted in New Jersey, New York, and Virginia found similar results on this question, although a plurality of residents in New Jersey and New York thought that stricter laws would make them safer. That poll also found similar results regarding the causes of mass shootings.[40]

As can be seen in Table 4.3, although strong majorities in each of those states supported a national gun registry, in no state did a majority think that stricter laws would make them more safe. Residents of New Jersey and New York were generally split between thinking stricter laws would make them more safe or make no difference, Virginians were more likely to choose the "no difference" response. When asked about the causes of mass shootings, weak gun laws finished third in New Jersey and fourth in New York and Virginia. At least twice as many respondents thought that mental illness policies were more responsible than weak gun laws (more than four times as many in Virginia). Clearly, there is doubt about the efficacy of stronger gun laws, even if a majority of citizens supports those laws.[41]

Previous research has shown that familiarity with firearms was the strongest determinant of how people assess the possible utility of various gun regulations. Familiarity was conceptualized as an index that combined several variables, including (1) self-reported knowledge of how firearms function, (2) if there was a gun in the household when the respondent was growing up, and (3) if the respondent owned a gun or lived with someone who did. This index was a more powerful predictor of one's views than an index comprised of gender, political party, and political ideology, three variables that are also strongly related to opinion regarding firearms.[42]

ACTIVISM AND INTENSITY GAPS

There is a "gun policy activism gap," insofar as those who support gun rights are more likely to vote and promote their position. A 2013 Pew Center study concluded, "There is a substantial gap between those who prioritize gun rights and gun control when it comes to political involvement. Nowhere is this gap larger than in making donations to activist organizations."[43] Gun-rights supporters were about four times as likely to have contributed money to a group that advocates their interest as compared to those who support gun control (25%–6%). The gap is not as great when looking at contacting an elected official about the policy (16%–11%) or discussing it on social media like Facebook or Twitter (19%–12%). On the important topic of influencing one's voting decision, the Pew survey found:

> People who own guns (46%) are more likely than those in households with no guns (33%) to view gun policy as an important voting issue. And among the vast majority of gun owners who support gun rights, 52% say they would not vote for a candidate with whom they disagreed on gun policy even if they agreed with them on most other issues. Among the much smaller share of gun owners who favor gun control, just 26% view gun policy as an important voting issue ... Among those in households with no guns, about as many who favor gun control (33%) as gun rights (32%) say they would not vote for a candidate who they disagreed with on gun policy but agreed with on most other issues.[44]

There is additional evidence for the activism gap carrying over into voting. One study found that voters in 19 of 25 states were more firmly committed to the NRA than to either the Democratic or Republican Parties. The overall percentage of voters in this category was not large—only about 10 percent—but, when many elections are decided by a margin much smaller than that, 10 percent can be the difference between winning and losing.[45] Some research, however, has suggested that, while opinion regarding gun control tends to be relatively stable, those who hold a gun-rights position may be more likely to change their minds than those who favor gun control.[46]

The Roanoke College–Rutgers University–Siena College three-state survey in 2014 provides some evidence of the intensity differences that reinforce the argument that gun-rights advocates think the issue is more important. As mentioned above, majorities in each state said they would vote to establish a national gun registry if they were a U.S. senator. As a follow-up, those who said they would vote for the hypothetical gun registry were asked how upset they would be if the bill did not pass. Similarly, those who said they would vote against the gun registry were asked how upset they would be if it passed. In each state, those who opposed the bill would be more upset if it passed.[47]

GUN CONTROL AND ELECTIONS

Like most issues, gun control is more important in some elections than in others. While it can be difficult to determine *the key* issue in any campaign, some issues are more prominent than others. Many groups, based on demographic characteristics or common interests, will be credited with a candidate's victory, or they may claim credit for themselves. Political pundits, talking heads, bloggers, academics, and journalists all espouse their own theory of why someone won or lost an election. Reality is usually much more complex than we are led to believe. Gun control can be an important issue, though it is rarely the determining issue in an election.

Most election analysts agree that the state of the economy is the most critical issue in presidential elections. Many political scientists subscribe to the retrospective voting theory, which posits that voters do a rough calculation in their head, comparing the state of the economy with its status four years prior—when the incumbent party won the White House. Economists and others run models using economic data several months prior to a presidential election to predict the winner, and their accuracy is impressive. The Bill Clinton campaign in 1992 coined the phrase, "It's the Economy, Stupid," and that remains relevant today. Certainly, the economy was the dominant issue in both the 2008 and 2012 presidential elections.

Gun control can be categorized with a group of social issues that are important in elections, but do not always rise to the level of being a critical issue. Other issues in this group would include abortion, gay rights, and immigration, to name a few. Gun control is rarely an issue in local elections, but it can be important in statewide elections, such as governor or U.S. senator, as well as in presidential elections. It can also be important in some states, but not in others in the same year.

Many analysts see the gun control issue in partisan terms. Democrats favor gun control, and Republicans favor gun rights. The partisan split on firearms issues is significant, but the urban/rural split may be even more important. These are often difficult to disentangle today because the two parties are so strongly aligned with that urban/rural dynamic. Nationally, and even within most states, Democrats are stronger in more urban areas, while Republicans predominate in more rural areas. It is often the suburban voters who are crucial in electoral contests, and they are the swing constituency on gun rights as well.

For example, the senators who defected from the parties' positions on the Manchin-Toomey amendment in 2013 were four Democrats from Republican-leaning rural states (Alaska, Arizona, Louisiana, and North Dakota) and Republicans from Democratic-leaning more urban states (Illinois, Pennsylvania) or "mavericks" (Arizona, Maine). Interestingly, one piece of research found that "party influence ... *never* occurs on gun control [emphasis in original]" in congressional roll-call voting.[48] That is a strong statement, but political party affiliation is not as important to gun control as many believe.

The differences between rural and urban areas are both cultural and environmental. Environmental, in this context, refers more to the crime environment. Think of the differences between states with stricter gun laws, such as Connecticut, Massachusetts, and New Jersey, and states with less strict laws such as Wyoming, Montana, and North Dakota. Violent crime is perceived to be more of a problem in urban areas, while hunting and sport shooting are much more common in rural areas. The gun experience, then, is at the extremes in these two environments. As a result, the views of firearms are very different as well. For urban dwellers, guns can easily be seen as a cause of the violence problem. Innocent people are caught in the cross-fire, and few residents own firearms for sporting purposes. A negative connotation is almost a reflex. At the other extreme, guns are a part of life for many who live in rural America. They are used for hunting, for recreational shooting, and for protection against predators—animal or human. They are respected, but they are not feared.

PRESIDENTIAL ELECTIONS

Election 2000

While the 2000 presidential election will be forever remembered for the debacle in Florida, how to determine when a vote is really a vote, and "hanging chads," gun control was an important issue in the 2000 presidential campaign because of the closeness of the outcome in states such as West Virginia, Tennessee, and Arkansas, which were carried by George W. Bush. Bush carried those three states—a traditional Democratic stronghold (West Virginia), the home state of Al Gore (Tennessee), and the home state of Bill Clinton (Arkansas). A victory in any of those states by Gore would have made the outcome in Florida a moot point.

> Gun control was not prominently featured in the campaign, although the candidates held very different views. Gov. George W. Bush had signed a permissive concealed carry law in Texas. Gore's position on firearms had evolved as he became more of a national figure in the Democratic Party. He supported President Clinton's gun initiatives, including the Assault Weapons Ban. During the campaign, he expressed support for background checks for all gun show purchases, a licensing requirement for those who wished to purchase a firearm, banning inexpensive handguns known as Saturday Night Specials, and limiting handgun sales to one per month. All of those were strongly opposed by the NRA and other gun rights groups.[49]

The NRA strongly supported Bush, even sending its president, Charlton Heston, "on tour" in West Virginia, Tennessee, and Arkansas. The NRA claimed credit for Gore's defeat, and some of it was probably deserved. An analysis of the 2000 election found that Gore received the support of about two-thirds of the voters who thought it should be much more difficult to purchase guns, a slight majority of those who thought it should be harder, and less than one-third of the rest.[50]

There was some discussion of gun control in the 2002 congressional elections, but the real lessons for Democrats had been learned by 2004. Doug Hattaway, Gore's 2000 campaign spokesman, and later a consultant to Americans for Gun Safety, a pro-control group, urged the Democrats to approach the issue with "a moderate rights and responsibilities" message "rather than throwing away elections on policies that are going nowhere."[51] Early in the primary election season, the *Washington Times* editorialized that "[A]side from same-sex 'marriage,' there is at least one other cultural issue no Democrat running against President Bush wants to touch: gun control."[52]

Several of the Democratic primary candidates in 2004 either backed away or deemphasized their support of gun control. Senator Joe Lieberman, Gore's running mate in 2000, said he opposed gun-owner licensing, although he did support expanded background checks and an Assault

Weapons Ban.[53] Former Vermont governor Howard Dean supported the
Assault Weapons Ban and instant background checks on all retail and gun-
show sales. Other regulations should be adopted or rejected by the states.

> If you say "gun control" in Vermont or Wyoming, people think it
> means taking away their hunting rifle. If you say "gun control" in
> New York City or Los Angeles, people are relieved at the prospect
> of having Uzis or illegal handguns taken off the streets. They're both
> right. That's why I think Vermont ought to be able to have a different
> set of laws than California.[54]

Election 2004

Clearly, gun control was, at best, a secondary issue in the presidential
contest of 2004, an election that heavily featured discussions of war and
terrorism. At the same time, social issues were thought to play a role in
the election, and firearms was one of those tertiary issues. Harold M.
Ickes, a former Clinton adviser who headed the 527 group MoveOn.org,
suggested: "I think we [Democrats] ignored in large measure the
three big cultural issues of this election: guns, abortion and gay
rights ... They really, really motivate people."[55] Other Democratic leaders, such as Democratic National Committee chairman Terry McAuliffe,
and one of the candidates to succeed him as DNC chair echoed those sentiments.[56] Numerous media outlets also picked up this theme, from the
Washington Post and the *New York Times* to *National Review*.[57]

Senator John Kerry (D-MA), the Democratic nominee, paid little attention to the gun-control issue throughout the campaign, except to try to
establish his bona fides as a sportsman. The Assault Weapons Ban expired
during the campaign, but it was barely discussed. It was mentioned briefly
during the third presidential debate, but it was mostly inconsequential.
President Bush said he would sign an extension of the ban if it were sent
to his desk, but he would not push for it.

Kerry emphasized that he was a hunter and fisherman, and he offered
interviews to several outdoor magazines. He also touted his support for
conservation measures that would protect the habitat for outdoor sports.
In one of Kerry's missteps during the campaign, he participated in a goose
hunt and photo-op in the battleground state of Ohio. A *New York Times*
reporter described the scene:

> Clad in camouflage clothing, a 12-gauge double-barreled shotgun
> under his arm, Senator John Kerry and three fellow hunters emerged

from an eastern Ohio cornfield Thursday morning with four dead geese and an image his aides hope will help shore up his macho bona fides among rural voters. "Everybody got one; everybody got one," said Mr. Kerry, his hands stained with goose blood, though he was the only member of the hunting party not carrying a carcass.[58]

The hunt turned out to be a poor attempt to connect with hunters and gun owners, and it probably won Kerry no votes among those who do not own firearms or hunt, either. The reporter's disdain is clear, but it is not clear if it was directed at Kerry, his staff, or those voters he was trying to impress. The event did provoke a response from the NRA in the form of an ad that spoofed the hunting trip.[59] As expected, the NRA challenged the Kerry candidacy with vigor and precision. They communicated their preference clearly in their publications and in targeted ads in specific states. For months, the NRA attacked Kerry in its *America's 1st Freedom* magazine.

The Brady Campaign communicated primarily through its Web site most likely due to its lack of funds. On October 1, 2004, the Brady Campaign and Million Mom March officially endorsed Kerry. Their press release focused more on the "failings" of the Bush administration for its individual-rights interpretation of the Second Amendment, its failure to renew the Assault Weapons Ban, its support for immunity for gun manufacturers, and for "turning his back on the victims of violent crime, on police officers gunned down on our streets, and on the fight against terrorists."[60]

The NRA noted the Bush victory with pride and touted a 95 percent success rate among endorsed congressional candidates. Of course, they did not make endorsements in every contest, and they often endorsed incumbents who would win with or without the NRA's support. Still, the NRA was clearly the victor in 2004. The passage of the Protection of Lawful Commerce in Arms Act of 2005 suggests that the few seats the NRA was able to gain in the Senate provided the impetus for pro-gun legislation to pass in Congress. In all, NRA spent about $20 million in the election.[61]

ELECTION 2008

While it may have been difficult for gun-rights supporters to rally behind John McCain, the Republican candidate in 2008, they found it much easier to oppose Democrat Barack Obama. Their problem was that few were listening to their cries. The economic crises of the past year dominated the campaign at the expense of all other issues.

President Bush's approval rating had plummeted to 25 percent just prior to the election.[62] Unemployment was at 6.5 percent in October 2008, its highest rate in 14 years. Public debt was skyrocketing as a result of the economic downturn. In that same month, more than $700 billion was committed to what was perceived to be a bailout for banks and businesses in the Troubled Asset Relief Program (TARP). Many Americans had lost significant equity in their homes when the housing bubble burst, sending home prices tumbling across the country. Gun control was barely on the radar screen for most voters.

There were clear differences between the two candidates on gun control, although then-Senator Obama tried his best to reassure gun owners. He had risked alienating them, as well as others, when at a San Francisco fund-raising event in April 2008, he uttered his famous quote:

> You go into these small towns in Pennsylvania and, like a lot of small towns in the Midwest, the jobs have been gone now for 25 years and nothing's replaced them. And they fell through the Clinton administration, and the Bush administration, and each successive administration has said that somehow these communities are gonna regenerate and they have not.
>
> And it's not surprising then they get bitter, they cling to guns or religion or antipathy toward people who aren't like them or anti-immigrant sentiment or anti-trade sentiment as a way to explain their frustrations.[63]

At a campaign event in Virginia in September, he said:

> I don't want any misunderstanding when you all go home, and you're talking to your buddies, and they say, "Aw, he wants to take my gun away." You've heard it here; I'm on television, so everybody knows it. *I believe in the Second Amendment. I believe in people's lawful right to bear arms. I will not take your shotgun away. I will not take your rifle away. I won't take your handgun away.* ... There are some common-sense gun safety laws that I believe in. But I am not *going to take your guns away.* So if you want to find an excuse not to vote for me, don't use that one. ... It just ain't true. [Emphasis in original][64]

It could be said that Obama's views on gun control had evolved over time. Just prior to the *Heller* decision by the Supreme Court, Obama was forced to backtrack on a statement made by an aide in 2007 to the *Chicago Tribune* regarding his view of the Washington, D.C., gun ban.

"He [Obama] believes that we can recognize and respect the rights of law-abiding gun owners and the right of local communities to enact common sense laws to combat violence and save lives. Obama believes the D.C. handgun law is constitutional." Obama often discussed an individual right, but he also talked about "common sense" gun laws that could be enacted by the states.[65] In response to the *Heller* decision, Obama issued the following statement:

> I have always believed that the Second Amendment protects the right of individuals to bear arms, but I also identify with the need for crime-ravaged communities to save their children from the violence that plagues our streets through common-sense, effective safety measures. The Supreme Court has now endorsed that view, and while it ruled that the D.C. gun ban went too far, Justice Scalia himself acknowledged that this right is not absolute and subject to reasonable regulations enacted by local communities to keep their streets safe . . .
>
> As president, I will uphold the constitutional rights of law-abiding gun-owners, hunters, and sportsmen. I know that what works in Chicago may not work in Cheyenne. We can work together to enact common-sense laws, like closing the gun show loophole and improving our background check system, so that guns do not fall into the hands of terrorists or criminals.[66]

Later in the campaign, Obama ran an ad in rural Pennsylvania in which a man wearing camouflage and carrying a shotgun and described as a NRA member says he is supporting Obama. The narrator says, "Barack Obama supports gun rights, our right to defend ourselves, and the Second Amendment. That's the truth."[67]

Obama's somewhat sparse legislative record prior to the election made it difficult to examine his record on gun control. There were few gun-related issues before Congress during his tenure, and he had been in the Senate for less than four years. Still, he had voted against immunity for gun manufacturers in 2005. He said he supported background checks at gun shows and the Assault Weapons Ban. He voted for a 2005 amendment that would have prohibited "armor-piercing" ammunition from being sold. He said he would vote to repeal the Tiahrt Amendment, which limits the ability of BATF to share gun-trace data. He declined to sign on to the amicus brief filed in the *Heller* case arguing that the D.C. law should be held unconstitutional. In contrast, John McCain's record had earned him a C+ grade from the NRA.[68]

Chris Cox, NRA-ILA executive director, offered the group's assessment of the elections of 2008. "Unfortunately, of course, Barack Obama won the presidential race, spending millions to hide his anti-gun record." NRA-backed candidates won 14 of 23 races for the Senate, and 216 of 248 candidates in the House of Representatives. Cox attempted to put a positive spin on the success rate, which was lower than in previous elections. "Your NRA-PVF does not just pick the easy battles ... [W]e get involved in every race where we can make a difference and this year was no exception." He noted that many of the pro-gun rights Republicans who did not win election lost their seats to pro-gun rights Democrats.[69]

Few, if any, candidates were willing to take on gun control directly. Paul Helmke, president of the Brady Campaign, told the media, "We know of no political candidate at any level, in any race, who lost because they supported sensible gun laws. That's because no political candidate at any level, in any race, would admit to supporting what the Brady Campaign considers 'sensible gun laws'—including Barack Obama!"[70]

The explanations for the relatively "poor" showing for the NRA and gun rights in 2008 are simple. The elections were not *about* gun control. Gun control was not an important factor in the election. The economy trumped all else, and the War in Iraq was important as well. Given the state of the economy, George W. Bush's abysmal approval rating, and a very unhappy electorate, people were ready for "Hope and Change." Barack Obama offered both, and he excited core Democratic constituencies, which increased voter turnout among minorities and youth significantly. Both of those groups voted heavily in favor of Obama.

Republicans were demoralized. McCain's choice of Sarah Palin as the vice-presidential candidate was designed to insert some excitement into the Republican base, and she was able to do that. But outside of that base, she was viewed negatively. To be sure, most gun-rights supporters voted for McCain and down-ticket Republicans and Democrats who agreed with them, but there was probably a degree of complacency there as well. Most of the battles of the previous decade had gone in the direction of gun rights. Success breeds complacency, while defeat can stoke fear and activism.

It was difficult to see how President Obama would push for gun control when there were other things he seemed to want more, such as health care reform and action on climate change, and things he had to do, such as address the economic situation. Beyond that, it was clear that no serious gun-control proposal would move through Congress. Even though Democrats controlled both houses from 2008 to 2010, no one other than the "usual suspects" was promoting the issue. It was reasonable to think that

Obama would have pushed for gun control if he thought he could win. It was not likely, however, that he would waste his time on initiatives and fights that he knew he would lose. With the Republican takeover of the House of Representatives in 2010, the fate of any gun control was sealed. It was simply "off the table."

In fact, the first Obama administration was not hostile to gun rights:

> Not only did a first-term Obama ignore the items on gun control advocates' wish lists, he also left those same advocates bewildered when he expanded gun rights by signing two bills into law—one that allowed the public to carry guns into national parks; another that let passengers carry guns in their luggage on Amtrak trains.
>
> Obama even boasted that his administration had expanded gun rights in a March 2011 op-ed in the Arizona Daily Star in an effort to prove to his gun rights opponents that he wasn't really a threat to their weapons, as he had been characterized.[71]

The potential threats of an Obama administration were not lost on gun owners or gun-rights supporters. Sales surged after his election in 2008, and they remained at a strong pace throughout his term. The number of background checks conducted by the FBI increased by 49 percent compared to the previous year in the week after his victory.[72] The number of federally licensed dealers increased as well, after a decade of decline. Obama, quite unintentionally, was an excellent gun salesman.[73] To place this in proper context, gun sales had been increasing throughout the decade, even prior to Obama's election, although the increases thereafter were even greater. Some of the increase is attributable to Obama's election, but some of it may have just been a continuation of guns becoming more popular.[74] There was a similar surge in sales following the 2012 elections, although later parts of that surge may have been due to the impact of the Newtown shootings.

Election 2012

The presidential election of 2012 seemed unlikely to prominently feature gun control. No Democrat challenged the renomination of President Obama. Mitt Romney emerged very quickly as the Republican frontrunner, and he survived challenges from a relatively large but somewhat lackluster field, including Rick Santorum, Ron Paul, Newt Gingrich, Herman Cain, Michele Bachmann, Rick Perry, Tim Pawlenty, and Jon Huntsman. With the presence of some very strong social conservatives such as

Santorum, Perry, and Bachmann; the conservative economic message of Ryan; and the Libertarian-leaning Paul, there was little discussion of fire-arms. There were numerous public debates and many attacks during that time, but guns were barely mentioned. The focus was on the economy and Obama's health care plan.

Complacency was also a potential problem for gun-rights advocates. Supporters of gun control had been largely silent for many years, particu-larly in elections. The gun-rights argument was in ascendance, and one term of Barack Obama's presidency, including two years with a Democrat-controlled Congress, had produced no gun-control measures. "Despite the perception that Mr. Obama is anti-gun rights, ... he has repeatedly reaffirmed the right to bear arms."[75]

Political defeat and fear are two important ingredients for any group, and they were largely missing from the 2012 elections. Outdoors writer Kyle Wintersteen summarized the "problem":

There's a reason gun owners make up one of the largest, most effec-tive voter blocs in American politics. We take our freedom seriously because we feel the impact of election wins and losses in our daily lives. But with concealed carry on the march and gun sales at all time highs, have you noticed a growing number of the politically compla-cent in our ranks? They apparently forget how long it took to dissolve the Gun Control Act of 1968; how closely the Clinton Assault Weap-ons Ban came to being permanent; and how closely the Supreme Court came to ruling that the Second Amendment doesn't really mean what it says.

Gun owners who sit out the 2012 election surely endanger all we've accomplished. If we don't "cling to our guns," to quote President Obama, but rather reelect him and bolster him with an assortment of anti-gun cronies in Congress, we're looking at a worst-case scenario. Power would be in the hands of those who wouldn't know the difference between an AR-15 and a sharp stick, yet want to know and control what's in your gun safe. If they win, you lose.[76]

Wintersteen's list of problems included Supreme Court appointees, defeat of concealed-carry reciprocity bills, banning of lead ammo, ballis-tic microstamping, and "blame" for gun deaths in Mexico resulting from the botched "Fast and Furious" overseen by the BATF. Noticeably absent, in retrospect, was any mention of expanded background checks.

Gun-rights advocates were never enamored of Romney, but, like many Republicans, they saw him as the candidate most likely to defeat Obama. When running for the Senate in Massachusetts and during his campaign for governor, Romney supported both the Brady Bill and the Assault Weapons Ban. He said he would not chip away at the strong gun laws in Massachusetts. In 1994, he said "I do not line up with the NRA." Like Obama, his views on guns evolved over time. In 2005, as governor, he declared a statewide "The Right to Bear Arms Day," and in 2006, he became a lifetime member of the NRA. During the 2012 campaign, he supported full enforcement of existing laws but was opposed to any new gun laws.[77]

Gun control was not the only, or even the most important, issue on which Romney had to prove his conservative bona fides. He fought the RINO (Republican In Name Only) label throughout the campaign. This is not surprising for a former governor of Massachusetts, one of the more liberal states in the country. A "true" conservative would be very unlikely to win statewide office there. The addition of Paul Ryan to the ticket helped with conservatives overall and with gun-rights supporters. Ryan, a Wisconsin representative, was an avid hunter and had a long history of strong support of gun rights.

While Obama continued to incur the wrath and scorn of the NRA and other supporters of gun rights, the issue never rose to the level of the economy or health care for most Americans. Given his lack of open hostility toward gun rights in his first term, the worst offense that could be ascribed to Obama was his *desire* to restrict gun rights. Regardless of the truth of the charges, there was a lack of hard evidence that four more years of Obama as president would be detrimental to gun owners. Early in his term, Obama received a grade of "F" from the Brady Campaign for his lack of support for gun control. It was reported that in early 2009, when Attorney General Eric Holder held a press conference and said the administration would push to renew the Assault Weapons Ban, White House chief of staff Rahm Emmanuel, no ally of the NRA, told him privately to "Shut the f—— up on guns."[78] While there had been suggestions that the White House would like to move on gun control, including Holder's statement and White House meetings with the Brady Campaign in 2011, many advisers, and likely the president himself, did not think the political cost was worth it.

Following the Aurora, Colorado, movie theater shooting, Obama called for "common sense" on the issue. "I believe the majority of gun owners would agree we should do everything possible to prevent criminals and fugitives from purchasing weapons, and we should check someone's criminal record before they can check out a gun seller," Obama said. "[So that] a mentally unbalanced individual should not be able to get his hands on a gun so easily."[79]

The day after that speech, however, Jay Carney, the White House press secretary, said that Obama was focused on action "short of legislation and short of gun laws," and that "tackling the broader issue of violence is not just about gun laws."[80] Even Senator Dianne Feinstein (D-CA), one of the strongest advocates of gun control in Congress, was pessimistic that gun control would be part of the election landscape. She noted that supporters of stricter laws had not "rallied in years" and that the election was not a good time for a new discussion.[81]

The January 8, 2011, mass shooting in Tucson in which Representative Gabrielle Giffords was wounded along with 12 others and six people were killed did little to push gun control to the forefront of the political debate. The shooter, Jared Lee Loughner, was subsequently diagnosed as a paranoid schizophrenic, although he was eventually found competent to stand trial, pleaded guilty to 19 charges, and was sentenced to life imprisonment without parole. Loughner used a legally purchased pistol in the attack.

Later, the Aurora movie theater shooting on July 20, 2012, in which 12 people were killed and 70 were wounded, did not move either candidate to call for new gun control laws. The shooter, James Holmes, used a shotgun, a rifle, and a handgun during a midnight screening of the film *The Dark Knight Rises*.

Press Secretary Carney said that Obama had supported extending the Assault Weapons Ban, "[b]ut given the stalemate in Congress, our focus is on steps that we can take to make sure criminals and others who should not have those guns, make sure that they cannot obtain them." Romney was quoted as saying, "I don't support new gun laws in our country ... the effort to continue to look for some law to somehow make violence go away is missing the point." The question of whether this was a bow to the NRA or a political ploy playing to the 55 percent of independent voters who thought it was more important to protect gun rights than to control guns was unanswered.[82]

Former Democratic adviser Robert Shrum suggested that as a political issue, gun control was "dead." "The Colorado massacre has prompted some calls for gun control. But the public doesn't support it. Romney, who flip-flopped on the issue once before, isn't about to take on the NRA. And Obama knows a quixotic fight for new regulations not only would fail, it would lose him the election."[83] Lamenting the unwillingness of anyone to propose new regulations, Shrum wrote, "The stark reality is that the half-century battle for gun control has been lost politically—again, and again, now perhaps permanently."[84] Expressing the frustration of gun-control supporters and the utter loss of hope for the future, he wrote of the evolution of Romney's thinking on gun control and reticence of others to speak up:

> Unfortunately, Romney's pretty close to where the public now is—and the Congress too—and even many Democrats. And many others who in their hearts may favor gun control now treat it as the issue that dares not speak its name. They're not cynical, they're practical. They believe, correctly, that they can't bend the arc of public opinion—and if they try, they will jeopardize not only the winning of elections, but the prospects for winning other great purposes such as economic justice and equal rights . . . The psychic satisfaction of being pure on gun control is not worth losing the election.[85]

Shrum recognizes a couple of important points regarding public opinion and the politics of gun control. First, opinion had shifted on the issue, so support for stricter measures was relatively low. Second, when candidates and elected officials failed to support or propose more gun laws, they were responding to the public and electoral will. Support for gun control was a losing issue, both in Congress and at the ballot box. To stand on that principle meant running the risk of losing an election with no chance of a policy gain, because no policy would be enacted anyway.

Toward the conclusion of the second presidential debate in October, a question was raised regarding gun control for one of the few times in the campaign. The response provides insight into Obama's view of the issue as well as the politics of the issue:

QUESTION: President Obama, during the Democratic National Convention in 2008, you stated you wanted to keep AK-47s out of the hands of criminals. What has your administration done or planned to do to limit the availability of assault weapons?[86]

OBAMA: We're a nation that believes in the Second Amendment, and I believe in the Second Amendment. We've got a long tradition of hunting and sportsmen and people who want to make sure they can protect themselves.

But there have been too many instances during the course of my presidency, where I've had to comfort families who have lost somebody. Most recently out in Aurora . . .

So my belief is that, (A), we have to enforce the laws we've already got, make sure that we're keeping guns out of the hands of criminals, those who are mentally ill. We've done a much better job in terms of background checks, but we've got more to do when it comes to enforcement.

But I also share your belief that weapons that were designed for soldiers in war theaters don't belong on our streets. And so what I'm trying to do is to get a broader conversation about how do we reduce the violence generally. Part of it is seeing if we can get an Assault Weapons Ban reintroduced. But part of it is also looking at other sources of the violence. Because frankly, in my home town of Chicago, there's an awful lot of violence and they're not using AK-47s. They're using cheap hand guns.

And so what can we do to intervene, to make sure that young people have opportunity; that our schools are working; that if there's violence on the streets, that working with faith groups and law enforcement, we can catch it before it gets out of control.

And so what I want is a—is a comprehensive strategy. Part of it is seeing if we can get automatic weapons that kill folks in amazing numbers out of the hands of criminals and the mentally ill. But part of it is also going deeper and seeing if we can get into these communities and making sure we catch violent impulses before they occur.[87]

Romney replied that we did not need new laws, but needed to enforce existing laws. His response moved the discussion toward the nature of gun violence as a social issue. He discussed education and children being raised in a two-parent family. He also referenced the "Fast and Furious" debacle in which the BATF allowed guns to be illegally sold and transported to Mexico. The hope was to trace the guns, but they were "lost" and some were used in crimes. When reminded by moderator Candy Crowley that he had signed an Assault Weapons Ban as governor of Massachusetts, Romney noted that it was a bipartisan bill that included enhanced opportunities for hunting as well. In response, Obama suggested that Romney had changed his views to gain the support of the NRA.

Still, there were differences between the positions of the two candidates. Obama's rhetoric may have been a reflection of his electoral strategy and his assessment of the political landscape. And, while Romney's position had clearly "evolved" over time, his record was not one of a gun-control crusader.[88]

Those differences had little resonance with most voters, whose attention was elsewhere—on the economy or the "47 percent."[89] The Obama election, however, was seen as important and as a harbinger of new gun regulations by some segment of the gun-rights public, which began pouring into gun shops and sporting goods stores, purchasing whatever firearms and ammo were available immediately after Election Day. Gun sales surged, and the stocks of gun manufacturers Sturm, Ruger & Co. and Smith & Wesson both gained 15 percent in a week while the overall market was down.[90] This spike in sales had been predicted by retailers who were anticipating a repeat of the surge in sales following Obama's victory in 2008.[91]

SPENDING IN THE 2012 ELECTIONS

Journalists and supporters of gun control often blame the NRA and the "gun lobby" for being obstructionist and blocking "common sense" measures supported by the public. They often look to the campaign contributions of the NRA as the evidence that candidates or elected officials are toeing the party line. Where the NRA is powerful, that power emanates largely from the organization's ability to turn out voters. Every candidate thrives on money, but the money is useless if it cannot be converted into votes. In certain constituencies around the country, the NRA can produce votes for or against a candidate. Votes are a more a valuable currency than money in that context. In areas where the group fails to influence enough voters, the amount of money it spends on a campaign is not nearly as important. If money was the only commodity with value, then Michael Bloomberg would be dictating firearms policy for the country. In short, money is important, but it is not determinative.

An examination of campaign spending by gun-control and gun-rights groups clearly demonstrates that the NRA dominated the field. NRA spent nearly $3 million in lobbying in 2012, to say nothing of the nearly $20 million it allocated to outside spending in the election or the mere $1 million–plus it donated directly to campaigns. On the other side, Mayors Against Illegal Guns and the Brady Campaign managed to scrape together less than $250,000 for lobbying.

While those totals may appear large, they pale in comparison to the spending of other groups (Table 4.4). In terms of outside spending, the Super PACs dwarfed every other group, and while the NRA spent almost $20 million, the League of Conservation Voters ($14 million) and Planned Parenthood (nearly $12 million) also spent considerable sums attempting to influence the election and public policy.[92]

The rise of Super PACs has coincided with a decline in the importance of contributions made to individual campaigns, but those contributions still receive attention from the news media and election watchdog groups. The NRA's total of $1.1 million did not even enable them to crack the top

Table 4.4   Election 2012 Outside Spending

Organization	Spending Rank	Total
American Crossroads/Crossroads GPS	1	$176,429,025
Restore Our Future	2	$142,097,336
Priorities USA/Priorities USA Action	3	$65,166,859
Majority PAC	4	$37,498,257
Americans for Prosperity	5	$36,352,928
US Chamber of Commerce	6	$35,657,029
National Rifle Association	10	$19,767,043
AFSCME	12	$18,012,198
League of Conservation Voters	17	$14,181,521
Planned Parenthood	19	$11,873,658
AFL-CIO	23	$8,992,291
National Association of Realtors	25	$8,210,268
National Education Association	30	$6,579,747

Source: OpenSecrets.org, "2012 Outside Spending, by Group," http://www.opensecrets.org/outsidespending/summ.php?cycle=2012&chrt=V&disp-0&type=U.

100 donors in 2012. That list was topped by the Las Vegas Sands Hotel with $52.4 million. The National Education Association was ranked fifth with $14.7 million. The National Beer Wholesalers Association contributed $3.6 million. Several universities also made the top 100, including the University of California ($3.2 million), Harvard ($2.5 million), and Stanford ($2.4 million).[93]

With regard to lobbying, the "gun lobby" total of about $5 million (including the NRA, Gun Owners of America, and National Shooting Sports Foundation) cannot even begin to match up against computer/Internet companies ($133 million), TV/movies/music ($118 million), or education (over $90 million). Even clergy and religious organizations spent $2.4 million in lobbying.[94]

When looking at spending, if the point of comparison is only groups involved in the gun-control issue, then the NRA and other gun-rights groups have dominated the field. That will change with the $50 million pledged by Michael Bloomberg to fight the NRA in the 2014 elections. If, however, one looks at overall spending, then even the NRA does not appear as significant. While it has been dubbed a "Heavy Hitter" by OpenSecrets.org, its spending totals over the years typically ranks it the 60s or 70s in terms of comparison with all other groups.

To provide greater context to campaign money, the Federal Election Commission has reported that presidential and congressional campaigns, political parties, and political action committees collected more than $7.1 billion and disbursed more than $7 billion in the 2011–2012 election cycle. For that same cycle, independent expenditures—that is, money spent independent of a party or candidate—totaled $1.25 billion. About half of that money was spent on the presidential election. Presidential election spending has more than doubled since 2000, and spending almost doubled since 2002 at the congressional level.[95]

How often do NRA-backed candidates win? Historically the NRA had a very high "winning" percentage, that is, a record of backing many more winners than losers. That record was not as stellar in 2012. Clearly, they lost the presidential election. By their own accounts, only 9 of 20 U.S. Senate candidates endorsed by the NRA won their election (45%), while their success rate was much higher in the House of Representatives (more than 80% of the 270 candidates they endorsed were winners).[96] Those numbers are lower than is typical, and there were many races in which they did not make an endorsement. Some of those involved two "A" candidates, while others involved two "F" candidates or pro-control candidates who ran unopposed. Regardless, they spun the result as best they could. "Prior to Tuesday, our country had an anti-gun president, a questionable U.S. Senate majority, and a pro-gun U.S. House majority. Today, America still has an anti-gun president, questionable U.S. Senate majority, and pro-gun U.S. House majority."[97] Using money spent as an indicator of electoral success, the NRA did not fare well at all in 2012. They backed a bare majority of winners (51.1%), and just over 5 percent of the money they spent aided a victorious campaign.[98]

There are several possible explanations for this apparent decline in success for NRA. First, they spent a great deal of money on the presidential election, and they lost. If President Obama had coattails, then he may have aided in the victories of some of the Senate and House candidates whom the NRA opposed. Second, perhaps the NRA did not spend enough money to make a difference, given the rapidly increasing amounts of money spent in national elections. Third, the relative unimportance of the gun-control issue in the election may have also lowered their success rate, assuming that their supporters were less concerned about gun control, which was not really on the national agenda, than they were about the economy. Finally, it is also possible that the NRA simply is not as powerful as it has been. The proof of that pudding would be borne out in future elections, as early as 2014. It should be much easier for the NRA to motivate its supporters in the midterm elections of 2014 given the conversations and proposed legislation at both the national and state levels in 2013 and 2014.

THE IMPACT OF THE 2012 ELECTIONS

Despite the fact that it was trying to spin the outcome, the NRA's description of the political scenery following the 2012 elections was mostly accurate. It was a status quo election in many ways. There would be a second Obama administration, although it was impossible to predict how hostile it would be to gun rights. It was a question of where and how they wished to spend their political capital. Would the president now move front and center in the debate, or would he concentrate more on other issues that had not yet been resolved—immigration, economic recovery, income inequality, etc.?

Congress was also essentially where it was before the election in terms of ideology and party control. The Republicans still controlled the House of Representatives, but they had failed to make gains in the Senate, primarily because they nominated some poor candidates in states where they had a realistic chance of winning some seats that had been held by Democrats. It seemed unlikely that supporters of stronger gun control in the Senate would seriously push for bills they were unlikely to pass in their own chamber and that stood no chance of passage in the House. Likewise, House members who supported gun rights understood they may be able to make small, incremental gains as they did in the first Obama administration, but major national legislation would have to wait. The stalemate that had been in place for several years appeared set to continue.

The Newtown shootings changed that equilibrium, if only for a short time. With public opinion moving against the prevailing trend that favored gun rights, supporters of gun control had the opportunity to exploit the backlash and enact legislation. With the support of two Senate moderates—Joe Manchin (D-WV) and Pat Toomey (R-PA)—the White House kept the issue in the news and attempted to move legislation. Still, the only regulation that could seemingly pass the Senate was expanded background checks.

As we have seen, that attempt was in vain. The bill's supporters failed to defeat the filibuster, and the fate of the legislation in the House of Representatives would have been very questionable, at best. Certainly, any legislation that could not make it out of the Senate would have been soundly defeated in the House. The idea floated by some analysts and journalists that passage in the Senate would have put sufficient pressure on members of the House to also approve the bill was misguided. Simply put, few, if any, conservatives in the House would have lost their seat in the next election if they had voted against any gun-control bill. On the contrary, assuming their districts are conservative (as most are), those Representatives would have risked their political futures if they had voted *for* gun control.

Newtown also set up the possibility of gun control being an important issue in the midterm elections of 2014 and even in the presidential contest in 2016. Three factors suggested that gun-rights supporters would do well in 2014. First, public opinion moved back in the direction of gun rights in the year following Newtown. Second, the activism gap between support-ers of gun regulations and gun-rights advocates boded well for gun rights. The real threats of Manchin-Toomey and the executive orders issued by President Obama brought gun rights advocates out of their political slum-ber. In recent U.S. history, their memories and staying power have exceeded those of their political opponents. Third, the historical trend of the party in control of the White House losing seats in the midterm boded well for gun-rights supporters.

It can be argued that the off-year victories in 2013 of Chris Christie (R-NJ) and Terry McAuliffe (D-VA) in gubernatorial contests suggest that gun control is in ascendance. Christie supports some gun-control measures, but he vetoed some regulations in the summer prior to his land-slide victory. New Jersey is a state with strong gun laws, so it is not sur-prising that even a Republican in that state would favor gun control.

The Virginia election should be more surprising. As recently as 2001, Mark Warner rewrote the Democratic playbook in that state to include tar-geted appeals to gun owners and even outreach to the NRA. Just over a de-cade later, McAuliffe bragged, "I don't care what grade I got from the NRA."[99] Michael Bloomberg and ARS invested in McAuliffe's cam-paign, and his Republican opponent, Attorney General Ken Cuccinelli, touted his A-rating from the NRA throughout the campaign and received $500,000 from the NRA. It appeared to many pundits that this was a vic-tory for gun control.[100] "It's clear to everyone that this is not your grand-father's Virginia," Larry Sabato, who heads the Center for Politics at the University of Virginia, wrote *Newsweek* in an e-mail. "That includes guns. Once upon a time, Virginia Democrats were almost indistinguishable from the state's Republicans in adherence to NRA views."[101]

Even with the memory of Newtown and an opponent with a strong gun-rights record, the McAuliffe victory was not related to gun control. Cucci-nelli's positions on same-sex marriage, abortion, and climate change were far more prominent in the campaign than his position on firearms. His record as attorney general was an issue, as was a scandal that had spread from Governor Bob McDonnell and his family and had tangentially touched Cuccinelli. In addition, there was bad blood between Cuccinelli and Lieutenant Governor Bill Bolling, another Republican, whom Cuccinelli outmaneuvered to gain the nomination.

Cuccinelli was a lightning rod for both sides, and numerous polls showed that the election was a referendum on the unpopular Cuccinelli. For his part, McAuliffe had registered more unfavorable ratings than favorable assessments from voters, but his were not as negative as Cuccinelli's. This was clearly a "lesser of the two evils" election for many Virginians. Still, with the state having gone for Obama twice and with McAuliffe's win, it is clear that gun issues are not always the "third rail" for Democrats in the state.

CONCLUSION

The public's perception of firearms and gun regulation is, in some ways, straightforward and, in other ways, more complex. While a majority of Americans favor numerous specific regulations of firearms and gun owners, bans of specific weapons are less popular. The public clearly supports the idea that there is an individual constitutional right to possess a firearm, although there is disagreement on the extent of that right.

Prior to the Newtown shootings, opinion had been incrementally moving for more than a decade in the direction of gun rights. There was a strong surge of support for gun control, specifically universal background checks, immediately after Newtown. Six months later, several, though not all, polls showed opinion returning to where it had previously been. In addition, support for the concept of expanded background checks did not directly translate into support for the bill that was defeated in the Senate.

The trend toward gun rights came at a time of apparent decline in overall gun ownership among Americans, although that trend had leveled off in the past decade. While the number of firearms sales had increased dramatically, evidence suggests that a steady or decreasing percentage of households contain a gun. Two trends help explain this apparent contradiction. First, those who own guns tend to own a larger number. In other words, those who are purchasing firearms are often already owners. Second, a rise in the number of households less likely to own a gun (single females, younger people, and minorities) also mitigates against overall increases in gun ownership.

Attitudes regarding gun control vary significantly by gun ownership, familiarity with firearms, where one lives, gender, race, age, and marital status. Those people most likely to own firearms are not the most likely to be involved in violent criminal activity.

In terms of influencing policy, supporters of gun rights have generally enjoyed an activism gap over those who prefer stricter gun laws. This gap can be seen in contacting decision-makers, fund-raising, and, most important, in voting. For decades, gun-rights groups enjoyed a significant funding advantage, allowing them to be more active in elections. That may change with Michael Bloomberg's decision to fund Everytown for Gun Safety with $50 million.

In national elections, the gun-rights argument had been so dominant that opponents had ceased to even raise the issue. Gun control had clearly damaged the electoral chances of Presidential candidates Al Gore in 2000 and John Kerry in 2004. By 2008, Barack Obama was campaigning on his support of an individual Second Amendment right, and he was reassuring gun owners that he would not take away their firearms. He did state support for some regulations, but his first term was notable for the absence of the issue from his agenda. In fact, the only gun-related bills he signed permitted owners to carry their firearms in national parks and in luggage on Amtrak trains, which earned him the ire of several gun-control groups. Gun control was a nonissue in the 2012 campaign.

No one has a crystal ball to predict the future, but it is difficult to imagine a scenario, short of another mass shooting like Newtown, in which the elections of 2014 or 2016 are influenced by the public demanding tighter controls on guns. Bloomberg will bankroll such a campaign, and it could be effective in some regions, but it is unlikely to be influential nationally. It is more logical to think that those who perceive their rights to be in jeopardy will again become mobilized.

NOTES

1. Weighting refers to the technique(s) used to modify the value of responses to fit a target population, which is usually derived from Census data, exit polls, or some other source.

2. Extended discussions of various aspects of polling may be found in Herbert F. Weisberg, Jon A. Krosnick, and Bruce D. Bowen, *An Introduction to Survey Research, Polling, and Data Analysis*, 3rd ed. (Thousand Oaks, CA: Sage, 1996); and Floyd J. Fowler Jr., *Survey Research Methods*, 4th ed. (Thousand Oaks, CA: Sage, 2008).

3. For example, in 2013, President Obama frequently referred to the will of the people when pushing for gun-control legislation, often citing the public's support for various measures, particularly universal background checks. At the same time, he did not discuss polls that showed that a majority of Americans were unhappy with the Affordable Health Care Act, a.k.a. Obamacare. On the other

hand, Republicans who opposed health care reform cited polling frequently, but they did not talk about public opinion when they opposed expanding background checks.

4. For a discussion of public opinion and democratic theory, see Barbara A. Bardes and Robert W. Oldendick, *Public Opinion: Measuring the American Mind* (Belmont, CA: Wadsworth, 2000), chap. 1.

5. U.S. Geological Survey, Information and Technology Report USGS/BRD/ ITR—2002-0002, "Americans' Attitudes toward Wolves and Wolf Reintroduction: An Annotated Bibliography," April 2002, https://www.fort.usgs.gov/sites/ default/files/products/publications/949/949.pdf.

6. Gallup, "Guns," 2012, http://www.gallup.com/poll/1645/guns.aspx.

7. U.S. Census Bureau, "Changing American Households," November 4, 2011, http://www.census.gov/newsroom/pdf/cah_slides.pdf.

8. Gary Kleck, "Measures of Gun Ownership Levels for Macro-Level Crime and Violence Research," *Journal of Research in Crime and Delinquency* 41, no. 1 (February 2004); Jens Ludwig, Philip J. Cook, and Tom W. Smith, "The Gender Gap in Reporting Household Gun Ownership,"*American Journal of Public Health* 88, no. 11 (November 1998): 1715–18; Ann P. Rafferty, "Validity of a Household Gun Question in a Telephone Survey," *Public Health Reports* 110, no. 3 (1995).

9. Robert M. Jiobu and Timothy J. Curry, "Lack of Confidence in the Federal Government and the Ownership of Firearms," *Social Science Quarterly* 82, no. 1 (March 2001): 77–88.

10. Anecdotally, the author has heard this from interviewers at the Institute for Policy and Opinion Research at Roanoke College. They often relate interviews in which the respondent expresses strong support for gun rights and excellent knowledge of firearms—two correlates of ownership—then will decline to answer the ownership question. Those respondents are also more likely to be male.

11. U.S. Fish and Wildlife Service, "Historical Hunting License Data," http://wsfrprograms.fws.gov/Subpages/LicenseInfo/Hunting.htm.

12. The question asked is, "What do you think is more important—to protect the right of Americans to own guns OR to control gun ownership?"

13. Pew Research Center for the People and the Press, "Gun Rights vs. Gun Control," May 23, 2013, http://www.people-press.org/2013/05/23/gun-rights -vs-gun-control/#total.

14. Pew Research Center for the People and the Press, "Political Polarization in the American Public," June 12, 2014, http://www.people-press.org/2014/06/ 12/political-polarization-in-the-american-public/.

15. Pew Research Center for the People and the Press, "Public Takes Conservative Turn on Gun Control, Abortion," April 30, 2009, http://people -press.org/report/513/public-takes-conservative-turn-on-gun-control-abortion/.

16. Gallup's question is, "In general, do you feel that the laws covering sale of firearms should be made more strict, less strict, or kept as they are now?"

Although this question is probably not as good an indicator of opinion as the one asked by the Pew Center, it is useful for both general orientations and/or analyzing tends over time.

17. Gallup, "Guns."

18. Pew Research Center for the People and the Press, "Mixed Reactions to Senate Gun Vote," April 24, 2013, http://www.people-press.org/2013/04/24/mixed-reactions-to-senate-gun-vote/.

19. Gallup, "Guns."

20. ABC News/*Washington Post* Poll, "Obama and 2014 Politics," January 26, 2014, http://www.langerresearch.com/uploads/1158a1Obamaand2014Politics.pdf.

21. Harry Wilson, "RC Poll: The Opinions of Virginians on Guns, Gun Policy, and Gun Violence," January 28, 2013, http://roanoke.edu/News_and_Events/News_Archive/RC_Poll_Jan_2013_Guns.htm.

22. Roanoke College Poll, Rutgers-Eagleton Poll, and Siena New York Poll. "Majority in Three States Favorable on Hillary Clinton; Give Former Sec of State 2016 Lead over Christie, Paul and Ryan," March 4, 2014, http://roanoke.edu/News_and_Events/News_Archive/Roanoke_Rutgers_Siena_Poll_0314.htm.

23. Pew Research Center, "Public Takes Conservative Turn."

24. Tom W. Smith, *1999 National Gun Policy Survey of the National Opinion Research Center: Research Findings* (Chicago: National Opinion Research Center, April 2000), http://www.consumerfed.org/pdfs/survey99.pdf.

25. Harry Wilson, *Guns, Gun Control, and Elections: The Politics and Policy of Firearms* (Lanham, MD: Rowman & Littlefield Publishers, 2007), 128.

26. William J. Vizzard, *Shots in the Dark: The Policy, Politics, and Symbolism of Gun Control* (Lanham, MD: Rowman & Littlefield Publishers, 2000), 69.

27. Maxwell E. McCombs and Donald L. Shaw, "The Agenda-Setting Function of Mass Media," *Public Opinion Quarterly* 36 (1972): 176–87; Roger W. Cobb and Charles Elder, *Participation in American Politics: The Dynamics of Agenda Building* (Baltimore, MD: Johns Hopkins University Press, 1983).

28. Donald P. Haider-Markel and Mark R. Joslyn, "Gun Policy, Opinion, Tragedy, and Blame Attribution: The Conditional Influence of Issue Frames," *Journal of Politics* 63, no. 2 (May 2001): 520–43.

29. Karen Callaghan and Frauke Schnell, "Assessing the Democratic Debate: How the News Media Frame Elite Policy Discourse," *Political Communication* 18 (2001): 183–212.

30. Pew Research Center, "Gun Homicide Rate Down 49% since 1993 Peak; Public Unaware," May 7, 2013, http://www.pewsocialtrends.org/files/2013/05/firearms_final_05-2013.pdf.

31. Ray Surette, *Media, Crime, and Criminal Justice: Images and Realities* (Pacific Grove, CA: Brooks/Cole, 1992).

32. Pew Research Center for the People and the Press, "Timeline: Top News Stories of 2012," December 20, 2012, http://www.people-press.org/2012/12/20/timeline-top-news-stories-of-2012/.

33. Wilson, *Guns, Gun Control,* chap. 6.

34. Mark Follman, Gavin Aronsen, and Deanna Pan, "A Guide to Mass Shootings in America," *Mother Jones*, updated May 24, 2014, http://www .motherjones.com/politics/2012/07/mass-shootings-map?page=1.

35. Pew Research Center, "Gun Homicide Rate Down 49%."

36. Smith, *1999 National Gun Policy Survey.*

37. Ibid.

38. Wilson, *Guns, Gun Control,* chap. 4.

39. Wilson, "Opinions of Virginians."

40. Roanoke College Poll, "Majority."

41. The 2014 three-state poll found differences between those with a gun in the household and those without regarding the potential benefit of stricter gun laws, although there were equally large differences for political ideology, political party, and, in some cases, gender. Those differences were smaller regarding support for a hypothetical gun registry, even smaller than the differences for other demographic variables. The gap reemerged on the intensity question, but it was again matched in some cases by ideology, party, and gender. Region (urban versus rural) was a factor is some cases, but not in others. While all of the differences were in the expected direction, the picture that emerges from that data is not completely clear. While probably not worthy of more explanation than a footnote here, all of those data are available from the author upon request.

42. Wilson, *Guns, Gun Control,* chap. 4.

43. Pew Research Center, "Mixed Reactions."

44. Pew Research Center for the People and the Press, "Gun Rights vs. Gun Control," May 23, 2013, http://www.people-press.org/2013/05/23/gun-rights -vs-gun-control/#total.

45. Ronald G. Shaiko and Marc A. Wallace, "Going Hunting Where the Ducks Are: The National Rifle Association and the Grass Roots," in *The Changing Politics of Gun Control*, eds. John W. Bruce and Clyde Wilcox (Lanham, MD: Rowman & Littlefield Publishers, 1998).

46. Smith, *1999 National Gun Policy Survey.*

47. In each of the three states, those who opposed the gun registry felt more strongly about the issue. For example, in New York among those who supported the gun registry, 46 percent would be very upset and 29 percent somewhat upset if it did not pass. Among those who opposed the registry, 56 percent would be very upset and 26 percent would be somewhat upset if it did pass. In Virginia, those numbers were 37 percent very upset and 34 percent somewhat upset if it did not pass and 50 percent very upset and 29 percent somewhat upset if it did pass. Still, when only including the high-intensity cluster of respondents, the registry was favored in New York (70–29%), New Jersey (78–20%), and in Virginia (58–39%).

48. James M. Snyder and Tim Groseclose, "Estimating Party Influence in Congressional Roll-Call Voting," *American Journal of Political Science* 44, no. 2 (April 2000): 203.

49. "The Election: Issues 2000: A Special Briefing; the Economy, Trade, Foreign Policy, Social Security, Health, Education, Death Penalty, Gun Control,

Poverty, Race, Campaign Finance, Environment, New Technology, Values," *Economist* 356 (September 30, 2000): 59–102.

50. Paul R. Abramson, John H. Aldrich, and David W. Rohde, *Change and Continuity in the 2000 and 2002 Elections* (Washington, DC: CQ Press, 2003), 144–48.

51. Sheryl Gay Stolberg, "A Swing to the Middle on Gun Control," *New York Times*, March 7, 2004, http://www.nytimes.com/2004/03/07/weekinreview/07stol .html.

52. "Democrats and Guns" (editorial), *Washington Times*, February 12, 2004, http://www.washingtontimesonline.com/op-ed/20040212-081232-1419r.htm.

53. "Joe Lieberman: Fighting Crime and Keeping Communities Safe," http:// www.joe2004.com.

54. Howard Dean, "Sensible Gun Laws," Howard Dean for America, http:// www.DeanForAmerica.com.

55. Adam Nagourney, "Baffled in Loss, Democrats Seek Road Forward," *New York Times*, November 7, 2004, http://www.nytimes.com/2004/11/07/ politics/campaign/07dems.html.

56. Adam Nagourney, "Democratic Leader Analyzes Bush Victory," *New York Times*, December 11, 2004, http://www.nytimes.com/2004/12/11/politics/ 11dems.html.

57. Terry M. Neal, "Election Reflections," *Washington Post*, November 4, 2004, http://www.washingtonpost.com/wp-dyn/articles/A24733-2004Nov4.html; Nicholas D. Kristof, "Time to Get Religion," *New York Times*, November 6, 2004, A19; Dave Kopel, "Arms Alive," *National Review Online*, November 3, 2004, http://www.nationalreview.com/articles/212801/arms-alive/dave-kopel.

58. Jodi Wilgoren, "Kerry on Hunting Photo-Op to Help Image," *New York Times*, October 22, 2004, http://www.nytimes.com/2004/10/22/politics/campaign/ 22kerry.html?_r=0.

59. NRA–Political Victory Fund, "If John Kerry Thinks the Second Amendment is about Photo-Ops, He's Daffy," NRA-PVF print advertisement, 2004.

60. Brady Campaign to Prevent Gun Violence, "The Morning After: Police, Victims, Democrats and Republicans Stood Up to an Extremist Agenda, Forced It Down," press release, March 3, 2004.

61. Chris W. Cox, "Your Tools for Victory," NRA-ILA, 2004, http://www .nraila.org/news-issues/articles/2004/your-tools-for-victory.aspx?s=%22Election +Volunteer+Coordinators%22&st=&ps.

62. "Presidential Approval Ratings—George W. Bush," Gallup, http://www .gallup.com/poll/116500/presidential-approval-ratings-george-bush.aspx.

63. Ben Smith, "Obama on Small-Town Pa.: Clinging to Religion, Guns, Xen-ophobia," *Politico*, April 11, 2008, http://www.politico.com/blogs/bensmith/0408/ Obama_on_smalltown_PA_Clinging_religion_guns_xenophobia.html.

64. "Obama's Gun Ban?" FactCheck.org, http://www.factcheck.org/2008/ 12/obamas-gun-ban/.

65. Alexa Ainsworth, "Obama Camp Disavows Last Year's 'Inartful' State-ment on DC Gun Law," June 26, 2008, http://abcnews.go.com/blogs/politics/2008/06/obama-camp-disa/.

66. Jonathan Martin, "Obama Careful on *Heller*," *Politico*, June 8, 2008, http://www.politico.com/blogs/jonathanmartin/0608/Obama_careful_on_Heller.html.

67. " 'Obama Supports Gun Rights': 2008 Campaign Ad Ran in Rural PA 10-13-2008," YouTube video, 0:29, http://www.youtube.com/watch?v=qmWhtaTdqB4.

68. "Election Center 2008: Guns," CNNPolitics.com, http://www.cnn.com/ELECTION/2008/issues/issues.gun.html.

69. Chris W. Cox, "Political Report: Election 2008 and the Long Road Ahead," NRA-ILA, December 22, 2008, http://www.nraila.org/news-issues/articles/2008/political-report-election-2008-and-the.aspx.

70. Ibid.

71. Frank James, "Obama Finding Gun Control Voice, Which Had Gone Quiet in the White House," NPR: It's All Politics, December 18, 2012, http://www.npr.org/blogs/itsallpolitics/2012/12/18/167562866/obama-finding-gun-control-voice-which-had-gone-quiet-in-white-house.

72. Kevin Bohn, "Gun Sales Surge after Obama's Victory," CNN.com, November 11, 2008, http://www.cnn.com/2008/CRIME/11/11/obama.gun.sales/.

73. The author has seen a clock with the face of the president (not a carica-ture) and the caption "Salesman of the Month" hanging in a gun shop in Roanoke, Virginia.

74. Frank Miniter, "What the Left Won't Tell You about the Boom in U.S. Gun Sales," *Forbes*, August 23, 2012, http://www.forbes.com/sites/frankminiter/2012/08/23/what-the-left-wont-tell-you-about-the-boom-in-u-s-gun-sales/.

75. Patrik Jonsson, "Briefing: Obama vs. Romney 101: 4 Ways They Com-pare on Gun Control," *Christian Science Monitor*, September 9, 2012, http://www.csmonitor.com/USA/DC-Decoder/2012/0909/Obama-vs.-Romney-101-4-ways-they-compare-on-gun-control/Second-Amendment.

76. Kyle Wintersteen, "9 Ways Gun Owners Can Lose in the 2012 Election," *Guns and Ammo*, February 27, 2012, http://www.gunsandammo.com/2012/02/27/how-gun-owners-can-lose-in-the-2012-election/.

77. Mackenzie Weinger, "Mitt Romney's Stance on Gun Control," *Politico*, July 20, 2012, http://www.politico.com/news/stories/0712/78767.html.

78. Andrew Kirell, "Norah O'Donnell Grills Rahm Emmanuel for Telling Obama AG to 'Shut the F**k Up' about Assault Weapons Ban," *Mediaite*, December 18, 2012, http://www.mediaite.com/tv/norah-odonnell-grills-emanuel-for-telling-obama-ag-to-shut-the-fk-up-about-assault-weapons-ban/.

79. Tracy Connor and Kristen A. Lee, "President Obama Calls for Action to Stop Gun Violence, but No New Laws," *New York Daily News*, July 26, 2012, http://www.nydailynews.com/news/election-2012/president-obama-calls-background-checks-purchasing-firearms-wake-aurora-colo-movie-theater-massacre-article-1.1122128.

80. Ibid.

81. "Dianne Feinstein on Guns: 2012 Election Year Not Ideal for Debate" (video), *Huffington Post*, July 22, 2012, http://www.huffingtonpost.com/2012/07/22/dianne-feinstein-guns-2012-election_n_1692994.html.

82. Tom Cohen, "Candidates Show Little Appetite for New Gun Control Laws," CNN, July 26, 2012, http://www.cnn.com/2012/07/26/politics/gun-control-debate.

83. Robert Shrum, "For Obama, Romney, and America, Gun Control Is Dead," *Daily Beast*, July 24, 2012, http://www.thedailybeast.com/articles/2012/07/24/for-obama-romney-and-america-gun-control-is-dead.html.

84. Ibid.

85. Ibid.

86. The question also demonstrates the lack of knowledge of the moderator. AK-47s are generally illegal because they can be set to fire as fully automatic rifles. Variants of the AK-47 that can be fired only in semiautomatic mode are legal. If the rifle was registered prior to 1986, then it may be purchased even if it is fully automatic; but they are not easy to locate and are quite expensive. While this may appear to be "only semantics," the confusion of fully automatic and semiautomatic firearms is both common and important to both opinion and policy.

87. Sarah Kliff, "Full Transcript of the Second Presidential Debate," *Washington Post* blog, October 16, 2012, http://www.washingtonpost.com/blogs/wonkblog/wp/2012/10/16/full-transcript-of-the-second-presidential-debate/?print=1.

88. Jonsson, "Briefing."

89. The "47 percent" refers to a[n] [in]famous reference made by Romney during the campaign. "There are 47 percent of the people who will vote for the president no matter what. All right, there are 47 percent who are with him, who are dependent upon government, who believe that they are victims, who believe the government has a responsibility to care for them, who believe that they are entitled to health care, to food, to housing, to you-name-it—that that's an entitlement. And the government should give it to them. And they will vote for this president no matter what. . . . These are people who pay no income tax. . . . [M]y job is not to worry about those people. I'll never convince them they should take personal responsibility and care for their lives." David Corn, "SECRET VIDEO: Romney Tells Millionaire Donors What He REALLY Thinks of Obama Voters," *Mother Jones*, September 17, 2012, http://www.motherjones.com/politics/2012/09/secret-video-romney-private-fundraiser.

90. Emily Miller, "Guns Blazing since Election: Obama's Second Term Driving Firearms Sales to New Heights," *Washington Times*, November 13, 2012, http://www.washingtontimes.com/news/2012/nov/13/guns-blazing-since-election/.

91. Shelly Banjo, "Gun Sales Hinge on Obama Re-Election," *Wall Street Journal*, September 14, 2012, http://online.wsj.com/article/SB10000872396390444433504577651393759726660.html.

92. OpenSecrets.org, "2012 Outside Spending, by Group," http://www.open secrets.org/outsidespending/summ.php?cycle=2012&chrt=V&disp-0&type=U.

93. OpenSecrets.org, "2012 Overview: Top Overall Donors," http://www .opensecrets.org/overview/topcontribs.php.

94. OpenSecrets.org, "Lobbying, Ranked Sectors," http://www.opensecrets .org/lobby/top.php?indexType=c&showYear=2012.

95. Federal Election Commission, "FEC Summarizes Campaign Activity of the 2011–2012 Election Cycle," April 19, 2013, http://www.fec.gov/press/ press2013/20130419_2012-24m-Summary.shtml.

96. NRA-ILA, "2012 Election Recap," November 9, 2012, http://www .nraila.org/news-issues/articles/2012/2012-election-recap.aspx.

97. Ibid.

98. OpenSecrets.org, "National Rifle Assn.," http://www.opensecrets.org/ outsidespending/detail.php?cmte=National+Rifle+Assn.

99. Timothy Johnson, "Terry McAuliffe Win Disproves Media Myth of NRA's Electoral Dominance," Media Matters for America blog, November 6, 2013, http://mediamatters.org/blog/2013/11/06/terry-mcauliffe-win-disproves -media-myth-of-nra/196755.

100. Ibid.

101. Pema Levy, "In Virginia Race, McAuliffe Runs against the NRA," *Newsweek*, October 25, 2013, http://www.newsweek.com/virginia-running -governor-and-against-nra-953.

FIVE

Interest Groups

Interest groups attempt to influence policy and represent the typically narrow concerns of those who belong to the group. Those policy interests may coincide or conflict with one's definition of the best interests of the larger society. Elected officials often adopt a delegate style of representation in which they act in accord with the wishes of their constituents, even if those interests, at times, conflict with what is in the best interest of the state or the nation. Interest groups, who are neither elected nor accountable to the public at large, operate in a similar fashion. All of us will find that we agree more with some groups than others. While elected officials must be concerned with a wide variety of issues, interest groups can, and, typically do, focus on one narrow policy area or issue. This allows them to concentrate their resources in pursuit of a single goal.

Interest groups are thought to influence policy and policy makers in a variety of ways. In a classic text on public policy, Thomas Dye lists five major ways in which this is done:

1. Direct lobbying at official hearings, direct contact with official offices, and assisting in writing legislation
2. Making campaign contributions through political action committees
3. Interpersonal contacts through travel, entertainment, social settings, or a "revolving door" between governmental offices and interest groups or lobbying firms that represent them
4. Litigation in the form of class-action suits or support of individual plaintiffs
5. Grassroots mobilization efforts to influence elected officials[1]

Groups that are active in the gun-control debate do little of item 3 above, but several groups on both sides of the issue are heavily involved in the other activities.

In Kingdon's revised "garbage can model" of policy making, interest groups are active in both helping to set the agenda and in identifying policy alternatives. Agenda setting can be either proactive, if an interest group seeks some type of favor, or more defensive, if it is trying to defend its position by blocking legislation. Group resources fall into the general categories of electoral advantages and disadvantages and group cohesion and strength. Groups that are better organized are, as we would expect, generally more successful than those that are not as well organized.[2]

Virtually all interest groups represent a "special interest." That term is used commonly and pejoratively by those who oppose a specific group. Yet, the term applies equally to nearly every group. This is true regardless of the nature of the group—whether it represents a general political ideology, an individual business, several businesses with similar interests, or a particular issue. While most interest groups argue that their views and issue positions, if adopted as policy, would benefit all of society, we know that is often not true. Even groups that we may view as more "benevolent" often represent a relatively narrow segment of society.

For example, some people think that AARP's[3] staunch protection of Social Security and Medicare comes with a price that is paid by others and that these entitlement programs must be modified to remain viable. AARP contends, "We're fighting to protect benefits that you've earned. These programs are crucial, and Washington should not undermine your health and retirement security."[4]

The American Medical Association (AMA) primarily represents the interests of medical professionals. Most of us would like to think that doctors have their patients' interests as paramount, but we know we do not always believe that to be true. For example, doctors are trained to prolong life, but there may be times that patients or their families would prefer to allow life to end to alleviate suffering. Doctors also understandably want to protect themselves from malpractice suits that many patients think should proceed through the courts with few or no limits on damage awards. The argument that lower malpractice insurance premiums would result in lower health care costs with little or no impact of the quality of health care for patients holds more merit for some of us than it does for others.

Few of us think of grandparents or doctors as bad people. On the contrary, we see them as enriching our lives and are generally supportive of both groups. We expect both AARP and AMA to represent the interests of their members, even though there may be times we disagree with their views. We know that there will be times that the interests of senior citizens or doctors will not be congruent with the best interest of everyone else, but we accept that these groups advocate on behalf of their members and that societal benefits may accrue from their activities. Many groups compromise when they have no alternative, but it is almost never their first choice.

Why, then, do many of us expect those who advocate for gun rights to accept "reasonable" restrictions on firearms and "common-sense" gun laws that will be in the country's "best interest" as defined by those who want to enact gun-control measures? We should not expect any of the gun-rights interest groups to present a nuanced discussion of the possible limits of the Second Amendment rights or even the nature of the rights. Rather, they are expected to assume that the right is absolute and to lobby for the legislative adoption of that position.

The unwillingness to accept any incursions into gun rights makes NRA appear incalcitrant to some, but the logic of their argument is virtually identical to that of most other interest groups. All engage to some extent in slippery-slope arguments. The NRA believes that any gun regulation inevitably leads to another and so on. In this regard, they are similar to any other group who advocates for what they define as rights—a woman's right to choose (National Organization for Women), the right to free speech (American Civil Liberties Union), the right to practice your religion, etc. For each of these groups the right is fundamental, and the proper role of the government is to protect the right, not trample on it.

Journalists rally around colleagues when they perceive the First Amendment to be under attack.[5] They even defend people with whom they disagree when they perceive the freedom of the press may be threatened. Many mainstream media outlets filed amicus briefs in support of *Hustler* magazine publisher Larry Flynt in the libel suit filed against him by Jerry Falwell that ended up in the Supreme Court. Similarly, groups who support abortion rights are absolute in their support, fearing that any restriction will inevitably lead to others. For example, Planned Parenthood opposed 2013 legislation that would have banned abortions after 20 weeks, calling it "dangerous and extreme . . . Abortion is a deeply personal, often complicated decision . . . These decisions should be made by a woman in consultation with her doctor, her family, and her faith—not by politicians."[6] Abortion-rights advocates view a variety of proposed restrictions—parental notification, abortion clinic and doctor regulations, waiting periods, required ultrasound examinations—as simply attempts to restrict abortions. They may well be correct in that assessment.

Is it, then, illogical, for gun-rights advocates to see many proposed fire-arms regulations as thinly veiled attempts to reduce the number of fire-arms? If, for example, Congress adopted universal background checks, would gun-rights groups declare victory and disband? Would they stop advocating additional gun regulations? Almost certainly not. If regulations are successful, then further regulations would be even more successful. If they fail, then they did not go far enough. Either way, gun-rights advocates feel that they lose. In their minds, they gain nothing by compromise.

Back in 1995, Senator Dianne Feinstein reflected on the passage of the Assault Weapons Ban on *60 Minutes*: "If I could've gotten 51 votes in the Senate of the United States for an outright ban, picking up every one of them—Mr. and Mrs. America turn 'em all in—I would have done it." Although the rhetoric has changed, many gun-rights advocates do not believe there has been a real change of heart.

We may disagree with the positions of gun-rights groups, but we should not expect those groups to be willing to compromise significantly from their basic position. Some gun-control groups have done that, but it can be easily argued that they adopted that approach for practical reasons, not ideological ones. While they may prefer a gun ban, they realize that it is not popular and that it has no chance of being enacted. Since the *Heller* decision, a gun ban would also almost certainly be unconstitu-tional. So, some groups say they are not working toward a gun ban, only "common-sense" regulations of firearms and gun owners. Semantics are also important here, as one person's "reasonable regulation" is another person's "right infringement."

Rhetoric is important to all groups and issues. The gun-control issue is no different. Groups compete to frame or to define issues. For example, viewing abortion through the lens of a "woman's right to control her body" is very different from seeing it as "ending the life of an unborn child." In the same way, "marrying who you love" is very different from "protecting the sanctity of the marriage." For gun control, it is about "common-sense regulations designed to protect innocent lives" versus protecting the "right of the individual to defend themselves and their families." Defining the ter-minology clearly goes a long way in winning the issue. It is far more than "just semantics."

"Gun lobby" is a term that is undefined but is frequently used in the news media and by elected officials. They often use the term to refer to the NRA, but it can be broader than just that group. Its connotation is often negative, as it is routinely utilized when referring to opposition to "common-sense" gun-control regulations. The media rarely refer to a "doctors' lobby" or a "seniors' lobby." Gun lobby is clearly a misnomer insofar as firearms are inanimate objects and have no interest to promote any more than airplanes, power tools, fine jewelry, or children's toys. Obviously, guns cannot vote and cannot lobby decision-makers. The term gun lobby helps to stigmatize the interests that are represented.[7] The interests being represented are those of firearms owners and collectors as well as, perhaps, gun manufacturers and dealers.

RESOURCES AND POWER

The news media often measure the strength of an interest group by looking at its finances and its campaign contributions. Such a limited analysis is not only myopic, but it can also be very misleading. A group's power can be a product of several factors. Perhaps the most influential interest group in the United States is AARP, which has successfully advocated on behalf of seniors for decades. AARP does not endorse candidates for office, nor does it contribute money to campaigns. It does, however, publish a Voter's guide, which contains references to candidates' statements on issues of importance to the group. It boasts about 38 million members, all of whom are 50 or older, and most of whom vote. Their power derives from their clout at the voting booth. What candidate would risk the ire of a large block of citizens whose voting turnout rates are very high? Of course, AARP also enjoys the benefit of advocating on behalf of everyone's grandmother. Who is big enough or bold enough to challenge Grandma? AARP communicates effectively and frequently with its members on issues of importance to seniors, and that is sufficient for them to be very successful in the policy arena.

Other interest groups, such as those that represent trial lawyers, doctors, and realtors, tend to lobby legislators behind the scenes. Their ability to influence policy is a result of their positions of power in society and their financial status. At the other end of the spectrum lies the so-called "Super PACs" that resulted from the U.S. Supreme Court decision in *Citizens United v. Federal Election Commission*.[8] That case, bemoaned by many as allowing wealthy individuals and groups to literally buy elections, prohibited the government from limiting the amount of money spent in independent expenditures (money *not* given to a candidate) in elections by corporations, associations, or labor unions.

Many groups were created in the wake of *Citizens United*, including the conservative group American Crossroads and its spinoff Crossroads Grassroots Policy Strategies, which were founded by Karl Rove, who served as chief of staff for former president George W. Bush. Those two groups spent about $175 million in the 2012 elections with abysmal success rates, demonstrating clearly that money alone does not equal success.[9]

Money is one very important weapon in an interest group's arsenal, but it is not the only one, nor is it necessarily the most important. Elections are determined by vote count, not dollars spent. Campaign dollars are spent in an attempt to convert them into votes. In short, votes are more valuable than dollars.[10] If your group can provide the votes, then money is less important. Of course, being able to provide both votes and campaign contributions and/or independent expenditures makes a group even more powerful. The power of an interest group is measured not only in dollars and votes, but also in terms of reputation. Some are powerful because of who they represent (realtors, doctors, attorneys, etc.) while others are powerful due to their size (AARP).

INTEREST GROUPS IN THE GUN-CONTROL DEBATE

National Rifle Association

When most people think of gun rights, they think of the National Rifle Association. Whether their view is favorable or unfavorable, virtually everyone recognizes the size and strength of the group. Journalists and legislators alike listen when the NRA speaks. With approximately 5 million members and its lobbying and electoral influence, the NRA is the lead group on firearms policy.

The NRA has separate branches for (1) lobbying, the Institute for Legislative Action (NRA-ILA); (2) electoral activity, the Political Victory Fund (NRA-PVF); (3) promoting sport shooting, grassroots outreach, and education activities, the NRA Foundation; and (4) litigation, the NRA Civil Rights Defense Fund (NRA-CRDF). In short, the NRA is a one-stop shop for influencing gun policy in just about every political facet and at every level of government—federal, state, and occasionally local.

Annual dues, which are $35 but are often discounted, provide about half the operating budget for the organization. As is common with various interest groups, membership benefits include: a magazine subscription; discounts for various services, i.e., travel, insurance; and numerous merchant discounts as well.

The Institute for Legislative Action (ILA) is the lobbying arm of the NRA. Established in 1975, ILA is committed to preserving the right of all law-abiding individuals to purchase, possess and use firearms for legitimate purposes as guaranteed by the Second Amendment to the U.S. Constitution.

ILA's ability to fight successfully for the rights of America's law-abiding gun owners directly reflects the support of NRA's nearly 5 million members—a number that has more than tripled since 1978. When restrictive "gun control" legislation is proposed at the local, state or federal level, NRA members and supporters are alerted and respond with individual letters, faxes, e-mails and calls to their elected representatives to make their views known . . .

These efforts include enacting laws that recognize the right of honest citizens to carry firearms for self-protection; preemption bills to prevent attacks on gun owner rights by local anti-gun politicians, and fighting for legislation to prevent the bankrupting of America's firearms industry through reckless lawsuits.[11]

The NRA Political Victory Fund (NRA-PVF) is NRA's political action committee. The NRA-PVF ranks political candidates—irrespective of party affiliation—based on voting records, public statements and their responses to an NRA-PVF questionnaire.

In 2008, NRA-PVF was involved in 271 campaigns for the U.S. House and Senate, winning in 230 of those races (85%). NRA-PVF also endorsed thousands of state legislative candidates that same year and achieved an 84% success rate in those elections . . .

NRA relies on a very simple premise: when provided with the facts, the nation's elected officials will recognize that "gun control" schemes are an infringement on the Second Amendment and a proven failure in fighting crime. The importance of this premise lies in the knowledge that, as one U.S. Congressman put it: "The gun lobby is people."[12]

The NRA Foundation is the country's leading charitable organization in support of the shooting sports, having awarded thousands of grants in support of educational programs since its inception in 1990. The NRA Foundation supports those organizations and programs that ensure the continuation of our proud shooting and hunting heritage.

Foundation grants provide essential program funding, ensuring the availability of quality training and educational opportunities nationwide. Grants benefit programs such as youth education, law enforcement training, hunter education, conservation, firearms and marksmanship training and safety, and much more.[13]

The NRA Civil Rights Defense Fund was established by the NRA Board of Directors in 1978 to become involved in court cases establishing legal precedents in favor of gun owners.

To accomplish this, the Fund provides legal and financial assistance to selected individuals and organizations defending their right to keep and bear arms.

Additionally, the Fund sponsors legal research and education on a wide variety of firearms related issues, including the meaning of the Second Amendment and nature of the right to keep and bear arms provisions in state constitutions.[14]

The four arms of the organization work together to secure members, raise funds, provide needed monies to numerous shooting clubs around the country, and defend their interests in the courts. All of this significantly enhances the group's power and reach. According to 2010 IRS filings, the National Rifle Association of America had nearly $228 million in revenue and $163 million in assets; NRA Foundation raised $21 million and held assets in excess of $80 million; CRDF had over $4 million in assets, and NRA spent nearly $10 million on the NRA-ILA.

The NRA is able to maintain and cultivate a vast membership, leading to gains in negotiation ability and funds from membership dues. They're able to ally with industry and serve as an intermediary between manufacturers and the public.

The NRA-ILA influences legislation and tries to recruit Congressional allies to push their goals through by leveraging the massive membership in the NRA. Then, the NRA-CRDF works to expand the interpretation of those laws in the courts. And the NRA Foundation, with funds from some of those corporate donors, recruits new gun users and NRA supporters, and loyal new members.[15]

The NRA was founded in 1871 as a small shooting association. It soon began to strengthen its ties with the government, first by being commissioned to help train members of the New York National Guard. In 1903, Congress created the National Board for the Promotion of Rifle Practice to assure that the population was militia-ready. Several members of the NBPRA board were also on the NRA board and helped secure passage of Public Law 149, which authorized the sale of military surplus weapons through NRA-sponsored clubs. This helped to resuscitate the organization, which had been in decline. Soon, Congress was giving away the surplus weapons and funding NRA shooting matches. As a result, NRA membership grew significantly.[16]

The NRA became active in national legislation during the 1930s. Its opposition to sections of the National Firearms Act led to the deletion of national gun registration from the bill, and its success in shaping that legislation led to a more active role in developing the Federal Firearms Act of 1938. While the NRA accepted some regulation in both instances, it resisted more extensive regulation and weakened the enforcement mechanisms included in the bills.[17]

Its tactics then foreshadowed the strategies of today. It distributed editorials and press releases, and it communicated with shooters and gun owners, urging them to write or send telegrams to their congressional representatives. This strategy was successful, in part because the NRA was the only game in town—there was no organized opposition.

The NRA continued its involvement with shooting sports and hunting, and returning soldiers from World War II increased its membership. These new members had more interest in hunting than gun control, and that, combined with a Congress that was not pushing gun-control legislation, led the NRA to devote more attention to that pursuit in the pages of its magazine *The American Rifleman*.[18] In 1958, the NRA's main entrance bore the slogan, "Firearms Safety Education, Marksmanship Training, Shooting for Recreation."[19]

The 1960s brought a stronger push for gun-control legislation in Congress, and the NRA responded in opposition. Still, resistance to the passage of the Gun Control Act (GCA) of 1968 was tepid by today's standards. The NRA even endorsed banning Saturday Night Specials—at least for a period of time.

The 1970s saw a schism develop within the ranks of the NRA. The passage of the GCA exacerbated the differences in goals advocated by the two factions within the organization. One group was primarily interested in promoting shooting sports, etc., while another was becoming increasingly interested in opposing gun-control legislation and protecting Second Amendment rights. The latter group gained both followers and intensity following the 1971 search for illegal firearms in which ATF agents shot a Maryland man after breaking down his door. No firearms were found, and the man, a NRA life member and *Washington Post* employee, was paralyzed.[20]

The American Rifleman published a series of articles and editorials discussing the dangers posed to gun owners by the GCA and criticizing the tactics employed by ATF. Still, most of the NRA leadership and membership was moderate on the gun-control issue. "Although the leadership did not favor gun control and was committed to opposing most gun-control proposals, it did not operate on an assumption that the infidels were at the gates or that gun prohibition was imminent."[21] The planned move of NRA headquarters to Colorado Springs from Washington, D.C., and the construction of an outdoor recreational complex in New Mexico indicated a lack of interest in political affairs, and it spurred an organized coup.

The more political wing of the organization, although constituting perhaps only 25 percent of its membership, was very well organized. Several of the group's leaders had been fired by the moderate leadership in 1976, ostensibly due to budget cuts, but it is more likely that they were the result of statements and publications that were critical of the leadership and its lukewarm opposition to gun control. They organized the Federation for the NRA in response to the leadership's agenda of working with groups such as the Sierra Club and Greenpeace on various conservation and wilderness protection initiatives.[22]

The takeover was led by former executive committee member and Border Patrol director Harlon Carter and firearms publisher Neil Knox and was carried out at the 1977 convention. The group took control of the board of directors by having Carter elected to chief operating officer. Carter, in turn, appointed Knox as director of the ILA. The coup was relatively easily accomplished because only life members who were present at the convention could vote in the board elections, and supporters of the Federation for the NRA were the members most highly motivated to attend the convention. Of course, the ability of the coup leaders to rally and organize their followers was essential to the takeover.[23] The new NRA had been born.

The group then embarked on recruiting new members to enhance its clout on Capitol Hill. NRA membership incentives were created, and the NRA became very successful in self-promotion. Although some of the old guard left, many more new members were added to the rolls. Prior to the 1977 convention, there were just over 1 million members. By 1983, that number had grown to 2.6 million. It increased to over 3.5 million by the early 1990s and now stands at about 5 million.[24] The NRA has also benefited from its relationship with the gun-manufacturing industry. While the NRA has, at times, done the political bidding of the gun industry, such as in its support for lawsuit immunity for gun manufacturers, it has also benefited from the relationship. It has gained advertising revenues from the industry, and it has likely gained members from inserts in product packaging.[25] There were some missteps in the 1990s with the "cop-killer bullets" and "plastic guns" issues that found the NRA in opposition to many law enforcement groups. Nonetheless, the NRA rebounded effectively from those setbacks, and Wayne LaPierre emerged as a strong and skillful leader.

With the eventual replacement of the Knox-Carter faction with the Wayne LaPierre–James Baker–Chris Cox–Charlton Heston group, the NRA maintained its strong anti-gun-control positions, and it added a more polished image. Heston, a former actor, was instrumental in portraying a more positive and mainstream image for the group.

In the early 1990s, the NRA became more active in state politics when it was evident that the national-level pendulum might be swinging toward gun-control advocates.[26] It focused successfully on right-to-carry laws and preemption laws, which prevent local governments from passing gun-control regulations. The NRA also began to focus more on alternative means of communication (Internet, e-mail, and its own radio station) because it believed it was not being treated equally by the news media. Finally, the group began to promote laws protecting gun dealers and manufacturers against certain lawsuits. That effort began at the state level, but the group focused more attention on Congress as it made electoral gains and its chances of success increased. With the passage of that legislation, the NRA reestablished itself as one of the most powerful interest groups in the country.

LaPierre steered the organization toward the harder-line stances favored by Knox and others, but his leadership, combined with Heston as president and eventually Chris Cox as the head of the lobbying arm of the group, was slightly smoother-edged than was the Knox regime. Still, there was no doubt that the group tended toward the no-compromise position on guns, and LaPierre's words would occasionally get him in trouble.

The group enjoyed increased interest and membership with the introduction of the Assault Weapons Ban and its eventual passage in 1994. President Bill Clinton proved to be a worthy opponent for the group, and worthy opponents are good for fund-raising. The NRA also made some political hay indirectly from the disastrous and deadly ATF raid on Ruby Ridge, Idaho, in 1992 and the raid on the David Koresh cult in Waco, Texas, a year later that resulted in the fiery death of 76 people, including many women and children.[27]

The April 1995 bombing of the Alfred P. Murrah Federal Building in Oklahoma City hurt the NRA, not due to any involvement on their part (there clearly was none), but because of a letter sent out by the group prior to the bombing in which LaPierre commented on the Assault Weapons Ban and referred to the law's giving "jackbooted Government thugs more power to take away our constitutional rights, break in our doors, seize our guns, destroy our property and even injure and kill us." Some in the media noted the rhetoric in the letter and the violence in Oklahoma City. Former president George H. W. Bush resigned his NRA membership, and the group was generally cast in a negative light.[28]

The NRA stagnated somewhat in the early 2000s. With George W. Bush in the White House and many victories at the state level, times were good for gun rights, but good times for gun rights do not necessarily mean better times for the NRA. Interest groups flourish when their members perceive danger and threats to their rights. There was little cause for concern until Barack Obama won the presidency in 2008. With the Democrats in control of the White House and both houses of Congress, the NRA again had a worthy foe. Membership rose as the threats were increasingly tangible.

The NRA never lacks for critics from both the left and the right. It is frequently criticized as being too mainstream, for example, for accepting more restrictions on machine guns in exchange for the benefits in the Firearms Owners Protection Act. There is always some group or groups trying to outflank them or gain membership by being more strident and demonstrating a complete unwillingness to compromise. This forces the NRA to the right, at times, even though there is no chance that it will be replaced as *the* gun-rights group. When the NRA lurches right, it is often at the behest of its members, or at least its most vocal members. The criticisms from the left are the essence of this book, so they need not be enumerated here. There is also criticism of the group from within, or from those who used to be members of the team. Two examples of this are Robert Ricker and Richard Feldman.

The first former insider to criticize the industry at large was Bob Ricker. Ricker had worked for several gun-rights groups, including as an attorney for NRA, a stint with Gun Owners of America–California, and Citizens Committee for the Right to Keep and Bear Arms (CCRKBA). Ricker also had ties to the Clinton White House and worked with the administration on gun-safety measures. This led to his ostracism by the gun-rights community. He then worked for the American Sports Shooting Council (ASSC), which was blended into the National Shooting Sports Foundation (NSSF), and he later headed a group called National Coalition of Firearms Retailers.

In 2002 he was part of a lawsuit against gun manufacturers. He filed an affidavit alleging that many in the industry knowingly allowed firearms to be sold to criminals by certain gun dealers and that they remained silent for fear of liability. Ricker claimed that there were conversations among representatives of gun manufacturers and within groups that represented the industry about these "rogue" dealers. The affidavit created a short-term firestorm and was described as a bombshell in many accounts. His allegations were denied by NSSF and other individuals, who said those conversations had never taken place and that it was not common knowledge which dealers did or did not sell to criminals or straw purchasers. They also questioned if it was the job of the industry to self-police or if that was a job better left to law enforcement (BATF). Ricker was alternately portrayed as a disgruntled former employee whose career had been ended by people at the NSSF and the NRA because of his views or as a "moderate in an industry dominated by hard-liners."[29]

Like many events, the Ricker affidavit was seen at that time as a watershed moment in which the underbelly of gun manufacturers and firearms politics was exposed. In the long run, it was much less than that. The lawsuits against dealers and manufacturers were indeed a major issue with the potential to do significant financial harm to the industry if not completely bankrupt it. Of course, all sides had attorneys, but the pockets of many gun manufacturers were not that deep, and protracted litigation could have been catastrophic. That was probably part of the plan—if the plaintiffs won the suits, that was great; but even if they lost, they still won in terms of inflicting financial harm on the firearms industry, and, in the process, raising the cost of guns. All of this became a moot point, however, when President Bush signed the Protection of Lawful Commerce in Arms Act in 2005. Ricker's allegations then became little more than a footnote in history.

Richard Feldman had worked for the NRA in one capacity or another for several years and for the gun industry for several years after that. As one of NRA's chief lobbyists, he was truly an insider. His criticisms of the group are generally less damning than those of Ricker. He describes an organization that is more concerned with self-preservation than in either "winning" or, more importantly, actually solving problems. He also notes that the top leaders in the group are extremely well compensated for their services, monies that are donated to the group by members who have been frightened into parting with their hard-earned cash to protect their rights, which they have been told time and time again are under siege.[30]

Feldman's split with the group resulted from both personal and professional differences. The latter were generally a result of his coming to believe that the NRA was at least as much interested, if not more so, in extending battles in order to attract more members and more funds to promote the longevity of the group and enrich its leaders. Feldman's problem-solving bent led him to work with the Clinton White House to broker a deal with Smith & Wesson to put trigger locks on their handguns. He believed this voluntary accommodation was preferable to governmental coercion, which he viewed as nearly inevitable. Similarly, as the leader of the ASSC, a gun-manufacturers group he joined after leaving the NRA, he tried to negotiate a deal with BATF to improve gun traces and to negotiate terms to end the lawsuits that had been filed against gun manufacturers in the early 2000s.[31] This made him a pariah to many in the gun-rights movement.

While important, Feldman's story did not significantly hurt the NRA. The NRA's actions in terms of self-promotion and paying its leaders very well is not uncommon among interest groups. Feldman himself noted that gun-control groups adopted the same tactics of trying to scare their members into making donations.[32] It is no secret that groups "do better" when they have an enemy to fight. Certainly real enemies are preferable, but imaginary enemies will suffice. This is also true of political parties and elected officials. Like it or not, this is American politics.

Similarly, many CEOs of charitable organizations are very well paid. In 2013, Wayne LaPierre's salary was reported at $972,000. This put him about $100,000 ahead of the CEOs of the American Heart Association and the American Cancer Society, but it placed him below the CEOs of United Way Worldwide, Cystic Fibrosis Foundation, Prostate Cancer Foundation, and Wildlife Conservation Society.[33]

A more recent criticism of NRA followed a group known as Open Carry Texas organized several demonstrations in which members legally carried weapons, including AR-style rifles, into various stores and restaurants. The stunts garnered publicity for the group, earned the scorn of Michael Bloomberg's new group Everytown for Gun Safety, and resulted in some photographs that may not have helped the gun rights cause. Even Gun Owners of America, a more hard-line organization, criticized the Texas group. The NRA responded to the dustup with an unsigned column which read, in part:

Recently, demonstrators have been showing up in various public places, including coffee shops and fast food restaurants, openly toting a variety of tactical long guns . . . [I]t is a rare sight to see someone sidle up next to you in line for lunch with a 7.62 rifle slung across his chest, much less a whole gaggle of folks descending on the same public venue with similar arms.

Let's not mince words, not only is it rare, it's downright *weird* and certainly not a practical way to go normally about your business while being prepared to defend yourself. To those who are not

acquainted with the dubious practice of seeing public displays of firearms as a means to draw attention to oneself or one's cause, it can be
downright *scary*. It makes folks ... question the motives of pro-gun
activists ...

Using guns merely to draw attention to yourself in public not only
defies common sense, it shows a lack of consideration and manners.
That's not the Texas way. And that's certainly not the NRA way.[34]

Just days later, Chris Cox, executive director of NRA-ILA, apologized
for the posting, which had been taken down from the NRA Web site, calling it a mistake and the opinion of one staff member, not the views of the
organization. He described it as a "poor choice of words."[35]

In the long run, this "family squabble" may prove to be unimportant,
but it demonstrates several points. First, the NRA is prone to mistakes
the same as any other group. Second, its "apologies" are also, like those
of other groups, barely believable. Third, the group does not dictate to
its members; on the contrary, it may be moved by members and others
to take positions that make it uncomfortable and that it believes may be
counterproductive. Still, this only detracts minimally from the group's
influence and importance.

Gun Owners of America

Gun Owners of America (GOA) has been described by former U.S.
representative Ron Paul has "the only no-compromise gun lobby in Washington."[36] Most observers would agree that GOA is more strident than
NRA and is less willing to accept *any* restrictions on firearms or gun
ownership.

GOA was formed in 1975 by NRA board member and California state
senator H. L. Richardson following his successful opposition to a proposed handgun ban in California. GOA boasts over 300,000 members.
Larry Pratt, a former Virginia legislator, has been executive director of
GOA for more than three decades. GOA argues that it was instrumental
in allowing the Assault Weapons Ban of 1994 to expire and "single-
handedly" prevented an expansion of background checks in 2006.[37]
GOA also has its own Political Victory Fund and foundation to facilitate
its involvement in elections and various legal battles. Candidate ratings
are available on its Web site. Annual dues are only $20 to encourage
membership.

GOA has pushed NRA to a more extreme position when it suggests
that NRA may be willing to compromise on a firearms-related issue.

For example, in 2004, GOA suggested that NRA might be willing to accept a renewal of the Assault Weapons Ban or enhanced background checks in exchange for limiting liability for gun manufacturers. The NRA immediately responded that it would not compromise. Similarly, there were suggestions, although they may not have originated from GOA, that the NRA was willing to compromise on background checks in 2013. Again, NRA distanced itself from any hint of compromise. GOA also enables the NRA to appear more "reasonable" to those involved in firearms policy and to outside observers. That may well be an unintended consequence of GOA's hard-line stances.

National Shooting Sports Foundation

The National Shooting Sports Foundation (NSSF) is the trade association for the firearms industry. It was formed in 1961 and currently has over 8,000 manufacturers, distributors, firearms retailers, shooting ranges, sportsmen's organizations and publishers as members.[38] Its mission statement is brief: "To promote, protect and preserve hunting and the shooting sports."[39] Various grants to state wildlife agencies and sporting groups support programs that promote sport shooting, hunting, and firearms safety. NSSF has its own political action committee, and it is involved with lobbying as well as providing its members with information and encouraging them to contact their elected officials on issues of importance to the industry.

NSSF generally flies under the radar of the news media, as it works behind the scenes and leaves the public outreach to other groups. This public invisibility should not be perceived as either impotence or irrelevance. Rather, NSSF works in a manner similar to most trade associations.

The NSSF Web site contains links to numerous "fact sheets," background information, state and federal gun law summaries, research reports, the economic impact of shooting sports, and advocacy for or against various laws. As one would expect, many of these are written from a particular perspective, but the information is presented in a different fashion from that of NRA or GOA. Geared toward the industry, the perspective is more that of a business, not a grassroots organization. Those links make clear NSSF's position on various gun-related issues, including that it does not oppose NICS checks or smart-gun technology, but it does oppose universal checks and mandating smart guns. It also links to "Don't Lie for the Other Guy," a program designed to aid law enforcement in helping to train firearms retailers how to better identify straw purchasers. At the very least, NSSF offers a look at how gun manufacturers and dealers view the issue of gun control. That view is part business model and part advocacy.

The Brady Campaign to Prevent Gun Violence

The Brady Campaign has a long history during which it has been transformed several times. It was founded as the National Council to Control Handguns (NCCH) in 1974 by Mark Borinsky, a victim of gun violence.[40] Pete Shields, a DuPont executive whose son had been killed in a random shooting, and retired CIA agent Ed Welles joined Borinsky in the new organization. Prior to this time, there was no significant *organized* gun-control movement. Borinsky and Shields sought to turn personal tragedies into policy changes.

In 1980 NCCH was renamed Handgun Control, Inc. (HCI). A fissure within the organization resulted in a change of philosophy from banning to controlling handguns. The shift was a pragmatic choice, not a philosophical epiphany. It was clear that neither the public nor Congress supported an outright ban and that pursuit of such a policy would be fruitless and, possibly, detrimental to the organization.

HCI, under the leadership of Shields, expanded its membership, attracted national publicity, and became active in lobbying and in political campaigns. By 1981, membership was over 100,000, and HCI had contributed $75,000 to congressional campaigns in the 1980 cycle.[41] Much of the increase in membership was due to the 1980 murder of former Beatle John Lennon and the 1981 assassination attempt on President Ronald Reagan.[42] Both of these shooters used a cheap handgun in their attacks, heightening awareness of the issue.

Two years later, Sarah Brady, the wife of Jim Brady, President Reagan's press secretary who was wounded in the assassination attempt on Reagan, became active in gun-control issues. Brady's decision to join the gun-control debate and HCI brought another injection of publicity and membership to the movement and the organization. Brady was an eloquent spokesperson and put a recognizable face on HCI. Often appearing with her husband, who was confined to a wheelchair and whose speech was slurred as a result of the wounds he sustained, Sarah Brady raised the profile of the group and opened doors that were previously closed. In 1989, the CPHV established the Legal Action Project to become active in the courts.

For more than 20 years, HCI/Brady Campaign was the most prominent gun-control group in the country. Its name was synonymous with the issue. Brady was credited with gaining passage of legislation at both the national level and within some states. Although it is dwarfed in size and resources by the NRA, HCI was a significant counterweight that took advantage of the opportunities it was given.[43] Its major accomplishment, passage of the Brady Bill in 1993, which institutionalized background checks, was the result of years of hard work, persistence, and understanding what was and was not possible, even with a somewhat friendly Congress and a very supportive President Clinton.

Despite the characterization of the Brady Bill as not signifying a major policy change and President Clinton's support as more political than substantive, there is no doubt that the bill was passed due to the tenacity of Sarah Brady and the relatively modest goals of the legislation and HCI.[44] "By seeking incremental gun laws, HCI has erased a perception of political ineptitude and shaken its loser image."[45] More important, passage of the Brady Bill indicated that the NRA could be defeated.

Buoyed by the passage of the Brady Bill, HCI sought more comprehensive gun-control legislation, pushing unsuccessfully for licensing of handgun owners, a firearms registration plan, licensing of ammunition sellers, and increasing the annual cost of a FFL from $200 to $1,000.

Described as "the gun control movement's *piece de resistance*,"[46] these regulations are comparable to those one would find in many European nations. Nothing like that had ever been passed in the United States, and HCI overplayed its hand in this case.

The 1994 midterm elections did not turn on the issue of gun control, but, nonetheless, with the Republicans gaining enough seats to claim a majority in the House of Representatives, the fate of "Brady II" was sealed. New House Majority Leader Newt Gingrich said that he would not move any gun control legislation.[47]

Yet, HCI had not lost all of its power. Another testament to Sarah Brady's influence was her speech at the 1996 Democratic National Convention in which she asked that anyone convicted of misdemeanor domestic abuse be added to the list of those who are ineligible to purchase a firearm. In September of that year, Congress included an amendment to the FY 1997 Omnibus Consolidated Appropriations Act, which prohibits gun ownership or possession by anyone convicted of domestic abuse.[48]

In June 2001, HCI was renamed the Brady Campaign to Prevent Gun Violence, and the CPHV was renamed the Brady Center to Prevent Gun Violence, maintaining its legal action and educational mission. In 2002, the Brady Campaign merged with the Million Mom March. The Million Mom March was a short-lived (1999–2002) organization that garnered a great deal of media attention when it organized a march in Washington,

D.C. in May 2000 that was attended by a reported 750,000 people. Later MMM events, however drew much smaller crowds, and the group never regained traction.

The Brady Campaign has persevered and survived through several name changes and even shifts in focus, but it has never been able to match the reach or clout of the NRA. The Bradys breathed new life into an organization that had plateaued, and they were able to move it forward and enhance its effectiveness for years. But decades later, the shooting of James Brady has faded from the collective memory, and it is now closer to history than current events for many Americans. The group served as the primary vehicle to promote gun control, and it was the go-to source for journalists when there was a gun-control story to be written. The group has been more reactive than proactive, and as a result, it has had a difficult time in passing its agenda. The Brady Campaign remains an important player in gun politics, but if it were truly powerful, then there would be less perceived need for other gun-control groups to arise.

Americans for Responsible Solutions

In many ways, Americans for Responsible Solutions (ARS) and the Brady Campaign are remarkably similar. Both groups were headed by a married couple following the shooting and near miraculous recoveries of prominent governmental officials. Representative Gabrielle Giffords (D-AZ) was shot on January 8, 2011, during a meeting with constituents at a supermarket near Tucson. Six people were killed and 13 wounded during the shooting spree by Jared Lee Loughner, who was mentally unstable. Remarkably, she survived a gunshot wound to the head, and she even returned to Congress for a short time prior to resigning on January 25, 2012, to focus on her continuing recovery.

Giffords and her husband, Mark Kelly, founded Americans for Responsible Solutions as a way to encourage elected officials to stand up for both the 2nd amendment and safer communities by communicating directly with the constituents that elect them. Giffords and Kelly will not let leaders across the country forget that Americans are demanding responsible solutions to this critically important issue.

Giffords, who was first a registered [R]epublican, considers herself a moderate [D]emocrat. She ran in six elections in Southern Arizona and won each of them. A third generation Arizonan, Giffords has long been a gun owner and believes in the constitutional right of all Americans to safe and responsible gun ownership.[49]

Giffords and Kelly formed ARS after the Newtown shootings to combat gun violence, emphasizing expanded background checks, limits on magazine capacity, restrictions on assault weapons, and stronger penalties for straw purchases and gun trafficking. Within six months of its formation and including receipts for its Super PAC and its nonprofit group, ARS reported having raised $11 million from more than 53,000 donors and having more than 350,000 members.[50] FEC reports stated the amount for the Super PAC was a much smaller but still significant $6.65 million.[51] Much of this total was earmarked for the 2014 congressional elections. The focus would be on seven Senate races and four House contests that were expected to be close, and it was reported that the group hoped to spend as much as $20 million, although that appeared to be a high estimate.[52]

They worked for passage of the Manchin-Toomey amendment to the Senate gun control legislation in 2013, and they ran ads following its defeat thanking several senators for their votes and attacking Senate Minority Leader Mitch McConnell (R-KY) and Senator Kelly Ayotte (R-NH) for their votes against it. The couple frequently emphasize that they are gun owners and have been photographed on shooting ranges. They have attended gun shows and shooting events. This is uncommon, although not unprecedented, among gun-control advocates. The effectiveness of that strategy has yet to be demonstrated, but it does inoculate them against the charge that they do not understand how firearms function, and therefore do not know how they should be regulated.

ARS faces several obstacles in its long-term efforts to influence gun policy. First, like the Brady shooting, the Giffords story will slowly recede from the public's consciousness. She will remain a heroic figure, but it will be difficult for her to remain in the public spotlight. In the short run, she has a significant amount of support and widespread personal admiration from both political allies and opponents. Her personal story is compelling. But when the story is not so fresh, she and the group seem likely to fit the mold of James Brady and the Brady Campaign. She and Kelly will try to keep themselves and the cause in the media, and thus in the public's mind. That is not a simple task, however. Numerous more timely stories compete for the news media's attention. Only time will tell if ARS will be relevant for the long term.

Mayors Against Illegal Guns

Mayors Against Illegal Guns (MAIG) was the creation of former New York City mayor Michael Bloomberg. Begun in 2006 with Boston mayor Thomas Menino, MAIG grew from 15 members to include more than 850 mayors from 44 states across the country in 2014. Their guiding principles focused on gun trafficking and straw purchase enforcement, holding dealers accountable, banning assault weapons, limiting the capacity of magazines, and making gun trace data readily available.[53]

MAIG's potential to rival the power of NRA derived from the involvement of Michael Bloomberg. With a net worth estimated at over $32 billion, Bloomberg was ranked as the seventh-wealthiest individual in the United States and was #16 on the Forbes most powerful list in 2014.[54]

In 2013, Bloomberg gave nearly $10 million as the sole donor to Independence USA PAC, and that organization spent about $3.5 million on a Democratic primary election for a congressional district in Chicago (Jesse Jackson Jr.'s former seat). About $1.5 million was spent supporting Robin Kelly, who won the election, and nearly $2 million was spent opposing two candidates, one of which, Debbie Halvorsen, was a former member of Congress who had earned an "A" rating from the NRA. Bloomberg also spent $12 million on an advertising campaign directed at 13 senators who were thought to be the key to passage of gun-control legislation in April 2013. Following the defeat of that package, MAIG ran ads criticizing some senators—Jeff Flake (R-AZ), Kelly Ayotte (R-NH), and Mark Pryor (D-AR)—for their vote against the bill.[55]

In short, whether it be through MAIG, a political action committee, or on his own, Bloomberg has the resources not only to match the NRA's spending, but to spend them into oblivion. He does not need any contributions from individuals or groups; he can do it on his own by using only a small portion of his available resources. Being over 70 years old and having retired as mayor of the nation's largest city, it was unclear if he had the ability or interest in doing so for the long term. MAIG was merged into Everytown for Gun Safety in mid-2014.

Everytown for Gun Safety

In April 2014, Michael Bloomberg announced that he was forming a new gun control group. The new organization was a blend of MAIG and Moms Demand Action for Gun Sense in America, a fledgling group formed just after the Newtown shootings. Simultaneously, he announced that he would spend $50 million to jump-start the effort and to influence voters in 2014. Envisioning a new way to fight the NRA, Bloomberg said that much of the money would be spent building a grassroots organization and the field operations necessary to support it. Bloomberg said the new group would be relentless and adopt what he sees as tactics employed by the NRA. "They say, 'We don't care. We're going after you ... If you don't vote with us we're going to go after your kids and your grandkids and your great-grandkids. And we're never going to stop.' "[56]

The plan is to model the group after Mothers Against Drunk Driving both in terms of outreach and in terms of targets. Bloomberg said the group would focus on expanding background checks rather than gun bans, targeting 15 states and attempting to recruit 1 million new supporters in addition to the 1.5 million the group claimed to have at that time. Women would be a particular focus of recruitment.

His tone as he discussed the commitment of $50 million was described "as if he were describing the tip he left on a restaurant check." When asked if his personality and other issue-related efforts such as banning large-sized soft drinks could negatively impact the group, Bloomberg said the reaction around the country to him was one of a "rock star." "Pointing to his work on gun safety, obesity, and smoking cessation, he said with a grin, 'I am telling you if there is a God, when I get to heaven I'm not stopping to be interviewed. I am heading straight in. I have earned my place in heaven. It's not even close.' "[57]

Bloomberg later said that the new effort "isn't gun control. This is simply making sure that people who everybody agrees should not be allowed to buy a gun—criminals, minors and people with psychiatric problems—make sure they can't buy guns." The group will work in elections. "[Candidates] have to be right on guns, and we're going to do everything we can . . . to make sure that we reward those who are protecting lives and make sure that those who are trying to keep people from being protected lose elections."[58]

MAIG was subsumed into Everytown, and its Web site redirected to Everytown. Moms Demand Action's site continued to function as a stand-alone, although it notes its partnership with MAIG. Begun as a Facebook page created by former Fortune 500 company PR-executive and current "stay-at-home-mom" Shannon Watts in Indianapolis in December 2012, the group established chapters in every state. The Moms Demand Action site states the group was formed to demand action from legislators, noting that no federal gun law has been passed in decades. "Moms Demand Action supports the 2nd amendment, but we believe common-sense solutions can help decrease the escalating epidemic of gun violence that kills too many of our children and loved ones every day."[59]

The Everytown site listed four issue areas—background checks, domestic violence, safe-storage laws (preventable deaths), and gun trafficking.[60] One of Everytown's first "reports" stated there had been at least 74 school shootings between the Newtown shootings and June 10, 2014.[61]

That figure seemed so high that it prompted a CNN investigation. CNN found that 15 of the incidents were "similar" to the violence in Newtown —a high number, but certainly much less than 74.[62] At the same time, a video/ad on the Everytown Web site portrayed a young girl and boy playing hide-and-seek while their mother was in the kitchen. While hiding, the girls discovered a loaded pistol in a box. She began to play with it, and when her brother entered the room, she playfully pointed it at him. Then the screen went blank and there was an audible gunshot and a woman's scream. Obviously an ad that was designed to have an emotional impact, it had nothing to do with background checks, but was focused on accidental deaths (as we have seen, a small number).

Assigning motives to the actions of others is rife with problems. The reasons a woman creates a Web page devoted to gun control following a mass shooting of children are most likely self-evident. The motives for a multibillionaire essentially shuttering a gun-control group he worked years to build in order to create a new one may lead to speculation. It is not unreasonable to surmise that MAIG was not having the desired effect, so Bloomberg sought to create what might be perceived as a grassroots effort. Why he partnered with a largely unknown group as opposed to contributing to ARS or even the Brady Campaign is less clear.

Given his view of himself as expressed in the *New York Times* interview, and his view that his works have clearly earned him entrance into heaven, one might surmise that he wants the limelight for himself and does not want to share it with Giffords and Kelly or Sarah Brady. Clearly, Shannon Watts did not have the name recognition of the others.

Gauging the potential impact of Everytown is also difficult, but, again, one can speculate. Bloomberg's money could be a game-changer. His pockets are deeper than those of the "gun lobby." This should, but probably will not, end the charges that the gun lobby "buys" the votes of elected officials. If money is all that matters, then Bloomberg wins, and he will buy more votes. That is generally not the way politics works. The lines are rarely so straight. This drama would play out in the midterm elections in 2014, and possibly beyond. It will most likely end when Michael Bloomberg tires of the cause, moves on to his next crusade, or simply recognizes that he cannot win.

HOW POWERFUL IS THE NRA AND WHY?

Over the past decade or more, several rankings have placed the NRA at the top or very near the top of the most powerful lobbying/interest groups in Washington. Any such ranking will be based on finances, membership, and, perhaps, the perceptions of Washington insiders. They have some value, but their value is clearly limited because power is very difficult to measure. Still, the NRA's results speak for themselves. By any measure, it is an extremely powerful group.

After the Newtown shooting, CBS News correspondent Bob Schieffer said, "Congress is literally afraid to take on the National Rifle Association because they know that if they make any kind of statement [that] even suggests some sort of limits on gun control, the NRA is going to pour, literally, hundreds of thousands of dollars in a campaign to defeat them." He stated that it was difficult to get elected officials to talk about gun control on *Face the Nation*, which he hosts.[63] Noting there are powerful lobbies working in Washington on behalf of senior citizens, energy companies, and others, Schieffer said, "I think the National Rifle Association is more feared than any of those associations."[64] Schieffer's comments touch on part of the power of the NRA, but the organization is much more than simply a money-funnel to campaigns.

"Because the NRA is simultaneously a lobbying firm, a campaign operation, a popular social club, a generous benefactor and an industry group, the group is a juggernaut of influence in Washington."[65] The NRA's reach extends far beyond the nation's capital to include many states as well. As with any group, its power is greater in some areas than in others. It is not equally influential in all states, or even within all parts of a particular state. For example, the NRA is more powerful in Texas than in New York, and its influence in New York would be felt upstate, not in New York City.

Its power emanates from its resources. Resources in this context should be defined to include more than money in the bank. Resources also include feet on the street, grassroots support, and the commitment level of its members. The NRA excels in all of these areas. Therefore, its power far exceeds its net worth, which, while significant, is not overwhelming in the current political environment in America.

Focus and emotion. The NRA focuses almost exclusively on gun control, which enables its leaders to doggedly pursue their legislative ends. Perhaps more important, many NRA members are as single-minded as the organization itself . . . [T]he NRA can reliably deliver votes. Politicians also fear the activism of NRA members. They're widely believed to be more likely to attend campaign events, ring doorbells, and make phone calls to help their favored candidates—or defeat their opponents—than senior citizens, members of labor unions, or public school teachers.[66]

This single-minded focus along with a willingness to say "No" to any and almost all gun-control legislation allows the NRA to never lose sight of its mission. "The NRA learned that controversy isn't a problem but rather, in many cases, a solution, a motivator, a recruitment tool, an inspiration. Gun-control legislation is the NRA's best friend."[67] While the NRA is hardly the only interest group to use fear as a motivator, it does use it effectively.

That is not easy to do when you are winning nearly all the battles, as NRA was in the late 1990s and early part of the new millennium. It is not nearly as difficult when you have the president of the United States and a billionaire former mayor as opponents. Two recent pleas for contributions will make the point:

> You need to look at the enclosed Gun Confiscation Notice. *This is real*. Notices like this are being issued right now to law-abiding gun owners in New York City, courtesy of former mayor and gun-hating billionaire Michael Bloomberg. And if you and I don't take action *right now* to stop Bloomberg from buying the U.S. Congress in this year's national elections . . . this notice could end up in *YOUR* mail box and you could lose *YOUR* guns before Barack Obama leaves office . . . [Y]ou and I have never faced an opponent like Bloomberg —and this is an election year that means *everything* for the survival of the Second Amendment [emphasis in original].[68]
>
> [B]ackground checks are NOT the real goal behind this effort. The Obama administration has clearly stated that once their plan is put into place, all law-abiding gun owners LIKE YOU must be forced to submit to mandatory 'gun registration' to enforce the new law. You read that right. GUN REGISTRATION. Not just for every gun you buy, but for every gun you already own! . . . how long do you think it will be before every firearm you own is *banned and confiscated*? [emphasis in original].[69]

Antitax advocate and NRA board member Grover Norquist summed up the message of gun control and its supporters as follows: "The D's [Democrats] keep coming back to this. This is so visceral to them. Again, it's an expression of contempt for Middle America. They don't like you and yours and don't think you should be in charge of the capacity to take care of yourself. They know they can't do this for you, but they've hired these nice people to draw chalk outlines of your kids, and that's supposed to make you feel better."[70]

Not all gun owners and not all NRA members respond positively to Cox's messages, nor do they necessarily share Norquist's reaction; but some, perhaps many, do. Fund-raising pleas like those above must be successful, or the NRA would take another approach. And, while Norquist's response may be over the top, the general sentiment is probably shared by many gun owners and NRA members who are more distrustful of the government than others. The condescension experienced by some is also quite real.[71] The threat of gun confiscation may seem distant to some, but the actions of Connecticut and New York make the threat quite tangible and imminent to others. Obama and Bloomberg are unquestionably more powerful real or potential foes than George Soros, the behind-the-scenes financial backer of numerous liberal causes including gun control, or the United Nations Arms Trade Treaty, which were the enemies of the early 2000s.

Should the NRA consider backing off hard-line stances, the lessons of others may be instructive. For example, Dick Metcalf, a longtime writer on firearms and gun culture, authored "The Backstop" column in *Guns & Ammo* magazine. In his December 2013, column he wrote:

[W]ay too many gun owners still seem to believe that any regulation of the right to keep and bear arms is an infringement. The fact is, all constitutional rights are regulated, always have been, and need to be ... I firmly believe that all U.S. citizens have a right to keep and bear arms, but I do *not* believe that they a right to use them irresponsibly. And I do believe their fellow citizens, by the specific language of the Second Amendment, have an equal right to enact regulatory laws requiring them to undergo adequate training and preparation for the responsibility of bearing arms.[72]

His column specifically addressed training requirements in order to get a concealed-carry permit. He did not address any gun bans or background checks, although one might infer support for the latter from his comments. The thrust of the column was gun safety, although he did talk about regulation as a means of achieving gun safety. Response to the column was both swift and severe. The editor of the Outdoor Wire Digital Network wrote: "[A]nother gun writer has weighed in ... to help those less knowledgeable better understand the constitution's second amendment. [G]un expert Dick Metcalf ... helps us understand that the second amendment was intended to be heavily regulated, and that onerous regulations are not infringements. Instead they simply reflect the wishes of the founding fathers."[73] Within days, two major firearms industry manufacturers informed Intermedia Outdoors, the parent company of *Guns & Ammo*, that they would not advertise with the company until it was restructured. Metcalf was fired by the magazine, and the editor Jim Bequette, who was already planning to step down, resigned immediately:

> As editor of "Guns & Ammo," I owe each and every reader a personal apology ... Dick Metcalf's "Backstop" column ... has aroused unprecedented controversy. Readers are hopping mad about it, and some are questioning "Guns & Ammo's" commitment to the Second Amendment. I understand why.
>
> Let me be clear: Our commitment to the Second Amendment is unwavering. It has been so since the beginning ... In publishing Metcalf's column, I was untrue to that tradition, and for that I apologize. His views do not represent mine—nor, most important, "Guns & Ammo's." It is very clear to me that they don't reflect the views of our readership either.
>
> Dick Metcalf has had a long and distinguished career as a gun-writer, but his association with "Guns & Ammo" has officially ended.[74]

The NRA spends a great deal of time and resources communicating with its members. In addition to the usual fund-raising letters (of which there are many), it also sends out endorsements in elections and regularly gets out its message through its monthly magazines, especially *America's 1st Freedom*, the periodical that focuses on gun policy and the Second Amendment.

The NRA may be decisively outspent by Michael Bloomberg, and there is no doubt that Barack Obama is more powerful than Wayne LaPierre, but neither Bloomberg nor Obama can motivate the same number of people on the sole issue of gun control as can the NRA. Within its sphere of influence, the NRA's power remains unmatched.

WHY "MIDDLE GROUND" GROUPS FAIL

A few so-called "middle ground" groups have sprung up in the gun-control debate, but they have generally not attracted much attention and have not been very successful. There are two major reasons for this. First, some of the groups are not truly in the middle regarding the issue. Second, if a group is in the middle, then they get little attention from the media and tend not to attract many members. Theoretically, if we assume that the position of most Americans is somewhere between virtually unlimited access to firearms and a total gun ban, then a group of this type should have the most followers. However, we know that people who join interest groups and are issue activists tend to be those who have positions closer to the extremes. People who are most excited about any issue are most often those who hold positions far from the middle option. Few people hold "intense moderate" views.

An example of what might be perceived as a true "middle" organization is the Independent Firearms Owners Association (IFOA), headed by Richard Feldman. For example, IFOA supported the Manchin-Toomey Amendment, but it generally opposes any assault weapons bans.[75]

> Without the NRA and Second Amendment Foundation and others we would have lost our Second Amendment Freedoms years ago. We are the future, not the past. We will work with anyone who will work with us—Republican, Democrat, Independent, Liberal or Conservative. We are prepared to chart a new course, with a new orientation, determined to achieve different results ...
>
> The firearm and related criminal justice issues have been subjected to juvenile politicized name-calling that do a disservice to intelligent gun owners, law enforcement professionals and our system of governance. There are no simple answers! This is a complex, multifaceted problem requiring thoughtful answers backed up by a serious organization that can provide a balance to the debate.[76]

To be sure, Feldman commands enough media attention that he gets called frequently to comment on gun issues, but IFOA is not a player on the same stage as NRA, the Brady Campaign, or Michael Bloomberg. Those groups provide more "newsworthy" comments, regardless of whether or not they are more informative. Middle groups are simply not as colorful. As important, they do not represent the interests of those most exorcised by gun control—one way or the other.

Other "middle groups" may not really be in the middle at all. One example was the short-lived American Hunters and Shooters Association (AHSA), which billed itself as a moderate gun-owners group devoted to protecting hunting lands and wildlife habitat without a radical political agenda. It was headed by Bob Ricker and several individuals who had been active in gun-control organizations. AHSA endorsed Barack Obama for president in 2008 and supported many gun-control measures. It was disbanded in 2010 after only five years in existence.[77]

Similarly, the Third Way is an organization involved in gun policy, as well as many other issues.

Third Way represents Americans in the "vital center"—those who believe in pragmatic solutions and principled compromise, but who too often are ignored in Washington.

Our mission is to advance moderate policy and political ideas. Our agenda includes: a series of grand economic bargains, a new approach to the climate crisis, progress on social issues like immigration reform, marriage for gay couples, tighter gun safety laws, and a credible alternative to neoconservative security policy.[78]

In its defense, Third Way does express support for tighter gun-safety laws, a fact that is borne out by its fact sheets, all of which favor the gun-control side of the debate. It is difficult to see how Third Way differs from Violence Policy Center, a think tank that strongly supports gun control. The group's title, as well its statement that it represents the "vital center," are both at least somewhat misleading. Third Way absorbed the defunct Americans for Gun Safety, a group that was formed by billionaire Andrew McKelvey and supported some restrictions on firearms and background checks, but not a total gun ban.[79] Both AHSA and Third Way are much more akin to gun-control groups than they are to gun-rights groups. Their positions do not seem to be true "middle" positions.

PROBLEMS FACING GUN-CONTROL GROUPS

A major impediment for gun-control groups is that supporters of gun control are not a large natural constituency in the way that gun owners are. Shooting victims, their families, and the families of those who died as a result of gun violence are often strongly and permanently committed to the cause. This is evidenced by the number of those people who are involved in leadership positions with the groups. Those, however, are very small constituencies when compared to gun owners. Many others have been touched more tangentially by gun violence, and they may also support gun-control measures. To be fair, some victims and families become advocates for gun rights.[80]

Many supporters of gun rights are thought to be less strongly committed to the cause and less likely to be single-issue voters.[81] For them, gun control is of some importance to them, but it is not the most important issue. Their support may be strong immediately following a mass shooting, but, as the event recedes in their memory, its salience may decline. For some, their position may change as the immediacy of the threat diminishes. The strategy for gun-rights supporters is to withstand the initial threat following a focusing event, and then "extend the political game" until they once again control the board.

Gun owners are a much more natural constituency. Certainly they are not monolithic—no group is—but they share an interest, and many share the concern that their rights are or could be threatened. Even assuming a low estimate of gun owners in the United States, that is a large base than can be, and often is, mobilized for grassroots actions. This consistent pressure allows groups like the NRA to work incrementally, exemplified by the gains made on concealed-carry laws in many states over the course of many years.

Kristin Goss argues that the gun-control movement has never succeeded, or even been a true "movement," for three important reasons. "Unlike other movements, such as those against tobacco, smoking, and abortion, the gun control campaign struggled to obtain patronage, to craft a resonant issue frame, and to settle on a strategy that could deliver movement-building victories."[82]

Goss suggests that several key ingredients have always been in place, including shootings and crime, as well the support of public opinion and groups that were capable of mobilizing the masses. Yet, it was never fully supported by the government because gun-rights groups were successful in employing a "defund, delegitimize, and deprive" strategy to keep gun control off the agenda. The polarizing nature of the issue kept both government and philanthropic groups at arm's length from the gun-control movement. Both interests had much to lose by getting involved and little to gain, politically or monetarily.

According to Goss, gun control has been framed as crime control, eschewing the more potentially popular and motivating frames of public health and protection of children. In some ways, this is natural, but it prevents expanding the issue into other areas, which would have increased the potential constituencies to support the cause. Crime is also multifaceted, so it does not lend itself to focusing on only one aspect of the problem, and it kept the debate within the realm of experts, not average citizens.

Finally, the legislative strategy favored bold initiatives at the national level that were much less likely to succeed. "Rather than organizing around modest measures and allowing policy regimes to expand by accretion, leading gun control advocates started out by seeking bans on handguns."[83]

Gun-rights advocates played very good defense at the national level, thwarting attempts at comprehensive gun control, and worked in state legislatures to weaken laws and to make gains on such things as concealed carry and the Castle Doctrine. Each of those wins was celebrated in the gun-rights community as a major victory, providing supporters with tangible proof that their efforts had been successful and encouraging them to continue the fight.

A GUN CONTROL STRATEGY THAT COULD WORK

One tactic open to gun-control advocates is to try to change public opinion by stigmatizing gun ownership. In fact, this may already be happening. This would be similar to efforts to change attitudes toward drinking and driving and smoking.

Founded in 1980, the mission of Mothers Against Drunk Driving (MADD) was "To aid the victims of crimes performed by individuals driving under the influence of alcohol or drugs, to aid the families of such victims and to increase public awareness of the problem of drinking and drugged driving." Four years later, that was modified to "create major social change in the attitude and behavior of Americans toward drunk driving." In 1985, it took a more regulation-focused approach, "to establish the public conviction that impaired driving is unacceptable and criminal, in order to promote corresponding public policies, programs and personal responsibility."[84] The purpose was to change attitudes before it changed laws. The group also took on underage drinking, but it never sought Prohibition or restricting drinking at home or even when out at a bar or restaurant as long as the person drinking did not drive. Even brewers promoted "drinking responsibly" and having a "designated driver." One of the major policy victories of MADD was the national lowering of the drunk driving standard to .08, signed into law by President Bill Clinton in 2000 and supported by about 70 percent of the public.[85] The percentage of highway deaths defined as alcohol-related declined from 50.6 percent in 1990 to 42 percent in 2009.[86]

Three crucial points differentiate drunk driving and gun control. First, few, if any, people argued in favor of drunk driving. There was no effort at prohibition, so no one's right to consume alcohol was abridged. The drinking age was raised, and there was some debate about that, but health statistics suggested that the measure would save lives. Second, there was no organized interest aligned in opposition to the drunk driving effort. Finally, it is nearly impossible to argue that there is any benefit to the individual from drinking and driving as can be argued for firearm possession. In short, it is an easier "sell."

Similarly, smoking rates have declined significantly as a result of government action, activism, publicity from the American Cancer Society and others, and changing public opinion. Research on the impact of secondhand smoke helped push legislatures across the country to restrict smoking in more areas over time. Taxes on tobacco were increased. Despite efforts by tobacco companies and the American Tobacco Institute (ATI) to dispute research findings, smokers have found their ability to smoke reduced over the past several decades. Public opinion has changed as well.[87] We moved from an era in which it was "cool" to smoke, and when television and movies often portrayed lead characters smoking, to a time when smokers are huddled together outside restaurants and office buildings because they are not permitted to smoke in public places or the workplace.

Again, smoking was not banned, though it has been severely restricted. Smokers argued, unsuccessfully, that their rights were being unnecessarily restricted. The only benefit they could demonstrate to smoking, however, was that it relaxed them. Once the link to potential injury to non-smokers was made, the issue's fate was sealed. Cigarette companies and ATI could easily be seen as less than truthful—and several whistleblowers asserted that they knew of the harmful effects for years—and there was no organized group that represented consumers of the product.

Firearms are clearly different. While some argue that the NRA represents gun manufacturers more than gun owners, most gun owners do not share that sentiment. NRA is seen positively by many people, especially those who own firearms.[88] Gun rights are constitutionally protected, at least to some degree. Even advocates of firearms regulations recognize that they can be and are used to protect lives and prevent crimes.

There is a path open to gun-control groups, however, to try to convince Americans that the costs of guns outweigh the benefits. There are academic studies supporting that claim, primarily in the public health field. Those studies are likely to increase as funding is restored to the Centers for Disease Control and Prevention to allocate for gun-violence research. Similarly, many schools now have a zero-tolerance policy regarding anything that resembles a firearm, thus helping to teach a new generation that guns are bad and are to be avoided. This is a long-term strategy that would require diligence, patience, and organization. Those qualities are not held in abundance by most gun-control groups. It remains to be seen if these qualities are attributes of Michael Bloomberg and Everytown.

INTEREST GROUPS AND GUN CONTROL

NRA generally represents the interests of its members. It may also represent the interests of firearms manufacturers, but there have been times when the organization has spoken out against individual manufacturers at the behest of activist members. Clearly, NRA draws significant funding from gun manufacturers in the forms of contributions to its various branches and advertising,[89] but still half of its funding comes from member dues.[90] It is only logical that firearms manufacturers would contribute to the group that most strongly represents shooting interests and that they would advertise in its publications. It would be shocking if they did not.

Others suggest that it is in fact the NRA that calls the shots and that gun manufacturers take their marching orders from the group's leaders.[91] When Smith & Wesson (S&W) brokered a deal with the Clinton administration, exchanging some safety features and marketing modifications for immunity from lawsuits aimed at holding manufacturers liable for some gun violence, the NRA helped spearhead a successful boycott of S&W. Sales declined, the company was sold at a steep discount, and rebounded only when it repudiated the deal.

It is reasonable to suggest that the views of interest groups and their members influence one another. No interest group perfectly represents the opinions of its membership, and the opinions of members are naturally influenced through communications from the group. This is true of the NRA, which communicates frequently with its members; but it is also true, for example, of AARP, which sends out mailers to its members asking if Social Security should be protected.[92]

We have already seen how the NRA ran into difficulty when it criticized the Texas Open Carry group. NRA's opposition to background checks during the 2013 Congress clearly ran counter to the opinions of gun owners as a whole and, possibly, a majority of its members. In both cases, however, it was most likely responding to a smaller, more vocal group of gun-rights activists. NRA members are more supportive of gun rights than gun-owning nonmembers.[93] A December 2012 Gallup Poll found that the NRA had an overall favorable rating of 54 percent (38% had an unfavorable view), with 71 percent of those who have a gun in the household holding a positive view of the group.[94] That 16-point spread was down from a high of 60 percent favorable and only 34 percent unfavorable in 2005, but given that this poll was taken shortly after Wayne LaPierre's much-maligned press conference following the Newtown shootings, the slippage was not significant.

Logically, any interest group whose lobbying and issues positions are opposed by its membership will eventually lose their support. NRA's membership increased significantly in early 2013, however. At the annual meeting in May 2013, Wayne LaPierre claimed that the number of members had passed 5 million, although that number could not be independently verified.

Gun owners felt that there were potential threats to their ability to purchase and possess firearms, accessories, and ammunition. Those challenges were coming from President Obama and Congress at the national level and, in many cases, from state legislatures as well. One need not look to public opinion data for evidence of this phenomenon. The empty shelves in gun shops and sporting goods stores in 2013 and 2014 strongly supported the notion that there was a shortage of firearms, ammunition, and shooting supplies.

It could easily have been predicted that AR-type rifles would have been in short supply. They were readily available prior to the presidential election in 2012. Supply began to diminish after Obama's reelection as fears of gun control rose. Those fears were stoked following the Newtown shooting, the president's speeches, and the introduction of national legislation.

By the time the Senate bills were defeated, AR-type rifles were extremely difficult to find. Prices had increased dramatically, and few were available. Gun shows, which previously had hundreds for sale, now had few, and they would sell out very quickly. Even the component parts were not easy to procure.[95] Online sellers were backordered on everything, with no expected date of availability.

This shortage extended far beyond ARs, though. Ammunition became scarce, prices rose, and materials for those who load their own rounds were difficult to find.[96] Even .22 ammo, which no elected official threatened to ban, was in short supply. Lines appeared at shops when the delivery truck arrived. Clerks did not have time to stock the shelves; buyers scooped up whatever was available as soon as it was unloaded from the truck. Many major sporting goods chains and local dealers instituted limits on the amount of ammunition a single buyer could purchase in order to allow more of their customers to purchase ammo.[97] Theories regarding the shortages ranged from large purchases by the Department of Homeland Security, hoarding by numerous gun owners, panic buying, or the inability of the manufacturers to respond to rapidly escalating demand.[98] The boom in sales was clearly good for gun and ammunition manufacturers as well as their employees.[99]

There is little to no evidence that the NRA was hurt by the aftermath of Newtown and the 2013 congressional debates. Legislation that surely would have been defeated in the House of Representatives never made it out of the Senate. Although Wayne LaPierre did not win any oratory awards for his performance after the Newtown shootings, his group gained members and flexed its muscles in early 2013.

The big question is the long-term impact and longevity of groups such as Americans for Responsible Solutions and, particularly, Everytown for

Gun Safety. The former seems likely not to be a significant long-term influence in the gun-control debate. At most, it could supplant the Brady Campaign as the fresh face for gun control for a new generation. That said, Brady was not a truly formidable opponent for the NRA.

Everytown poses a more serious threat to NRA and could influence gun-control policy. Despite the argument made early in this chapter that money alone does not equal success for an interest group, with Michael Bloomberg's seemingly limitless financial backing, Everytown can have the staying power that many gun-control groups lack. At its core, though, it is an elite group and not a grassroots group. It relies solely on the largesse of its patron, not the support of the comparatively paltry donations of millions of members. That, however, could change.

In addition, Bloomberg can be both a positive actor and a detriment to any cause.[100] Somewhat mercurial and with many interests, it is never certain that he will concentrate on firearms rather than soda size, the environment, or some other cause. In addition, his support, while very helpful in some areas of the country, can be a negative factor in others.

One thing is certain: No gun-control group will match the NRA in terms of number of members or intensity. The NRA's influence was on display when it helped defeat the Manchin-Toomey amendment in 2013. While the NRA does not win every battle in which it engages, it has an enviable win-loss record in producing votes in the legislative arena and at the ballot box.

NOTES

1. Thomas Dye, *Understanding Public Policy*, 14th ed. (Boston: Pearson Education, Inc., 2013), 44.

2. John Kingdon, *Agendas, Alternatives, and Public Policies*, updated 2nd ed. (New York: Longman Publishing Group, 2011), 48–53.

3. AARP is now known only by the acronym. That was an abbreviation for American Association of Retired Persons.

4. AARP, "It's Time for Responsible Solutions to Social Security and Medicare," direct mail, May 2013.

5. Steve Simpson, "We Don't Need a 'Media Shield' Law for Fox and AP; We Already Have the First Amendment," *Forbes*, June 19, 2013, http://www.forbes.com/sites/realspin/2013/06/19/we-dont-need-a-media-shield-law-for-fox-and-ap-we-already-have-the-first-amendment/.

6. Planned Parenthood, "Planned Parenthood: Extreme 20-Week Abortion Ban Takes Personal Medical Decisions Out of the Hands of Women and Their Doctors," November 7, 2013, http://www.enewspf.com/opinion/commentary/47729-planned-parenthood-extreme-20-week-abortion-ban-takes-personal-medical-decisions-out-of-the-hands-of-women-and-their-doctors.html.

7. While some would argue this is only semantics, the nomenclature used when discussing policy and interest groups is clearly important. There is a reason why those who oppose abortion refer to themselves as "pro-life," while those who advocate for abortion rights call themselves "pro-choice." In the same way, there are significant differences in the implications of "gay rights" and "homosexual agenda."

8. *Citizens United v. Federal Election Commission*, 558 U.S. 310 (2010).

9. Michael Martinelli, "Crossroads' $175 Million Strikeout," OpenSecrets.org blog, November 8, 2012, http://www.opensecrets.org/news/2012/11/despite -dropping-millions-crossroads-strikes-out.html.

10. See the discussion on this topic in Chapter 4.

11. NRA–Institute for Legislative Action, "About NRA-ILA," http://www .nraila.org/about-nra-ila.aspx.

12. NRA–Political Victory Fund, "About PVF," http://www.nrapvf.org/ about-pvf.aspx.

13. NRA Foundation, "About Us," http://www.nrafoundation.org/.

14. NRA Civil Rights Defense Fund, "About Us," https://www.nradefense fund.org/about-us.aspx.

15. Walter Hickey, "How the NRA Became the Most Powerful Interest in Washington," *Business Insider Politics*, December 18, 2012, http://www.business insider.com/nra-lobbying-money-national-rifle-association-washington-2012-12.

16. Gregg Lee Carter, *The Gun Control Movement* (New York: Twayne Publishers, 1977), 66.

17. Carter, *Gun Control Movement*, 68; William J. Vizzard, *Shots in the Dark: The Policy, Politics, and Symbolism of Gun Control* (Lanham, MD: Rowman & Littlefield Publishers, 2000), 59.

18. Edward F. Leddy, *Magnum Force Lobby* (Lanham, MD: University Press of America, 1987), 197.

19. Carter, *Gun Control Movement*, 71.

20. Vizzard, *Shots in the Dark,* 60.

21. Ibid., 60–61.

22. Carter, *Gun Control Movement*, 79–80.

23. Vizzard, *Shots in the Dark,* 61; Carter, *Gun Control Movement*, 80.

24. Carter, *Gun Control Movement*, 81.

25. Robert J. Spitzer, *The Politics of Gun Control*, 5th ed. (Chatham, NJ: Chatham House Publishers, 2004), 94.

26. Carter, *Gun Control Movement*, 108–9.

27. Any rogue or botched operations by BATF benefit the NRA, whether they comment on them or not in the same way that mass shootings benefit gun-control groups. They stir up the base.

28. Joel Achenbach, Scott Higham, and Sari Horwitz, "How the NRA's True Believers Converted a Marksmanship Group into a Mighty Gun Lobby," *Washington Post*, January 12, 2013, http://www.washingtonpost.com/politics/

how-nras-true-believers-converted-a-marksmanship-group-into-a-mighty-gun
-lobby/2013/01/12/51c62288-59b9-11e2-88d0-c4cf65c3ad15_story.html.

29. Dave Workman, "Ricker Deposition 'without Foundation,' " *Gun Week*, February 20, 2003, http://www.gunweek.com/2003/ricker0220.html; Fox Butterfield, "Gun Industry Ex-Official Describes Bond of Silence," *New York Times*, February 3, 2003, http://www.nytimes.com/2003/02/04/national/ 04GUNS.html.

30. Richard Feldman, *Ricochet: Confessions of a Gun Lobbyist* (Hoboken, NJ: John Wiley & Sons, Inc., 2008).

31. Feldman described his friend Bob Ricker has having gone over to the "dark side" a little bit when commenting on Ricker's affidavit. Feldman suggested that everyone in the country knew there were rogue dealers, but he also suggested it was the job of law enforcement, not the industry, to police them. Workman, "Ricker."

32. Feldman, *Ricochet*, 120–21.

33. American Institute of Philanthropy, "Top 25 Compensation Packages," CharityWatch.org, 2013, http://www.charitywatch.org/hottopics/Top25.html. The reader can decide if those salaries are appropriate.

34. Reid J. Epstein, "NRA Splits with Open Carry Texas amid Chipotle Beef," *Wall Street Journal*, June 2, 2014, http://blogs.wsj.com/washwire/2014/ 06/02/nra-splits-with-open-carry-texas-amid-chipotle-beef/.

35. Michael Muskal, "NRA Apologizes for Calling Texas Open-Carry Gun Demonstrators 'Weird,' " *Los Angeles Times*, June 4, 2014, http://www.latimes .com/nation/nationnow/la-na-nn-nra-apologize-texas-long-gun-open-carry-20140 604-story.html.

36. Gun Owners of America, https://gunowners.org/.

37. Ibid.

38. National Shooting Sports Foundation, http://nssf.org/.

39. Ibid.

40. Brady Campaign to Prevent Gun Violence, Organizational history, http:// www.bradycampaign.org/our-history.

41. Spitzer, *Politics of Gun Control,* 111–12.

42. Carter, *Gun Control Movement,* 83; Diana Lambert, "Trying to Stop the Craziness of This Business," in *The Changing Politics of Gun Control,* ed. John M. Bruce and Clyde Wilcox (Lanham, MD: Rowman & Littlefield Publishers, 1998), 184.

43. Spitzer, *Politics of Gun Control,* 111–12.

44. Vizzard, *Shots in the Dark,* 135–36. It is true that the Brady bill was modified significantly from what was originally introduced and that the waiting period provision was rendered impotent by the introduction of the instant background check.

45. Lambert, "Trying to Stop the Craziness," 184.

46. Carter, *Gun Control Movement,* 84.

47. Ibid., 85–86.

48. Lambert, "Trying to Stop the Craziness," 184.

49. Americans for Responsible Solutions, "About Gabrielle Giffords," http://americansforresponsiblesolutions.org/about/gabrielle-giffords/.

50. Manu Raju and Anna Palmer, "Gabrielle Giffords Guns Group Raises $11 Million," *Politico*, May 8, 2013, http://www.politico.com/story/2013/05/gabrielle-giffords-guns-group-fundraising-91074.html.

51. Federal Election Commission, "FEC Disclosure from 3 for Americans for Responsible Solutions," filed July 31, 2013, http://query.nictusa.com/cgi-bin/dcdev/forms/C00540443/883049/.

52. "Gabby Giffords' Group Announces 2014 Election Strategy," CNN Politics Political Ticker, June 4, 2014, http://politicalticker.blogs.cnn.com/2014/06/04/gabby-giffords-group-announces-2014-election-strategy/.

53. Mayors Against Illegal Guns. http://www.mayorsagainstillegalguns.org/html/home.

54. "Michael Bloomberg," Forbes.com, 2014, http://www.forbes.com/profile/michael-bloomberg/.

55. Kevin Bohn and Gabriella Schwarz, "Bloomberg Gun Group Hits a Democrat," CNN Politics Political Ticker, May 24, 2013, http://politicalticker.blogs.cnn.com/2013/05/24/bloomberg-gun-group-hits-a-democrat/?hpt=po_c2.

56. Jeremy W. Peters, "Bloomberg Plans a $50 Million Challenge to the N.R.A.," *New York Times*, April 15, 2014, http://mobile.nytimes.com/2014/04/16/us/bloomberg-plans-a-50-million-challenge-to-the-nra.html?referrer=.

57. Ibid. Several news media repeated Bloomberg's afterlife musings, and his self-image was also recounted. Yet, coverage of the creation of Everytown, his financial support, and his statements did not dominate news coverage. Certainly, had Wayne LaPierre suggested that his work in supporting those who are protecting lives while opposing those who are trying to prevent people from protecting lives (claims he makes implicitly, if not always explicitly) had assured his place in heaven, the coverage would have been more extensive and more negative.

58. Lucy McCalmont, "Michael Bloomberg Plans $50M Gun Effort," *Politico*, April 16, 2014, http://www.politico.com/story/2014/04/michael-bloomberg-nra-gun-effort-105745.html.

59. Moms Demand Action for Gun Sense in America, http://www.momsdemandaction.org/about/.

60. Everytown for Gun Safety, http://everytown.org/who-we-are/.

61. "School Shootings in America since Sandy Hook," Everytown.org, June 2014, http://everytown.org/article/schoolshootings/.

62. Ashley Fantz, Lindsey Knight, and Kevin Wang, "A Closer Look: How Many Newtown-Like School Shootings since Sandy Hook?" CNN, June 12, 2014, http://www.cnn.com/2014/06/11/us/school-shootings-cnn-number/index.html.

63. Schieffer's difficulty in getting elected officials and others to talk about gun control is not an isolated incident. This author was unable to get several U.S. senators or any staff members to discuss the issue. One office, which was

not directly involved in gun-control legislation, would not speak even when offered an "off the record" conversation and after a request from another staffer in the office. One declined an e-mail request in less than five minutes. Other offices simply did not return messages. The same was true for the NRA, which also did not respond to a request for an interview. The logic is relatively straightforward: there is no political gain from talking, while there is potential risk.

64. "Schieffer: NRA the Lobby Most Feared by Congress," CBS News, December 15, 2012, http://www.cbsnews.com/news/schieffer-nra-the-lobby -most-feared-by-congress/.

65. Hickey, "How the NRA."

66. Brian Palmer, "Why Is the NRA So Powerful? How the Gun Lobby Leverages Modest Resources into Outsized Influence," *Slate*, December 18, 2012, http://www.slate.com/articles/news_and_politics/explainer/2012/06/eric _holder_charged_with_contempt_how_did_the_nra_swing_the_votes_of_so_many _democrats_.html.

67. Achenbach et al., "NRA's True Believers."

68. Chris Cox, Letter from NRA–Political Victory Fund, February 28, 2014.

69. Chris Cox, "National Campaign to Stop Gun Registration," Letter from NRA–Institute for Legislative Action, March 7, 2014.

70. Achenbach et al., "NRA's True Believers."

71. Recall the dubious distinction afforded gun owners as creating the most unhappiness among consistent liberals if a family member married one. See Pew Research Center for People and the Press, "Political Polarization in the American Public," June 12, 2014, http://www.people-press.org/2014/06/12/ political-polarization-in-the-american-public/.

72. Dick Metcalf, "Let's Talk Limits: Do Certain Firearms Regulations Really Constitute Infringement?" The Backstop, *Guns & Ammo*, December 2013.

73. Paul Erhardt, "Between the Berms: Paging Uncle Ted," *Shooting Wire*, November 6, 2013, http://www.shootingwire.com/features/228219.

74. Jim Bequette, "Our Response to the December 2013 Backpage Column," *Guns and Ammo*, November 6, 2013, http://www.gunsandammo.com/2013/11/ 06/response-december-2013-backpage-column/.

75. Independent Firearms Owners Association, http://www.independentfire armowners.org/2013/.

76. Ibid.

77. David E. Petzal and Phil Bourjaily, "Meet the American Hunters and Shooters Association," *Field and Stream*, September 7, 2006, http://www .fieldandstream.com/pages/meet-american-hunters-and-shooters-association.

78. Third Way, "About Us," http://www.thirdway.org/about_us.

79. Dick Foster, "Billionaire Backs Gun-Curb Measure," *Rocky Mountain News: Election 2000*, January 7, 2000, http://denver.rockymountainnews.com/ election/1002mons5.shtml.

80. A prominent example of this is Suzanne Gratia Huff, who was present when her parents and 18 others were killed in a restaurant shooting in Killeen,

Texas, in 1991. Although she had a concealed-carry permit, she was required by law to leave her firearm in her car. As a result, she was unable to confront the shooter. She subsequently became active in the gun-rights movement to the point of winning a seat in the Texas state legislature.

81. See the "Activism and Intensity Gaps" discussion in Chapter 3.

82. Kristin A. Goss, *Disarmed: The Missing Movement for Gun Control in America* (Princeton, NJ: Princeton University Press, 2006), 191.

83. Ibid., 192–93.

84. "About Us," Mothers Against Drunk Driving, http://www.madd.org/about-us/.

85. Kelly Maybury, "Most Americans Favor Tougher Drunk Driving Law," Gallup, October 26, 2000, http://www.gallup.com/poll/2395/Most-Americans-Favor-Tougher-Drunk-Driving-Law.aspx.

86. Matthew Chambers, Mindy Liu, and Chip Moore, "Drunk Driving by the Numbers," Bureau of Transportation Statistics, 2012, http://www.rita.dot.gov/bts/sites/rita.dot.gov.bts/files/publications/by_the_numbers/drunk_driving/index.html.

87. Julianna Pacheco, "Trends—Public Opinion on Smoking and Anti-Smoking Policies," *Public Opinion Quarterly* 75, no. 3 (Fall 2011): 576–92.

88. Pew Research Center for the People and the Press, "Broad Support for Renewed Background Checks Bill, Skepticism about Its Chances: Gun Rights Proponents More Likely to Vote on Issue," May 23, 2013, http://www.people-press.org/2013/05/23/broad-support-for-renewed-background-checks-bill-skepticism-about-its-chances/; Frank Newport, "NRA has 54% Favorable Image in U.S.," Gallup Politics, December 27, 2012, http://www.gallup.com/poll/159578/nra-favorable-image.aspx.

89. Walter Hickey, "Here's Who the NRA REALLY Represents," *Business Insider Politics,* December 19, 2012, http://www.businessinsider.com/the-nra-has-sold-out-to-the-gun-industry-to-become-their-top-crisis-pr-firm-2012-12.

90. Eugene Kiely, "Do Assault Weapons Sales Pay NRA Salaries?" FactCheck.org, January 15, 2013, http://www.factcheck.org/2013/01/do-assault-weapons-sales-pay-nra-salaries/.

91. Paul M. Barrett, "Why Gun Makers Fear the NRA," *Bloomberg Businessweek*, March 14, 2013, http://www.businessweek.com/articles/2013-03-14/why-gun-makers-fear-the-nra.

92. AARP, "It's Time."

93. Pew Research Center, "Broad Support."

94. Newport, "NRA has 54% Favorable Image in U.S."

95. For example, a gun show in Roanoke, Virginia, in December 2012 had a 40-minute wait to purchase tickets to enter. Less than two hours after opening, there were no AR rifles available, and the component parts were sold out within another hour. One dealer reported selling more than 30 .223 AR rifles in the first hour.

96. The author tried unsuccessfully to purchase ammunition for an M-1 carbine .30 caliber World War II military surplus rifle in February 2013. Previously,

this was readily available in local shops and online. By early 2013, it was back-ordered everywhere, and it was not available anywhere. Similarly, attempts to locate the components for reloading a cartridge for a .300 Winchester Magnum (a large-caliber hunting rifle) yielded results only after numerous online searches and purchasing bullets and primers from different sellers. Gunpowder was also scarce during that time. A local big-box store had none of the items listed above. Extending into 2014, there was a continuing shortage of .22 ammo even as other calibers became available. Reloading supplies were still scarce as well. By mid-2014, ARs were back in stock and prices had receded to previous levels.

97. Aaron Smith, "Gun Shops Face Massive Ammunition Shortage," CNN Money, March 12, 2013, http://money.cnn.com/2013/03/12/news/companies/guns-ammo-shortage/index.html.

98. Kristina Shevory, "Bullet Blitz: Demand from Public, Government Leave Ammo Shelves Empty," Fox News, May 12, 2013, http://www.foxnews.com/us/2013/05/12/bullet-blitz-demand-from-public-government-leaves-ammo-shelves-empty/?test=latestnews.

99. Aaron Smith, "Guns and Ammo Sales Spark Jobs Boom," CNN Money, March 25, 2013, http://money.cnn.com/2013/03/25/news/companies/guns-ammo-jobs/index.html?hpt=hp_t2.

100. For example, more than one of the senators he targeted with ads criticizing their vote on Manchin-Toomey responded with ads of their own welcoming the disapproval of the (former) New York City mayor.

SIX

Conclusion

Many authors know the general conclusions of their book before they begin to write. The research has been done, and they have formulated their argument. That was not the case with this book. While the direction of gun-control policy was fairly clear in late 2012 when this book was proposed, the path took several turns after Adam Lanza fatally shot 20 children and six staff members at Sandy Hook Elementary School before taking his own life on December 14, 2012. Thus, the conclusion begins where the introduction began—with an examination of the impact of the Newtown shootings on gun control policy.

By 2012, policy had been moving incrementally, but clearly in the direction of gun rights for over a decade. Many of the gains had been made in the states, with a few significant victories, but more of a stalemate at the national level. The Assault Weapons Ban of 1994 had expired in 2004 with little more than a national whimper. There were a few people shouting, perhaps, but they were the proverbial tree falling in the forest with no one else there to hear them or to intervene politically. Within many states, restrictions on concealed carry of firearms were being eased, and Castle Doctrine and Stand Your Ground laws were becoming increasingly common.

Numerous polls indicated that public opinion was moving in the direction of gun rights as well. According to the Pew Research Center, a 22 percent margin in favor of controlling gun ownership over protecting gun rights existed in 1993, but it had completely dissipated by early 2012. Opinion shifted back in favor of gun control after the New-town shooting, but it was about evenly split again six months later.[1]

Violent crime rates continued to fall, even as gun sales rose dramatically with the election and reelection of Barack Obama as president. The overall rate of violence declined significantly in the latter part of the 1990s and continued the downward trend through 2010. Nonfatal victimizations in 2011 were about one-third the number seen in 1993; firearm homicides declined by about 40 percent during the same time.[2] The "more guns, more crime" thesis appeared much less plausible in 2014 than it did 25 years previously.

The first Obama administration produced no major laws regulating firearms, even though Democrats controlled both houses of Congress for the first two years of that term. The usual suspects introduced the usual bills, but it was generally understood they would not pass, and they were largely ignored by the media and by legislators. Many Democrats appeared to be running away from the issue, and those who were not in full-scale retreat were at least reluctant to raise the issue of gun control or cast a vote on the record. Several mass shootings in the previous few years had failed to generate sufficient support to pass serious gun-control legislation.

The National Rifle Association was, essentially, the only player in town in terms of influencing gun policy. Enjoying a period of growth and success, its major problems seemed to be guarding against creeping complacency among its members and finding a sufficiently frightening "bogey man" to heighten awareness, create some fear, and raise some money. The Brady Campaign remained the primary voice arguing for gun control, but there is little doubt its power had diminished.

When the U.S. Supreme Court weighed in with two landmark decisions that generally favored the rights of gun owners, the die was seemingly cast. Although the opinions in those cases clearly stated that individuals have a constitutional right to possess firearms for their personal protection, they also clearly stated that many, if not most of the current gun regulations were constitutional. Gun bans were out, but gun regulations could well be in. Narrowly decided, and with many caveats, they were still widely interpreted as protecting gun rights.

VIOLENCE AND FIREARMS POLICY

Miles's law, which states "Where you stand depends on where you sit," certainly applies to both gun laws and their perceived efficacy. Just as the nation has become more polarized between blue and red states, those who support stricter gun laws appear to have never seen a regulation they did not like, while their political opponents appear to believe that the Second Amendment states there can be no regulation of firearms. There are certainly many people between those opposing positions, but the political battles often feature those diametrically opposed views.

For one side, gun laws have failed to reduce violence because criminals do not obey laws. For the other side, gun laws have not been more effective because there are so many loopholes that we have not really restricted firearms in any meaningful way. Neither side pays much attention to the reductions in gun violence, although gun-rights advocates do note declining crime rates when they refute the "more guns, more crimes" thesis. The decline has been significant and enduring; it is important.

With over 300 million firearms in circulation, disarming the nation is not possible even if one thinks that would be an efficacious policy. By everyone's admission, the vast majority of those firearms will never be used in a crime, in a suicide, or as part of an accidental shooting. Some, however, will. The Unites States has a much higher homicide rate than most other developed nations. The suicide rate is not particularly high in international comparisons, but the gun-related suicide rate is, not surprisingly, quite high. The question is if that violence is driven by the presence of firearms or by socioeconomic and cultural factors.[3] In the face of conflicting views by respected scholars, how can the average citizen who does not hold a PhD in statistics make sense of the claims?

Perhaps some logical reasoning can help. First, students in introductory social science research methods classes learn that correlation does not equal causation. The United States has a higher murder rate than many countries with lower rates of gun ownership. That does not prove that fewer guns means less crime. The U.S. murder rate has declined as gun sales have soared. That does not prove that more guns means less crime. So, should we disregard statistics? Of course not. Rather, we should look at empirical evidence and temper our conclusions with common sense.

Logic suggests that firearms make killing easier. Logic also suggests that firearms are used to prevent crimes and lethal violence. Eliminating guns would not eliminate crime, lethal violence, or suicide. Controlling guns will, inevitably, result in the prevention of some bad acts. It would also prevent those guns from being used to stop other bad acts. Some crimes, although the number is disputed, are deterred through armed citizens. Whether more crimes would be prevented and lives would be saved as a result of further gun restrictions, or if there would be a net increase in one or both, is an important question. In addition, the issue of a law-abiding citizen's right to defend themselves and others against crime and violence must be considered.[4] It is also quite reasonable to consider the recreational benefits of firearms as we do with other objects, i.e., swimming pools and automobiles, which are sometimes related to death.

A cursory examination of violent crime and homicide rates reveals that both declined during an economic downturn, a phenomenon most criminologists find almost inexplicable. Gun sales have soared in the past decade, although the rate of gun ownership has remained steady or, perhaps, even declined slightly. While many of the firearms sold during that time were semiautomatic handguns and "assault rifles"—guns that the public most often associates with violence—crime rates declined. Clearly, the selling of those guns did not result in more crime. Simultaneously, gun laws were made incrementally less strict. If nothing else, that should cause everyone to question the more-guns-equals-more-crime theory. That does not imply, however, that we should arm everyone in order to achieve a quiescent state.

Could we reduce crime further with more controls on guns and gun owners? If so, can we enact those regulations without infringing upon the rights, constitutionally guaranteed or societally recognized, of gun owners? To address the first question, the best evidence regarding the effectiveness of gun laws is equivocal. Two national panels assembled for the purpose of evaluating the effectiveness of gun laws both decided that the evidence was insufficient to draw any conclusions. To be sure, neither panel could in any way be described as having been organized to promote gun rights. While they did not say that gun laws do *not* work, they could not find evidence that they *do* work.[5] The second question is, in some ways, more difficult to answer. No one is opposed to "common-sense" regulations of firearms. That said, different people define common-sense regulations in very different ways. Regarding the efficacy of gun control, public opinion suggests that fewer of us are optimistic about the potential impacts of stricter gun regulations even though we may favor various restrictions. Our ambivalence is understandable, given that we tend not to think that guns are the cause of violence.

The tension between supporters of gun control and those who wish to protect gun rights seems intractable. It is difficult to conceive of a gun regulation that will effectively reduce criminal violence without the creation of some form of national gun registry. Gun traces are effective only if they can truly be traced to the owner. Background checks are effective only if everyone who should be prohibited from purchasing a firearm is actually on the prohibited list and if checks are conducted in all transactions. We know that a small percentage of mental health records are in the NICS database, and predicting violent behavior is an extremely imprecise science.

To ensure that all transactions have been conducted properly, some entity would have to maintain a database of all firearms. A memo from the deputy director of the National Institute of Justice was found and published by the NRA.[6] The memo included several assertions that future regulations would have to be more stringent than those passed previously in order to impact gun violence. Universal background checks would have to be accompanied by a permanent gun registry, magazine bans would have to include surrender of those currently owned, and assault weapon bans would have little impact. A gun registry is the worst fear of most gun-rights supporters because they believe it could lead to gun confiscation. Some argue that the fear is unfounded or irrational, but the fear is real nonetheless.[7]

Perhaps, most important, criminals will not go through regular channels to procure their weapons. They may not disobey all laws, but they will certainly ignore gun laws when it is to their benefit to do so. Black markets exist to serve needs that cannot be met through legal channels. To assume that the black market for firearms would not expand to meet the needs of organized crime and street-level criminals willing to pay the price flies in the face of basic economics.

In summary, the effectiveness of gun laws is questionable at best. It is not even necessary to address the possibility that stricter laws will actually increase crime by preventing access by law-abiding citizens.

WHAT GUN-CONTROL SUPPORTERS SEEK AND GUN-RIGHTS ADVOCATES FEAR

Proponents of stricter gun regulations define the problem as one of crime control and suicide prevention and argue that they only want reasonable, common-sense regulations. Gun-rights advocates define the problem as potential infringement of rights they hold dear. It is the difference between *needing* a gun and the *right* to possess a firearm. This difference is not impossible to bridge, but it is difficult to do in the absence of trust. Trust is often missing in this relationship.

Both elected officials and gun-control groups reassure gun owners that they do not want to take away firearms from law-abiding citizens. They simply want to keep them away from people who should not have guns—criminals and people who are mentally unstable. Again, gun-rights groups and owners say they are not opposed to this in theory, but the mechanisms can be problematic. Some think that gun-rights groups create fear where none should exist, distort the potential impact of regulations, and engage in straw-man and slippery-slope arguments. Those who argue for gun rights would dispute those charges and suggest that the ultimate goal of gun control is to take away firearms.

The underlying motives for those who support stronger gun laws seem quite apparent. They see tragic and inexplicable mass shootings. They read that guns are responsible for the deaths of 30,000 Americans each year with many thousands more wounded. Maybe they have a friend or relative who was the victim of gun violence, or they may have been a victim. We should not accept these statistics, to say nothing about the lives that are taken and the others seriously impacted. There *has* to be way to reduce the carnage. We have to do *something*; we cannot sit back and do nothing.

Many, though certainly not all, see no need for a private citizen to own a firearm; at the least, they should be strictly regulated like other dangerous items. Whose responsibly is it to assure the safety of the people? That is a proper role for government. Government has both the ability and the duty to regulate guns. Guns are not the solution; guns are the problem.

Why do some people think that gun control means that firearms will ultimately be confiscated? First, recall that gun-rights supporters tend to be distrustful of the government. They do not believe that government should know or has the right to know who has firearms, how many, and what type. They point to "Fast and Furious," Ruby Ridge, the storming of the Branch Davidian compound in Waco, Texas, etc., as evidence that the government is not to be trusted. Even though it is not related to firearms, the controversy regarding the National Security Agency and spying on American citizens only fuels these fires.

Also, the logic of gun-control supporters and their solutions have changed over time and do not always appear to match the problem. At one point, the focus was on handguns, specifically the inexpensive Saturday Night Specials. Although those proposed regulations (and bans) were opposed by many in the gun-rights community, there was logic to the argument. Most homicides were and are committed with handguns.

Over time, the focus shifted to "assault rifles." Poorly defined in the Assault Weapons Ban of 1994, many in the gun community saw this as an attempt to ban all semiautomatic firearms. Combined sales of semiautomatic rifles and handguns currently comprise about more than half of gun sales. For supporters of gun control, these are weapons designed for the military that have no place on the streets or in American homes. For gun owners, they are the sporting guns, the guns they own for personal protections, and, in some cases, for hunting. They also account for a very small percentage of homicides in the United States. The language of the Assault Weapons Ban led many supporters of gun rights to the conclusion that those who wish to more strictly regulate firearms do not understand how guns work or care about the rights of gun owners.

Other restrictions on firearms have been proposed. For example, trigger locks must now be included in all sales of new handguns by a dealer. They are also included with some long guns. Safe-storage laws are thought to protect children and others unfamiliar with firearms who could find a loaded gun and accidentally shoot themselves or someone else. However, if one owns a gun for personal protection, then that firearm must be readily accessible when needed. An intruder will not wait while you retrieve your gun from the safe and load it in order to confront them. Responsible gun ownership would dictate that the owner must assess the relative risks of where the gun is stored and make their own decision accordingly. Of course these laws are virtually unenforceable without permitting the police to make unannounced checks of homes they know contain a gun (again, the specter of a gun registry).

Following the shooting at Columbine, the proposed solution was background checks at gun shows. The perpetrators, Eric Harris and Dylan Klebold, obtained their guns from friends.[8] With the benefit of hindsight and research, though, we now know that this was not a planned firearm attack. "In fact, the pair's suicidal attack was planned as a grand—if badly implemented—terrorist bombing that quickly devolved into a 49-minute shooting rampage when the bombs Harris built fizzled."[9] They planned the attack for over a year building about 100 bombs and gathering the firearms. They brought two duffel bags with propane tank bombs into the cafeteria. They walked outside and waited for the bombs to explode, planning to shoot the survivors who would flee. Had the cafeteria bombs exploded, they may have collapsed the entire school building, killing nearly everyone inside. Fortunately, they were not adept at bomb making.

The Virginia Tech shootings similarly spurred much lobbying to close the gun-show loophole. Here, though, the links are not even tenuous. Sung Hui Cho purchased his guns from an FFL, and he passed the background checks, which were properly conducted. He even waited a month between handgun purchases as was then required under Virginia state law. He did not make any known purchase at a gun show. The NICS Improvement Amendments did, however, address mental health records, a direct connection with Cho.

As noted in the Introduction, Adam Lanza stole his firearms from his mother, who had purchased them legally in a heavily regulated state. She passed the required background checks. A national universal check system could not have possibly prevented that tragedy. When you put all these incidents together, some gun-rights proponents see solutions in search of a problem, not vice versa, and they question the actual motives and goals of those who propose the solutions.

Combined with the efforts of the Obama Administration to regulate firearms after it promised a comprehensive review of gun violence in the
wake of Newtown, these examples fuel skepticism among gun-rights
advocates. The White House said it would look at all sources of violence,
but the regulations it proposed and executive orders it issued involved
only firearms. There was nothing about video games, and nothing regarding violence in the media. As Joseph Heller wrote in *Catch-22*, "Just
because you're paranoid doesn't mean they aren't after you."

THE SHORT-TERM FUTURE

Given that policy change did not result from the previous recent mass
shootings, perhaps it should not be a surprise that national firearms policy
changed little as a result of Newtown. A determined President Obama was
unable to rally sufficient support in the Congress to pass new gun legislation. It is now difficult to see a situation in which that status quo would be
shaken. Public opinion changed for a time, but it soon began to return to
the pattern of moving in the direction of gun rights. Beyond that, violent
crime, while still a concern of the public, continues to remain steady or
decline. We may well be at the end of the era of crime decline, but there
is no reason to suspect any sort of spike in gun violence in the near future.
Mass shootings will always generate a great deal of attention and short-
term support for gun control, but the fervor fades over time. And, while
the public supports various gun measures, particularly universal background checks, many surveys suggest that that same public holds less
hope that new gun laws will solve any of the problems. Is violent crime
in the United States a gun problem, or a mental health and culture problem? There is no definitive answer.

Supporters of gun rights, perhaps having been lulled into a false sense
of security in the early 2000s, appear to be once again mobilized to fight
the necessary battles. Even as President Obama announced executive
orders that would increase restrictions on guns and gun owners, Congress
declined to follow with legislation that would codify those actions.

New interest groups formed (Americans for Responsible Solutions and
Everytown for Gun Safety), but their ability to influence policy was limited. In Congress, the votes were simply not there. Their strategy of
attacking the Senate Democrats who voted against universal background
checks is not a strategy to get more supporters of gun control elected
any more than Tea Partiers challenging mainstream Republicans results
in more conservatives in elective office. As President Obama stated, the
change will have to come from the American people. There are not

enough people dedicated to the cause for a sufficient amount of time to create that change.

Gun-control supporters were able to make gains in several states. Generally, those states, e.g., Connecticut, New York, and New Jersey, already had strict gun regulations. Some combination of gun registration, owner licensing, universal background checks, and bans on "assault weapons" is now the law in several states. We are seeing some evidence of civil disobedience in those states as gun owners protest the restrictions by refusing to register their restricted firearms or dispose of them. What happens to these recalcitrant citizens remains to be seen.

At the same time, other states continue to have fewer restrictions on firearms and gun owners. Several moved further in the direction of gun rights after Newtown, while most simply kept the laws that were already on the books. Some passed so-called nullification laws that prevented some gun laws from being enforced in the state, although their constitutionality is questionable.

A year after Newtown, the national policy window had closed. Another tragic shooting could reopen the window, but, it is reasonable to ask, if Newtown did not result in national legislation, then what would? The national agenda is full of important and large items, including ongoing debates over health care policy and immigration, and an economy that spits and sputters toward recovery. Those are the major issues on which elections are decided. Gun control is a tertiary issue that is of great importance to a smaller percentage of the electorate. That group is comprised of a larger number of gun-rights supporters than those who want stricter gun laws. The intensity and activism gaps favor gun rights.

THE LONGER-TERM FUTURE

Long-term predictions in any profession are fraught with stipulations, caveats, and a high probability of error. Gun control is no different. Still, it is reasonable to examine some trends and see where they may lead.

As is the case for most issues, the battle lines are first drawn with children. How and what children are taught about guns helps to determine future firearms policy. There is disagreement over if or when children should be taught gun safety versus simply avoiding guns. With the policy in many schools moving toward zero tolerance of anything gun-related and teaching children that guns are "bad," one would also expect the number of gun owners to decline over time. Educational philosophy is open to change, and it is not monolithic across the country. It is difficult to envision moving from an era in which students are suspended for wearing a

T-shirt with a depiction of a gun, chewing a Pop Tart into the shape of a gun, or pointing a finger at another student and saying "bang," to a situation in which students are taught that guns can be used for recreation and self-defense. At the same time, it is almost inconceivable that we would see guns disappear from popular culture—television, movies, and video games.

The percentage of the population that owns or is familiar with firearms is also extremely important for policy. We have seen that the owner/ non-owner, gun-in-household/no-gun, and rural/urban dichotomies strongly influence both public opinion and gun policy. Therefore, demographic shifts are crucial.

Some projected demographic changes seem to favor the gun-control side. The United States continues to experience population growth, and while its population is aging, it is expected to see continued higher fertility rates than many other nations. Population growth is likely to be fueled by immigration and higher fertility rates among minorities—groups that are less likely to own firearms. If there is a move away from the suburbs and rural areas to a resurgence of inner cities, that could also contribute to fewer gun owners. Of course, those predictions and trends are subject to change.[10]

Following a period of decline, the percentage of the population that hunts has increased over the past decade. Hunting, in particular, but also gun owning, is more prevalent among whites than among other demographic groups.[11] Having an ally in the White House is critical in getting national legislation enacted and signed into law. President Obama may not have been everything gun-control supporters had hoped for (at least during his first administration), but it was certain he would never sign serious gun-rights legislation. If Hillary Clinton is elected president in 2016, we should expect to see much the same. The wild card of Michael Bloomberg being a force for gun control means the hope/specter of stricter regulations will stay on the horizon. Finally, the near inevitability that some future mass shooting will at least temporarily fuel the movement ensures that the battle over guns will not end.

Gun rights continue to have the momentum, although it was interrupted by the Newtown shootings. The recent Supreme Court decisions in the *Heller* and *McDonald* cases have allowed the movement to continue, even while recognizing the legitimacy of some gun regulations. Public opinion had been shifting in favor of gun rights prior to Newtown, and many polls have found that trend returning. The unparalleled power of the NRA continues as well, although the Bloomberg threat is ever-present. Many elected officials who may actually favor gun control have been taught, correctly or not, that challenging gun rights may cost them their careers. The failure of Manchin-Toomey will likely dissuade others from attempting to pass gun-control legislation. All of these conditions point to continued success at the national level for gun rights. So long as the crime rate remains relatively stable or declines, and absent a mass shooting that provokes a prolonged visceral response, it is difficult to envision gun rights losing the national battle. A federal-level stalemate or incremental movement toward gun rights is more likely.

Supporters of gun rights have demonstrated their ability to fend off national legislation, even in the face of a heart-wrenching national tragedy, with the defeat of the Manchin-Toomey amendment in the U.S. Senate. They have been able to largely resist, executive orders notwithstanding, pressure from a president who was committed to gun-policy change. If and when they are able to count on a friend in the White House, they can begin to play offense once again.

The NRA remains ever-vigilant for possible incursions of the rights of gun owners. Fear is a great motivator for any group, and in 2014, there were enough legitimate causes for fear that there was little need to create any. The previous, somewhat distant threat of the United Nations' Arms Trade Treaty had been replaced by President Obama calling for universal background checks, a renewed and stronger assault weapons ban, and magazine restrictions, and several states enacting very strict laws. Hillary Clinton as a candidate and/or president would make an equally compelling foil. The possible impact of Michael Bloomberg was also more tangible than the threat of the less well-known George Soros.

The Supreme Court will continue to set the boundaries within which regulations will be debated. Using the *Heller* and *McDonald* decisions as guides, it is safe to say that most, perhaps not all, current gun regulations would be judged to comport with constitutional requirements. More onerous restrictions regarding who may possess firearms and many gun bans may be struck down. Universal background checks would almost certainly pass judicial scrutiny.

Individual states will continue to chart their own courses, and they are likely to continue to take different directions. With little action from Washington, some states will continue to enact stricter regulations, while others will loosen their gun laws. This will satisfy no one completely, but a majority of residents of most states may take solace in the fact that their state has the "right idea," even as their neighbors may enact very different policies.

While this may not be a solution that results in street celebrations, it is quite reasonable and rational in a federalist system of government.

A national consensus does not exist, and it is doubtful that one can be reached. It makes no sense to enact restrictive gun legislation when the best evidence is that most gun laws have little practical impact. Making people feel better is not inherently a bad thing for governments to do. Making some people feel better while restricting the rights and sense of well-being of others is hardly a reasonable tradeoff.

If states with more restrictive laws begin to see tangible results that can be identified, then other states and the country as a whole may reevaluate their policies. Conversely, if those laws do not have an impact or are even counterproductive, then we can see that as well. Of course, this would mean that one side, or even both, would have to put their preconceived notions aside, look at the evidence, and support policies they do not like or abandon policies they do like. Unfortunately, there is little reason to be hopeful that policy analysis will produce unequivocal findings, or that those results would then be accepted by all and acted upon accordingly. If that were the case, then we have little need for *politics*. All things considered, the gun-rights argument can be expected to win most, but certainly not all, of the battles.

There can never be a long-term truce in the battle over gun control. Short-term accommodations can be reached, and there is a middle ground that would be acceptable to most Americans. The exact parameters of that deal would have to be negotiated, but they would probably include some form of enhanced background checks, some limits on some types of fire-arms, and guarantees against total bans and a government-maintained fire-arms database. Many observers have suggested that such provisions would be minimally intrusive on the rights of law-abiding gun owners and would allow for some of the regulations favored by those who want stronger control on guns and gun owners.

That deal will not be struck, though, because of the more extreme positions of both sides—both interest groups and the attentive public. Both sides benefit from the current and future battles. Interest groups survive and, in some cases, flourish, in the current environment. Elected officials and candidates gain from taking up a particular cause. Citizens feel that their efforts are focused on protecting innocent lives or protecting cherished freedoms. The job is not finished until all unnecessary deaths are prevented or until rights are properly and permanently protected. Neither state is a realistic scenario. One side will doggedly pursue more regulations to prevent gun-related deaths, while the other side will relentlessly argue in favor of protecting rights and loosening policies to allow the law-abiding to protect themselves and their families. There are extremely few concessions to be made in this debate. Neither side will surrender even if their opponents win most of the battles. That is the political and societal realty. More important, such a "grand deal" would have little, if any, impact on either accidental or intentional shootings.

If such a deal were struck, when the next mass shooting occurred, the next young child was accidentally shot, or when violent crime rose—all of which are inevitable—there would be more calls for stronger gun-control measures. They would come from interest groups, elected officials, concerned citizens, and relatives of the victims. On the other side, interest groups, elected officials, concerned citizens, and many gun owners would unite behind the "more guns, less crime" hypothesis and argue for a relaxation of gun regulations.

Returning to the logical argument, we should balance the benefits of the regulations against the level of infringement of the right.[12] Ultimately, elected officials and courts decide where the line is drawn between infringing upon gun rights and enacting gun-control regulations. Most of us would agree that rights should be infringed only when there is evidence that the infringement will be of benefit to society. Even then, there must be some balancing.[13] Absent evidence that gun-control laws effectively reduce violent crime or suicides, then only very unobtrusive regulations are acceptable. Regulations with little to no chance of impacting crime or gun violence should be rejected.[14]

It is unrealistic to expect that gun-rights supporters will reach a point where they say that stricter laws are necessary. Similarly, those who support stricter laws will never conclude that we have sufficiently regulated firearms and that we must accept that we cannot reduce violence any further by regulating guns. One side believes that guns are the problem and government is the solution, while the other thinks that government is the problem.

Given the current state of research in the field, we should not expect to see any definitive answers from academia or governmental research. Research to this point is, at best, ambiguous. Research will and should continue to attempt to find answers to the questions regarding the effectiveness of various policies. That is not just an obligatory promotion of academic work; it is recognition that unbiased research is the best and perhaps only hope we have to find those answers. They certainly will not be found in preconceived notions and platitudes. We already have plenty of each of those.

While this may appear to be a pessimistic view of the future, it need not be viewed through that prism. Important political, economic, and social issues are rarely settled "once and for all." Debates continue within society with varying degrees of intensity, and the political world often struggles to find acceptable policies to deal with problems. Simply put, the important problems are not easily solved, or they would not be so contentious.

The argument throughout this book has been that the success of the gun-rights movement derives from the number and fervor of its supporters. This is exemplified by the reach and resources of the NRA. It is doubtful that those who favor gun control can match the numbers or strength of support of their counterparts. Everytown is the only group that can out-spend the NRA. It is virtually certain that no other gun-control group can command the resources and, hence, media attention that Bloomberg can provide. If he can't take down the NRA, then who can? Who would even try? If this is the "final showdown," so to speak, we may be seeing the true end of the gun-control debate in the United States.

NOTES

1. Pew Research Center for the People and the Press, "Gun Rights vs. Gun Control," May 23, 2013, http://www.people-press.org/2013/05/23/gun-rights-vs-gun-control/#total.

2. Bureau of Justice Statistics, *National Crime Victimization Survey, 1993–2011*; and Centers for Disease Control and Prevention, National Center for Injury Prevention and Control, Web-based Injury Statistics Query and Reporting System (WISQARS), 1993–2010, http://www.cdc.gov/ncipc/wisqars.

3. For different perspectives, evidence, and answers to this question, see Don B. Kates and Gary Mauser, "Would Banning Firearms Reduce Murder and Suicide? A Review of International and Some Domestic Evidence," *Harvard Journal of Law and Public Policy* 30, no. 2 (2007): 650–694; and Harvard Injury Research Control Center, "Firearms Research: Homicide," http://www.hsph.harvard.edu/hicrc/firearms-research/guns-and-death/.

4. There is a similar current national debate about the wisdom of lengthy criminal sentences and incarceration. Without question, there is a high cost of incarceration. Logically, it is also makes sense that by selectively incapacitating individuals who commit many crimes, we will prevent some crimes from occurring. As a society we have to decide how we will balance the economic costs, determine fairness in sentencing, and estimate possible impacts on crime rates.

5. Charles F. Wellford, John V. Pepper, and Carol V. Petrie, eds., *Firearms and Violence: A Critical Review* (Washington, DC: National Academies Press, 2004); Robert A. Hahn et al., "First Reports Evaluating the Effectiveness of Strategies for Preventing Violence: Firearms Laws: Findings from the Task Force on Community Preventive Services," Centers for Disease Control, October 3, 2003, http://www.cdc.gov/mmwr/preview/mmwrhtml/rr5214a2.htm.

6. Greg Ridgeway, "Summary of Select Firearm Violence Prevention Strategies," January 4, 2013, http://www.nraila.org/media/10883516/nij-gun-policy

-memo.pdf. Although the White House subsequently claimed it was a draft and only the thinking of one person, it did not deny the memo's authenticity, and Dr. Ridgeway remained in his position.

7. Fears related to the National Security Agency tapping phone conversations or government entities wanting to know Web sites visited or library books read may also be unfounded. The reader can make those judgments.

8. They bought one (a TEC-9 assault rifle) from a friend and persuaded a female acquaintance to purchase three other guns for them at a gun show. She made the purchase from an individual seller who was not required to make her complete the paperwork and conduct background check (which she would have passed). She later said that if she was required to fill out the form, then she would not have made the purchase.

9. Greg Toppo, "10 Years Later, the Real Story behind Columbine," *USA Today*, April 14, 2009, http://usatoday30.usatoday.com/news/nation/2009-04 -13-columbine-myths_N.htm.

10. Joel Kotkin, "The Changing Demographics of America," *Smithsonian Magazine*, August 2010, http://www.smithsonianmag.com/40th-anniversary/ the-changing-demographics-of-america-538284/.

11. U.S. Fish and Wildlife Service, *2011 National Survey of Fishing, Hunting, and Wildlife-Associated Recreation*, revised February 2014, 21–33, http:// www.census.gov/prod/2012pubs/fhw11-nat.pdf.

12. This "balance test" may or may not reflect the method that will be used by the courts in the future.

13. For example, would (or should) society be willing to accept "profiling" based on race or ethnicity even if it was demonstrated that it would reduce crime?

14. The executive order issued by President Obama in August 2013, which banned the re-importation of surplus military firearms, falls into the category of a regulation that imposes a burden on some with no overall benefit. Described by the White House as "two new common-sense executive actions to keep the most dangerous firearms out of the wrong hands and ban almost all re-imports of military surplus firearms to private entities," (The White House, Office of the Press Secretary, "FACT SHEET: New Executive Actions to Reduce Gun Violence," August 29, 2013, http://www.whitehouse.gov/the-press-office/2013/08/29/fact-sheet-new -executive-actions-reduce-gun-violence) the reality is that the "military-grade" weapons at stake here are almost exclusively from the World War II and Korean War era. While often very serviceable firearms, they are of significant value to collectors but of little use to criminals. They are almost never used in crimes. The benefit to society cannot be seen as anything other than negligible.

EPILOGUE

The Midterm Elections of 2014

While the midterm elections of 2014 were not *about* gun control, they were critical to the future of the issue. The elections were generally seen as either a referendum on President Barack Obama, or the Republicans' "war on women," or a commentary on race relations in the United States. Many federal, state, and local elections impacted gun laws, but none of them were focused on that issue. There were competing ballot initiatives in the state of Washington regarding background checks. While those who favor stricter gun laws won the initiative battle in Washington, gun-rights candidates mostly won the competitive electoral contests. Regardless of how one views an electoral map that favored Republicans, the GOP was clearly victorious in what many called a "wave election." Those Republican wins boded well for gun rights.

A year and a half after the failure of Manchin-Toomey and nearly two years after the Newtown shootings, the familiar pattern for the public returned. The economy was uppermost in the minds of most voters and, for the majority, gun control was no longer an important issue. That did not deter the interest groups from becoming involved in the election. The NRA was spending about as much money as it typically does in elections, but that was more than matched by Everytown for Gun Safety and Michael Bloomberg, and by Americans for Responsible Solutions.

Regarding endorsements for the U.S. Senate, Everytown endorsed candidates in 16 races, 11 of whom were virtual locks for their candidate, while five were thought to be competitive. The NRA endorsed a total of 28 candidates, six in competitive races and six who were almost certain to lose. Although the Virginia Senate election provided the closest margin of victory, it was not seen as competitive prior to Election Day.

The competitive head-to-head states were Colorado, Iowa, Louisiana, and North Carolina. The NRA also endorsed in Arkansas, Georgia, Kansas, and Kentucky. In fairness, foresight may not have predicted that Kansas and Kentucky would have been competitive. Still, the NRA took the tougher route to victory. NRA-supported candidates won all those elections, with Louisiana headed to a runoff and likely victory for the NRA candidate. Everytown-backed candidates lost three of the close races (Colorado, Iowa, and North Carolina) and perhaps Louisiana. They won only in New Hampshire.

Simply endorsing a candidate, however, does not mean that maximum effort was expended on behalf of the candidate. The NRA spent most heavily ($1 million or more) on Senate races in Arkansas, Colorado, Georgia, Iowa, Kansas, Kentucky, and Louisiana. Everytown invested in candidates at several levels of office and most heavily in the Washington referendum where they reportedly accounted for about $4 million of the over $10 million spent by gun-control supporters, including Bill and Melinda Gates. Governors who had signed stricter gun legislation in the wake of Newtown survived close calls in Colorado and Connecticut, but strong supporters of gun control lost in Illinois and Maryland.

American for Responsible Solutions also did not fare well. They spent most heavily (about $2 million) in the House of Representatives seat previously held by Gabrielle Giffords. The incumbent, her former aide who was wounded in the Tucson shooting, won a close victory in 2012. As this is written, the Republican challenger appeared to be the winner, but a legal challenge was possible and a recount was certain.

ARS also invested in the Senate contests in Maine, New Hampshire, North Carolina, Colorado, Iowa, and Louisiana as well as two House of Representatives seats in New Hampshire (supporting two incumbents, one of whom lost). They did not cherry-pick races, but their won-lost record was not impressive.

Voters in Washington State approved Initiative 594, which mandated background checks for all gun purchases in the state, except for antique firearms and transfers between immediate family members. At the same time, voters rejected Initiative 591, which would have prohibited the state from implementing enhanced background checks until a national standard was established. The NRA opposed Initiative 594 and supported Initiative 591, but the group spent little money in the state, perhaps perceiving that it could not win.

THE IMPACT OF THE 2014 ELECTIONS

Democrats had to defend more seats in the Senate and several of those were in strong Republican states. In addition, the party that controls the White House typically loses seats in midterm elections, particularly in the sixth year of a presidential term. Republicans, however, were thought to be at a advantage in many governors' races. Overall, the midterm elections of 2014 were a resounding victory for Republicans.

At the national level, gun rights, although they were not a major issue in most campaigns, were also big winners. With Republicans in control of both houses of Congress, the odds of passage of a revived Manchin-Toomey bill or anything like it were infinitesimal. No such bill could pass in either the House or the Senate. Outside of the Washington initiative, which was a clear victory for gun control, there was almost no mention of firearms in election analyses. It was no longer on the agenda, and the policy window was tightly shut. The absence of the issue from governmental agendas should be seen as a win for gun rights.

States will continue to chart their separate courses, as was evidenced by the Washington initiative victory. While more than a dozen states allow for citizen-written initiative, many of those are in the West and South, areas that are not likely to approve gun-control measures. Such measures could pass in a few states, such as Oregon and, perhaps, Maine, but this tactic seems to have limited, albeit important, reach. Republicans won governorships in several traditionally Democratic-leaning states, including Massachusetts, Maryland, and Illinois, while the Democrats made a gain in Pennsylvania. The Democrats held the governor's seat in Colorado in a close contest, but they lost the U.S. Senate seat there.

It was not immediately clear what impact, if any, those changes would have on gun laws. Most likely, we will continue to see some states pursue stricter laws while others will move to strengthen gun rights. That dance will continue, but at least in the short-term future, and probably beyond, the national debate over stricter gun laws is over.

The NRA emerged from the elections as strong, if not stronger than ever. Their won-lost record improved from recent elections, and, more important, they won almost every national race that could reasonably be seen as winnable. They nearly won a couple of contests that were not viewed as even possible victories.

For the major gun-control groups, the future was less clear. Americans for Responsible Solutions did not fare well, and the group may struggle to remain relevant to the issue. For Everytown, the future depends upon the wishes and the checkbook of Michael Bloomberg. They were clearly unable to muster any sort of a national surge of support for stricter gun laws. Many of their endorsed candidates won, but that was more due to their selection of candidates in safe seats rather than their campaigning acumen. When they went head-to-head with the NRA, their candidates generally lost, even if their defeat was not directly linked to firearms regulations.

The political landscape was not favorable toward gun-control supporters due to the number of seats the Democrats had to defend. At the same time, the elections were held less than two years after the Newtown shootings. That tragic event was the best opportunity for gun-control supporters to make their case to the nation for stricter laws. In the first national election after the shootings, they failed to make guns an issue, and they failed to elect candidates who would enact stricter laws.

This was, arguably, the most receptive climate for stricter gun laws since the passage of the Gun Control Act of 1968. The country was not quite two years away from arguably the most horrific mass murder in its history. Stricter laws were supported by the president. A tragically wounded former Congresswoman had survived and helped create a new organization to advocate for gun-control policies and support like-minded candidates. A billionaire former New York City mayor merged his group of mayors with a newly formed grassroots organization to create the first interest group that could not only match, but actually exceed the spending of the NRA. They joined the Brady Campaign, which still retained national influence. If this was the perfect storm for gun control, then it was weathered quite well by supporters of gun rights. In fact, they emerged largely unscathed.

The reality is that Everytown, ARS, and the Brady Campaign could not raise the profile of the gun-control issue with a major focusing event and a significant amount of money. Perhaps the tens of millions of dollars spent by Bloomberg and by the NRA are now paltry sums when one considers the costs of contested elections ($4 billion for all 2014 congressional and gubernatorial races, with over $100 million in North Carolina and just under $100 million in the Colorado Senate election). If the money has become less important, then the NRA's five million members have become even more important. The gun control groups cannot match the NRA's membership or loyalty. The old strength of the NRA may be the new strength of the NRA.

Bibliography

AARP. "It's Time for Responsible Solutions to Social Security and Medicare."
Direct mail. May 2013.

ABC News/*Washington Post* Poll. "Obama and 2014 Politics." January 26, 2014.
http://www.langerresearch.com/uploads/1158a1Obamaand2014Politics.pdf.

Abramson, Paul R., John H. Aldrich, and David W. Rohde. *Change and Continuity in the 2000 and 2002 Elections*. Washington, DC: CQ Press, 2003.

Achenbach, Joel, Scott Higham, and Sari Horwitz. "How the NRA's True
Believers Converted a Marksmanship Group into a Mighty Gun Lobby."
Washington Post, January 12, 2013. http://www.washingtonpost.com/
politics/how-nras-true-believers-converted-a-marksmanship-group-into-a
-mighty-gun-lobby/2013/01/12/51c62288-59b9-11e2-88d0-c4cf65c3ad15
_story.html.

Ainsworth, Alexa. "Obama Camp Disavows Last Year's 'Inartful' Statement on
DC Gun Law." ABC News, June 26, 2008. http://abcnews.go.com/blogs/
politics/2008/06/obama-camp-disa/.

Amar, Akhil Reed. "Comment: *Heller*, *HLR*, and Holistic Legal Reasoning."
Harvard Law Review 122, no. 1 (2008): 145–90.

American Institute of Philanthropy. "Top 25 Compensation Packages."
Charitywatch.org, 2013. http://www.charitywatch.org/hottopics/Top25
.html.

Americans for Responsible Solutions. "About Gabrielle Giffords." http://
americansforresponsiblesolutions.org/about/gabrielle-giffords/.

Assault Weapons Ban of 2013. S. 150, 113th Congress. https://www.govtrack.us/
congress/bills/113/s150/text.

Associated Press. "Pro-gun voters Put Heat on Democratic Senators." Fox News,
March 9, 2013. http://www.foxnews.com/politics/2013/03/09/pro-gun
-voters-put-heat-on-democratic-senators/?intcmp=related.

Ayres, Ian, and John Donohue. "Nondiscretionary Concealed Weapons Law: A Case Study of Statistics, Standards of Proof, and Public Policy." *American Law and Economics Review* 1 (1999): 436–70.

Ayres, Ian, and John Donohue. "Shooting Down the More Guns, Less Crime Hypothesis." *Stanford Law Review* 55 (2003): 1193–312.

Baker, Peter, and Michael D. Shear. "Obama to Put 'Everything I've Got' Into Gun Control." *New York Times*, January 16, 2013. http://www.nytimes .com/2013/01/17/us/politics/obama-to-ask-congress-to-toughen-gun-laws .html?pagewanted=all.

Banjo, Shelly. "Gun Sales Hinge on Obama Re-Election." *Wall Street Journal*, September 14, 2012. http://online.wsj.com/article/SB10000872396390444 433504577651393759726660.html.

Bardes, Barbara A., and Robert W. Oldendick. *Public Opinion: Measuring the American Mind*. Belmont, CA: Wadsworth, 2000.

Barrett, Paul M. "Are 3D Plastic Guns Really a Threat? Four Blunt Points." *Bloomberg Businessweek*, November 21, 2013. http://www.businessweek.com/ articles/2013-11-21/are-3d-plastic-guns-really-a-threat-four-blunt-points.

Barrett, Paul M. "Why Gun Makers Fear the NRA." *Bloomberg Businessweek*, March 14, 2013. http://www.businessweek.com/articles/2013-03-14/why -gun-makers-fear-the-nra.

Beccaria, Cesare. "On Crimes and Punishment." In *On Crimes and Punishment and Other Essays,* edited by Richard Bellamy, translated by Richard Davies, 101. New York: Cambridge University Press, 1995.

Bell, Larry. "Why The Centers for Disease Control Should Not Receive Gun Research Funding." *Forbes*, February 12, 2012. http://www.forbes.com/ sites/larrybell/2013/02/12/why-the-centers-for-disease-control-should-not -receive-gun-research-funding/.

Bennett, Matthew. "A Symposium on Firearms, the Militia and Safe Cities: Merging History, Constitutional Law and Public Policy: Article: Public Policy Approach: Misfire: How the Debate Over Gun Rights Ignores Reality." *Albany Government Law Review* 1, no. 2 (2008): 482–95.

Bequette, Jim. "Our Response to the December 2013 Backpage Column." *Guns & Ammo*, November 6, 2013. http://www.gunsandammo.com/2013/11/06/ response-december-2013-backpage-column/.

Black, Dan, and Daniel Nagin. "Do 'Right to Carry' Laws Deter Violent Crime?" *Journal of Legal Studies* 27 (January 1998): 209–19.

Blair, J. Pete, and M. Hunter Martaindale, "United States Active Shooter Events from 2000 to 2010: Training and Equipment Implications." Advanced Law Enforcement Rapid Response Training, Texas State University, 2013. http://alerrt.org/files/research/ActiveShooterEvents.pdf.

Blumenthal, Michael. "Gun Control Polls Show Longterm Decline in Support, despite Columbine Bump." *Huffington Post*. July 20, 2012. http://www .huffingtonpost.com/2012/07/20/gun-control-polls-aurora-shooting_n_169 0169.html.

Bohn, Kevin. "Gun Sales Surge after Obama's Victory." CNN, November 11, 2008. http://www.cnn.com/2008/CRIME/11/11/obama.gun.sales/.

Bohn, Kevin, and Gabriella Schwarz. "Bloomberg Gun Group Hits a Democrat." CNN Politics Political Ticker, May 24, 2013. http://politicalticker.blogs .cnn.com/2013/05/24/bloomberg-gun-group-hits-a-democrat/?hpt=po_c2.

Brady Campaign to Prevent Gun Violence. Legal Action Project (LAP) of the Brady Center. http://www.gunlawsuits.org/docket/docket.php.

Brady Campaign to Prevent Gun Violence. Million Mom March. http://brady campaign.org/?q=programs/million-mom-march/state-gun-laws/.

Brady Campaign to Prevent Gun Violence. "The Morning After: Police, Victims, Democrats and Republicans Stood Up to an Extremist Agenda, Forced It Down." Press release, March 3, 2004.

Brady Campaign to Prevent Gun Violence. Organizational history. http://www .bradycampaign.org/our-history.

Brady Campaign to Prevent Gun Violence. "Senate Votes Down Immunity for Gun Industry." Press release, March 2, 2004.

Brady Campaign to Prevent Gun Violence. "Special Protection for the Gun Industry: State Bill." http://www.bradycampaign.org/facts/issues/?page =immun_state.

Brady Campaign to Prevent Gun Violence. "2013 State Scorecard." December 9, 2013. http://bradycampaign.org/?q=2013-state-scorecard.

Bureau of Alcohol, Tobacco, Firearms and Explosives. Department of the Treasury. "Annual Firearms Manufacturing and Export Report 2009." January 20, 2011. http://www.atf.gov/files/statistics/download/afmer/ 2009-firearms-manufacturers-export-report.pdf.

Bureau of Alcohol, Tobacco, Firearms and Explosives. Department of the Treasury. "Annual Firearms Manufacturing and Export Report 2010." January 30, 2012. https://www.atf.gov/files/statistics/download/afmer/ 2010-final-firearms-manufacturing-export-report.pdf.

Bureau of Alcohol, Tobacco, Firearms and Explosives. Department of the Treasury. "Annual Firearms Manufacturing and Export Report 2011." January 7, 2013. https://www.atf.gov/files/statistics/download/afmer/ 2011-final-firearms-manufacturing-export-report.pdf.

Bureau of Alcohol, Tobacco, Firearms and Explosives. Department of the Treasury. "Annual Firearms Manufacturing and Export Report 2012." January 17, 2014. https://www.atf.gov/sites/default/files/assets/pdf-files/ afmer_2012_final_web_report_17jan2014.pdf.

Bureau of Alcohol, Tobacco, Firearms and Explosives. Department of the Treasury. "Commerce in Firearms in the United States." February 2000.

Bureau of Justice Statistics. "About 1.4 Million Guns Stolen during Household Burglaries and Other Property Crimes from 2005 through 2010." November 8, 2012. http://www.bjs.gov/content/pub/press/fshbopc0510pr .cfm.

Bureau of Justice Statistics. National Crime Victimization Survey, 1993–2011.

Butterfield, Fox. "Gun Industry Ex-Official Described Bond of Silence." *New York Times*, February 3, 2003. http://www.nytimes.com/2003/02/04/national/04GUNS.html.

Callaghan, Karen, and Frauke Schnell. "Assessing the Democratic Debate: How the News Media Frame Elite Policy Discourse." *Political Communication* 18 (2001): 183–212.

Carter, Gregg Lee. *The Gun Control Movement*. New York: Twayne Publishers, 1977.

Carter, Gregg Lee. ed. *Guns in American Society: An Encyclopedia of History Politics, Culture, and the Law*. 2nd ed. Santa Barbara, CA: ABC-CLIO, 2012.

Centers for Disease Control and Prevention. "FastStats, 2013." http://www.cdc.gov/nchs/fastats/homicide.htm.

Centers for Disease Control and Prevention. National Center for Injury Prevention and Control, Web-Based Injury Statistics Query and Reporting System (WISQARS), 1993–2010. http://www.cdc.gov/ncipc/wisqars.

Centers for Disease Control and Prevention. National Center for Injury Prevention and Control, Web-Based Injury Statistics Query and Reporting System (WISQARS). "Fatal Injury Reports, 1999–2010, for National, Regional, and States." http://webappa.cdc.gov/cgi-bin/broker.exe.

Chambers, Matthew, Mindy Liu, and Chip Moore. "Drunk Driving by the Numbers." *Bureau of Transportation Statistics*. 2012. http://www.rita.dot.gov/bts/sites/rita.dot.gov.bts/files/publications/by_the_numbers/drunk_driving/index.html.

Chasmar, Jessica. "Calif. Elementary School Offers Toy Gun Buyback." *Washington Times*, June 10, 2013. http://www.washingtontimes.com/news/2013/jun/10/calif-elementary-school-offers-toy-gun-buyback/.

Cicero. "In Defense of Titus Annius Milo," In *Selected Political Speeches of Cicero,* edited and translated by Michael Grant, 215–78. New York: Penguin Books, 1969.

Citizens United v. Federal Election Commission, 558 U.S. 310 (2010).

City of Akron v. Akron Center for Reproductive Health, 462 U.S. 453 (1983).

CNN Politics Political Ticker. "Gabby Giffords' Group Announces 2014 Election Strategy." CNN Politics, June 4, 2014, http://politicalticker.blogs.cnn.com/2014/06/04/gabby-giffords-group-announces-2014-election-strategy/.

"CNN Poll: Support for Stricter Gun Control Fades." CNN, December 4, 2013. http://politicalticker.blogs.cnn.com/2013/12/04/cnn-poll-support-for-stricter-gun-control-fades/?iref=allsearch.

Cobb, Roger W., and Charles Elder. *Participation in American Politics: The Dynamics of Agenda Building*. Baltimore: Johns Hopkins University Press, 1983.

Cohen, Michael, James March, and John Olsen. "A Garbage Can Model of Organizational Choice." *Administrative Science Quarterly* 17 (March 1972): 1–25.

Cohen, Tom. "Candidates Show Little Appetite for New Gun Control Laws." CNN, July 26, 2012. http://www.cnn.com/2012/07/26/politics/gun -control-debate.

Confessore, Nicholas, and Jeremy W. Peters. "Bloomberg Asks Donors to With-hold Gifts over Gun Votes." *New York Times*, June 12, 2013. http://www .nytimes.com/2013/06/12/nyregion/bloomberg-urges-no-gifts-to-democrats -who-blocked-gun-bill.html?pagewanted=1&tntemail0=y&emc=tnt.

"Congress and the Gun Lobby" (editorial). *New York Times*, March 3, 2004. http://www.nytimes.com/2004/03/03/opinion/03WED2.html.

Congressional Research Service. "Submission of Mental Health Records to NICS and the HIPAA Privacy Rule." April 15, 2013, http://www.fas.org/sgp/crs/ misc/R43040.pdf.

Connor, Tracy, and Kristen A. Lee. "President Obama Calls for Action to Stop Gun Violence, but No New Laws." *New York Daily News*, July 26, 2012. http://www.nydailynews.com/news/election-2012/president-obama-calls -background-checks-purchasing-firearms-wake-aurora-colo-movie-theater -massacre-article-1.1122128.

Cook, Philip J., and Jens Ludwig. "Defensive Gun Uses: New Evidence from a National Survey." *Journal of Quantitative Criminology* 14, no. 2 (1998): 111–31.

Cook, Philip J., and Jens Ludwig. *Guns in America: Results of a Comprehensive National Survey on Firearms Ownership and Use.* Washington, DC: Police Foundation, 1996.

Cook, Philip J., and Jens Ludwig. *Gun Violence: The Real Costs.* New York: Oxford University Press, 2000.

Cook, Philip J., and Jens Ludwig. "The Limited Impact of the Brady Act." In *Reducing Gun Violence in America,* edited by Daniel W. Webster and Jon S. Vernick, 21–32. Baltimore: Johns Hopkins University Press, 2013.

Cooper, Alexia, and Erica L. Smith. "Homicide Trends in the United States, 1980–2010." Bureau of Justice Statistics, November 2011. http://www. bjs.gov/content/pub/pdf/htus8008.pdf.

Cork, Daniel L., John E. Rolph, Eugene S. Meieran, and Carol V. Petrie, eds. *Ballistic Imaging.* Washington, DC: National Academies Press, 2008.

Corn, David. "SECRET VIDEO: Romney Tells Millionaire Donors What He REALLY Thinks of Obama Voters." Mother Jones, September 17, 2012. http://www.motherjones.com/politics/2012/09/secret-video-romney-private -fundraiser.

Cornell, Saul. "Commonplace or Anachronism: The Standard Model, the Second Amendment, and the Problem of History in Contemporary Constitutional Theory." *Constitutional Commentary* 16 (1999): 221–46.

Cornell, Saul. Introduction, in *Whose Right to Bear Arms Did the Second Amendment Protect?* Boston: Bedford/St. Martin's, 2000.

Cornell, Saul. "A Symposium on Firearms, the Militia and Safe Cities: Merging History, Constitutional Law and Public Policy: Article: Historical

Approach: The Ironic Second Amendment." *Albany Government Law Review* 1, no. 2 (2008): 293–311.

Cottroll, Robert J., and Raymond T. Diamond. "The Second Amendment: Toward an Afro-Americanist Reconsideration." *Georgetown Law Journal* 80 (1991): 309–61.

Cox, Chris W. Letter from NRA–Political Victory Fund, February 28, 2014.

Cox, Chris W. "National Campaign to Stop Gun Registration." Letter from NRA–Institute for Legislative Action. March 7, 2014.

Cox, Chris W. "Political Report: Election 2008 and the Long Road Ahead." NRA-ILA, December 22, 2008. http://www.nraila.org/news-issues/articles/2008/political-report-election-2008-and-the.aspx.

Cox, Chris W. "Your Tools for Victory." 2004. http://www.nraila.org/news-issues/articles/2004/your-tools-for-victory.aspx?s=%22Election+Volunteer+Coordinators%22&st=&ps.

Cress, Lawrence Delbert. "An Armed Community: The Origins and Meaning of the Right to Bear Arms." *Journal of American History* 71 (June 1984): 22–42.

Davidson, Osha Gray. *Under Fire: The NRA and the Battle for Gun Control.* Iowa City: University of Iowa Press, 1998.

Dean, Howard. "Sensible Gun Laws." Howard Dean for America. http://www.DeanForAmerica.com.

"Democrats and Guns" (editorial). *Washington Times*, February 12, 2004. http://www.washingtontimesonline.com/op-ed/20040212-081232-1419r.htm.

Denning, Brannon P., and Glenn H. Reynolds. "Five Takes on *McDonald v. Chicago*." *Journal of Law and Politics* 26 (Winter 2011): 273–303.

DeSilver, Drew. "Suicides Account for Most Gun Deaths." Pew Research Center, May 24, 2013. http://www.pewresearch.org/fact-tank/2013/05/24/suicides-account-for-most-gun-deaths/.

Dewar, Helen. "Bush Opposes Additions to Gun Bill." *Washington Post*, February 26, 2004.

"Dianne Feinstein on Guns: 2012 Election Year Not Ideal for Debate" (video). *Huffington Post*, July 22, 2012. http://www.huffingtonpost.com/2012/07/22/dianne-feinstein-guns-2012-election_n_1692994.html.

Diedrich, John, and Raquel Rutledge. "ATF Uses Rogue Tactics in Storefront Stings across Nation." *Milwaukee Journal Sentinel*, December 7, 2013. http://www.jsonline.com/watchdog/watchdogreports/atf-uses-rogue-tactics-in-storefront-stings-across-the-nation-b99146765z1-234916641.html.

District of Columbia v. Heller, 554 U.S. 510 (2008).

Doherty, Carroll. "Did Newtown Really Change Public Opinion about Gun Control?" CNN, December 6, 2013. http://globalpublicsquare.blogs.cnn.com/2013/12/06/did-newtown-really-change-public-opinion-about-gun-control/?iref=allsearch.

Donohue, John J. "The Impact of Concealed-Carry Laws." In *Evaluating Gun Policy,* edited by Jens Ludwig and Philip J. Cook, 287–344. Washington, DC: Brookings Institution Press, 2003.

Dorf, Michael C. "Symposium on the Second Amendment: Fresh Looks: What Does the Second Amendment Mean Today?" *Chicago-Kent Law Review* 76 (2000): 291–347.

Drash, Wayne, and Toby Lyles. "States Tighten, Loosen Gun Laws after Newtown." CNN, June 8, 2013. http://www.cnn.com/2013/06/08/us/gun-laws-states/index.html?hpt=hp_t1.

Ducat, Craig R. *Constitutional Interpretation*. 7th ed. Belmont, CA: West, 2000.

Duggan, Mark. "More Guns, More Crime." *Journal of Political Economy* 109 (October 2001): 1086–114.

Dye, Thomas. *Understanding Public Policy*. 14th ed. Boston: Pearson Education, Inc., 2013.

Editorial Board. "The NRA's Simplistic Response to Newtown: 'Good Guy with a Gun.'" *Washington Post*, December 21, 2012. http://articles.washingtonpost.com/2012-12-21/opinions/36017867_1_gun-violence-gun-owners-and-manufacturers-wayne-lapierre.

Eisenberg, Pablo. "On Gun Control, White House Fails to Tap Power of (Its Own and Other) Nonprofits." *Huffington Post*, April 2, 2013. http://www.huffingtonpost.com/pablo-eisenberg/post_4592_b_2999416.html.

"The Election: Issues 2000: A Special Briefing; the Economy, Trade, Foreign Policy, Social Security, Health, Education, Death Penalty, Gun Control, Poverty, Race, Campaign Finance, Environment, New Technology, Values." *Economist* 356 (September 30, 2000): 59–102.

"Election Center 2008: Guns." CNNPolitics.com. http://www.cnn.com/ELECTION/2008/issues/issues.gun.html.

Engelhardt, Christopher R., Bruce D. Bartholow, Geoffrey T. Kerr, and Brad J. Bushman. "This Is Your Brain on Violent Video Games: Neutral Desensitization to Violence Predicts Increased Aggression following Violent Video Game Exposure." *Journal of Experimental Social Psychology* 47, no. 5 (September 2011): 1033–36.

Epstein, Reid J. "NRA Splits with Open Carry Texas amid Chipotle Beef." The Wall Street Journal. June 2, 2014. http://blogs.wsj.com/washwire/2014/06/02/nra-splits-with-open-carry-texas-amid-chipotle-beef/.

Epstein, Richard A. "Justice for Trayvon Martin?" *Hoover Institution Journal*, July 22, 2013. http://www.hoover.org/publications/defining-ideas/article/152351.

Erhardt, Paul. "Between the Berms: Paging Uncle Ted." *Shooting Wire*, November 6, 2013, http://www.shootingwire.com/features/228219.

Everytown.org. "School Shootings in America since Sandy Hook." June, 2014, http://everytown.org/article/schoolshootings/.

Everytown.org. "We Are Everytown for Gun Safety." http://everytown.org/who-we-are/.

Fantz, Ashley, Lindsey Knight, and Kevin Wang, "A Closer Look: How Many Newtown-Like Shootings since Sandy Hook?" CNN, June 12, 2014. http://www.cnn.com/2014/06/11/us/school-shootings-cnn-number/index.html.

Federal Bureau of Investigation. "National Instant Criminal Background Check System (NICS) Operations 2012." http://www.fbi.gov/about-us/cjis/nics/reports/2012-operations-report.

Federal Bureau of Investigation. "Total NICS Background Checks: November 30, 1998–January 30, 2014." http://www.fbi.gov/about-us/cjis/nics/reports/1998_2014_monthly_yearly_totals-013114.pdf.

Federal Election Commission. "FEC Disclosure from 3 for Americans for Responsible Solutions." Filed July 31, 2013. http://query.nictusa.com/cgi-bin/dcdev/forms/C00540443/883049/.

Federal Election Commission. "FEC Summarizes Campaign Activity of the 2011–2012 Election Cycle." April 19, 2013. http://www.fec.gov/press/press2013/20130419_2012-24m-Summary.shtml.

Feldman, Richard. *Ricochet: Confessions of a Gun Lobbyist.* Hoboken, NJ: John Wiley & Sons, Inc., 2008.

Ferner, Matt. "Gun Violence in Colorado: From Columbine to Aurora, Mass Shootings Reignite Gun Control Debate." *Huffington Post*, December 17, 2012. http://www.huffingtonpost.com/2012/12/17/gun-violence-in-colorado-_n_2316633.html.

Follman, Mark, Gavin Aronsen, and Deanna Pan. "A Guide to Mass Shootings in America." Mother Jones. Updated May 24, 2014. http://www.motherjones.com/politics/2012/07/mass-shootings-map?page=1.

Follman, Mark, Gavin Aronsen, Deanna Pan, and Maggie Caldwell. "US Mass Shootings, 1982–2012: Data from Mother Jones' Investigation." September 16, 2013. http://www.motherjones.com/politics/2012/12/mass-shootings-mother-jones-full-data.

Foster, Dick. "Billionaire Backs Gun-Curb Measure." *Rocky Mountain News: Election 2000*, January 7, 2000. http://denver.rockymountainnews.com/election/1002mons5.shtml.

Fowler, Floyd J., Jr. *Survey Research Methods.* 4th ed. Thousand Oaks, CA: Sage, 2008.

Fox, James Alan. "Top 10 Myths about Mass Shootings." Boston.com, December 19, 2012. http://www.boston.com/community/blogs/crime_punishment/2012/12/top_10_myths_about_mass_shooti.html.

Gallia, Anthony. " 'Your Weapons, You Will Not Need Them,' Comment on the Supreme Court's Sixty-Year Silence on the Right to Keep and Bear Arms." *Akron Law Review 33* (1999): 131–62.

Gallup. "Guns." 2012. http://www.gallup.com/poll/1645/guns.aspx.

Gallup. "Presidential Approval Ratings—George W. Bush." http://www.gallup.com/poll/116500/presidential-approval-ratings-george-bush.aspx.

Gonyea, Don. "Gun Control Advocates Say Little After Navy Yard Shootings." NPR, September 18, 2013. http://www.wbur.org/npr/223627238.

Goss, Kristin A. *Disarmed: The Missing Movement for Gun Control in America.* Princeton, NJ: Princeton University Press, 2006.

Gun Owners of America. https://gunowners.org/.

Haar, Dan. "Dan Haar: Untold Thousands Flout Gun Registration Law." *Hartford Courant,* February 10, 2014. http://touch.courant.com/#section/-1/article/p2p-79243214/.

Hahn, Robert A., Oleg O. Bilukha, Alex Crosby, Mindy Thompson Fullilove, Akiva Liberman, Eve K. Moscicki, Susan Snyder, Farris Tuma, and Peter Briss. "First Reports Evaluating the Effectiveness of Strategies for Preventing Violence: Firearms Laws: Findings from the "Task Force on Community Preventive Services." Centers for Disease Control, October 3, 2003. http://www.cdc.gov/mmwr/preview/mmwrhtml/rr521 4a2.htm.

Haider-Markel, Donald P., and Mark R. Joslyn. "Gun Policy, Opinion, Tragedy, and Blame Attribution: The Conditional Influence of Issue Frames." *Journal of Politics* 63, no. 2 (May 2001): 520–43.

Halbrook, Stephen P. *That Every Man Be Armed: The Evolution of a Constitutional Right.* Oakland, CA: The Independent Institute, 1994.

Hamilton, Alexander. "The Federalist No. 28." In *The Federalist,* edited by Sherman F. Mittell, 173. Washington, DC: National Home Library Foundation, 1938.

Hamilton, Alexander. "The Federalist No. 29." In *The Federalist,* edited by Sherman F. Mittell, 176, 178–79. Washington, DC: National Home Library Foundation, 1938.

Hardaway, Robert, Elizabeth Gormley, and Bryan Taylor. "The Inconvenient Militia Clause of the Second Amendment: Why the Supreme Court Declines to Resolve the Debate over the Right to Bear Arms." *St. John's Journal of Legal Commentary* 16 (Winter 2002): 41–164.

Harvard Injury Research Control Center. "Firearms Research: Homicide." http://www.hsph.harvard.edu/hicrc/firearms-research/guns-and-death/.

Hawley, Francis Frederick. "Gun Culture." In *Guns in American Society: An Encyclopedia of History Politics, Culture, and the Law,* edited by Gregg Lee Carter, 2nd ed., 341–46. Santa Barbara, CA: ABC-CLIO, 2012.

Hayes, Benjamin. "Stolen Guns: Why You Should Worry." *Crime Report,* September 10, 2013. http://www.thecrimereport.org/viewpoints/2013-09-stolen-guns-why-you-should-worry.

Healy, Jack. "Colorado Lawmakers Ousted in Recall Vote over Gun Law." *New York Times,* September 11, 2013. http://www.nytimes.com/2013/09/11/us/colorado-lawmaker-concedes-defeat-in-recall-over-gun-law.html?emc=edit_tnt_20130911&tntemail0=y.

Hemenway, David. *Private Guns Public Health.* Ann Arbor: University of Michigan Press, 2004.

Hemenway, David. "Risks and Benefits of a Gun in the Home." *American Journal of Lifestyle Medicine* (2011): 7. http://www.iansa.org/system/files/Risks+and+Benefits+of+a+Gun+in+the+Home+2011.pdf.

Henigan, Dennis A. "Lawsuits against Gun Manufacturers." In *Guns in American Society: An Encyclopedia of History Politics, Culture, and the Law,* edited by Gregg Lee Carter, 2nd ed., vol. 2, 491–500. Santa Barbara, CA: ABC-CLIO, 2012.

Hickey, Walter. "Here's Who the NRA REALLY Represents." *Business Insider Politics*, December 19, 2012. http://www.businessinsider.com/the-nra-has-sold-out-to-the-gun-industry-to-become-their-top-crisis-pr-firm-2012-12.

Hickey, Walter. "How the NRA Became the Most Powerful Interest in Washington." *Business Insider Politics*, December 18, 2012. http://www.business insider.com/nra-lobbying-money-national-rifle-association-washington-2012-12.

Higginbotham, Don. "The Federalized Militia Debate: A Neglected Aspect of Second Amendment Scholarship." *William and Mary Quarterly* 55 (1998): 39–58.

Horwitz, Joshua, and Casey Anderson. "Public Policy Approach: The Insurrectionist Idea and Its Consequences." Symposium on Firearms, the Militia and Safe Cities: Merging History, Constitutional Law and Public Policy. *Albany Government Law Review* 1, no. 2 (2008): 497–515.

Houston v. Moore, 5 Wheat, 1, 24 (1820).

Independent Firearms Owners Association. http://www.independentfirearm owners.org/2013/.

Institute of Medicine of the National Academies. "Priorities for Research to Reduce the Threat of Firearm-Related Violence." June 2013. http://www .iom.edu/~/media/Files/Report%20Files/2013/Firearm-Violence/Firearm Violence_Insert.pdf.

Jacobs, James B. *Can Gun Control Work?* New York: Oxford University Press, 2002.

James, Frank. "Obama Finding Gun Control Voice, Which Had Gone Quiet in the White House." NPR: It's All Politics, December 18, 2012. http:// www.npr.org/blogs/itsallpolitics/2012/12/18/167562866/obama-finding -gun-control-voice-which-had-gone-quiet-in-white-house.

Jervis, Rick. "Newtown on NRA Speech: 'Completely Off the Mark.' " *USA Today*, December 21, 2012. http://www.usatoday.com/story/news/nation/ 2012/12/21/nra-guns-newtown-reaction/1784957/.

Jiobu, Robert M., and Timothy J. Curry. "Lack of Confidence in the Federal Government and the Ownership of Firearms." *Social Science Quarterly* 82, no. 1 (March 2001): 77–88.

Johnson, Timothy. "Terry McAuliffe Win Disproves Media Myth of NRA's Electoral Dominance." Media Matters for America blog, November 6, 2013. http://mediamatters.org/blog/2013/11/06/terry-mcauliffe-win -disproves-media-myth-of-nra/196755.

Jones, Jeffrey M. "Men, Married, Southerners Most Likely to Be Gun Owners." Gallup Politics. February 1, 2013. http://www.gallup.com/poll/160223/ men-married-southerners-likely-gun-owners.aspx.

Jonsson, Patrick. "Briefing: Obama vs. Romney 101: 4 Ways They Compare on Gun Control." *Christian Science Monitor*, September 9, 2012. http://

www.csmonitor.com/USA/DC-Decoder/2012/0909/Obama-vs.-Romney
-101-4-ways-they-compare-on-gun-control/Second-Amendment.

Jonsson, Patrick. "Gun Debate: Is Price of an Armed America a More Dangerous
America?" *Christian Science Monitor*, February 2, 2014. http://www
.csmonitor.com/USA/2014/0202/Gun-debate-Is-price-of-an-armed-America
-a-more-dangerous-America-video.

Kates, Don B. "Introduction, the Second Amendment: A Right to Personal Self-
Protection." In Gary Kleck and Don B. Kates, *Armed: New Perspectives
on Gun Control,* 343–56. Amherst, NY: Prometheus Books, 2001.

Kates, Don B. "Symposium: The Second Amendment and the Right to Bear
Arms after *D.C. v. Heller*: A Modern Historiography of the Second
Amendment." *UCLA Law Review* 56 (2009): 1211–32.

Kates, Don B., and Gary Mauser. "Would Banning Firearms Reduce Murder
and Suicide? A Review of International and Some Domestic Evidence."
Harvard Journal of Law and Public Policy 30, no. 2 (2007): 650–94.

Kates, Don B., Henry E. Schaffer, and William B. Waters IV. "Public Health Pot
Shots." *Reason.* April 1997.

Kellermann, Arthur L., and Donald T. Reay. "Protection or Peril? An Analysis of
Firearm Related Deaths in the Home." *New England Journal of Medicine*
314 (1986): 1557–60.

Kellermann, Arthur L., Grant Somes, Frederick P. Rivara, R. K. Lee, and J. G.
Banton. "Injuries and Deaths Due to Firearms in the Home." *Journal of
Trauma* 45 (1998): 263–67.

Kellman, Laurie. "Trayvon Martin's Mother Testifies at Senate Hearing on
'Stand Your Ground' Laws." *Washington Post*, October 29, 2013. http://
www.washingtonpost.com/politics/trayvon-martins-mother-testifies-at
-senate-hearing-on-stand-your-ground-laws/2013/10/29/94285480-40c6
-11e3-a624-41d661b0bb78_story.html.

Kessler, Glenn. "The Fact Checker: The Claim That the Brady Law Prevented
1.5 Million People from Buying a Firearm." *Washington Post,* January 24,
2013. http://www.washingtonpost.com/blogs/fact-checker/post/the-claim
-that-the-brady-law-prevented-15-million-people-from-buying-a-firearm/
2013/01/23/77a8c1d4-65b4-11e2-9e1b-07db1d2ccd5b_blog.html.

Kiely, Eugene. "Do Assault Weapons Sales Pay NRA Salaries?" Factcheck.org,
January 15, 2013. http://www.factcheck.org/2013/01/do-assault-weapons-
sales-pay-nra-salaries/.

Kingdon, John. *Agendas, Alternatives, and Public Policies.* 2nd ed. New York:
Longman, 2003.

Kingdon, John. *Agendas, Alternatives, and Public Policies.* Updated 2nd ed. New
York: Longman Publishing Group, 2011.

Kirell, Andrew. "Norah O'Donnell Grills Rahm Emmanuel for Telling Obama
AG to 'Shut the F**k Up' about Assault Weapons Ban." *Mediaite*, December 18, 2012. http://www.mediaite.com/tv/norah-odonnell-grills-emanuel
-for-telling-obama-ag-to-shut-the-fk-up-about-assault-weapons-ban/.

Kleck, Gary. "Impossible Policy Evaluations and Impossible Conclusions: A Comment on Koper and Roth." *Journal of Quantitative Criminology* 17, no. 1 (March 2001): 75–80.

Kleck, Gary. "Measures of Gun Ownership Levels for Macro-Level Crime and Violence Research." *Journal of Research in Crime and Delinquency* 41, no. 1 (February 2004): 3–36.

Kleck, Gary. "The Nature and Effectiveness of Owning, Carrying, and Using Guns for Self-Protection." In Gary Kleck and Don B. Kates, *Armed: New Perspectives on Gun Control*, 285–342. Amherst, NY: Prometheus Books, 2001.

Kleck, Gary, and Miriam A. DeLone, "Victim Resistance and Offender Weapon Effects in Robbery." *Journal of Quantitative Criminology* 9, no. 1 (1993): 55–81.

Kleck, Gary, and Marc Gertz. "Armed Resistance to Crime: The Prevalence and Nature of Self-Defense with a Gun." *Journal of Criminal Law and Criminology* 86, no. 1 (Fall 1995): 150–87.

Kliff, Sarah. "Full Transcript of the Second Presidential Debate." *Washington Post* blog, October 16, 2012. http://www.washingtonpost.com/blogs/wonkblog/wp/2012/10/16/full-transcript-of-the-second-presidential-debate/?print=1.

Kopel, Dave. "Arms Alive." *National Review Online*, November 3, 2004. http://www.nationalreview.com/script/kopel/kopel200411031134.asp.

Kopel, Dave. *The Truth about Gun Control.* New York: Encounter Books, 2013.

Koper, Christopher S., and Jeffrey A. Roth. "The Impact of the 1994 Assault Weapons Ban on Gun Violence Outcomes: An Assessment of Multiple Outcome Measures and Some Lessons for Policy Evaluation." *Journal of Quantitative Criminology* 17 (March 2001): 33–74.

Kotkin, Joel. "The Changing Demographics of America." *Smithsonian Magazine*, August 2010. http://www.smithsonianmag.com/40th-anniversary/the-changing-demographics-of-america-538284/.

Kristof, Nicholas D. "Time to Get Religion." *New York Times*, November 6, 2004.

Krouse, William J. *Gun Control Legislation*. Congressional Research Service, November 14, 2012. http://www.fas.org/sgp/crs/misc/RL32842.pdf.

Lambert, Diana. "Trying to Stop the Craziness of This Business." In *The Changing Politics of Gun Control,* edited by John M. Bruce and Clyde Wilcox, 172–95. Lanham, MD: Rowman & Littlefield Publishers, 1998.

Landler, Mark, and Peter Baker. "'These Tragedies Must End,' Obama Says." *New York Times*, December 16, 2012. http://www.nytimes.com/2012/12/17/us/politics/bloomberg-urges-obama-to-take-action-on-gun-control.html?pagewanted=all.

Landler, Mark, and Erica Goode. "Obama's Cautious Call for Action Sets Stage to Revive Gun Debate." *New York Times*, December 12, 2012. http://www

.nytimes.com/2012/12/15/us/politics/obamas-reaction-to-connecticut
-shooting-sets-stage-for-gun-debate.html?pagewanted=1&_r=0.

LaPierre, Wayne. Appearance on *Meet the Press.* September 22, 2013.

LaPierre, Wayne. "NRA: Full Statement by Wayne LaPierre in Response to
Newtown Shootings." *Guardian*, December 21, 2012. http://www.
theguardian.com/world/2012/dec/21/nra-full-statement-lapierre-newtown.

Leddy, Edward F. *Magnum Force Lobby.* Lanham, MD: University Press of
America, 1987.

Lee, Matthew R. "Reconsidering Culture and Homicide." *Homicide Studies* 15,
no. 4 (2011): 319–40.

Levinson, Sanford. "The Embarrassing Second Amendment." *Yale Law Journal*
99 (1989): 637–59.

Levy, Pema. "In Virginia Race, McAuliffe Runs against the NRA." *Newsweek*,
October 25, 2013. http://www.newsweek.com/virginia-running-governor
-and-against-nra-953.

Levy, Robert A. "Challenging the D.C. Gun Ban." Cato Institute. http://www
.cato.org/publications/commentary/challenging-dc-gun-ban.

Lieberman, Joe. "Joe Lieberman: Fighting Crime and Keeping Communities
Safe." http://www.joe2004.com.

Lott, John R., Jr. *More Guns, Less Crime.* Chicago: University of Chicago Press, 1998.

Lott, John R., Jr. *More Guns, Less Crime: Understanding Crime and Gun Control Laws.* 2nd ed. Chicago: University of Chicago Press, 2000.

Lott, John R., Jr., and David B. Mustard. "Crime Deterrence and Right-to-Carry
Concealed Handguns." *Journal of Legal Studies* 26 (January 1997): 1–68.

Ludwig, Jens. "Concealed-Gun-Carrying Laws and Violent Crime: Evidence
from State Panel Data." *International Review of Law and Economics* 18
(1998): 239–54.

Ludwig, Jens. "Gun Self-Defense and Deterrence." *Crime and Justice* 27 (2000):
363–417.

Ludwig, Jens, Philip J. Cook, and Tom W. Smith. "The Gender Gap in Reporting
Household Gun Ownership." *American Journal of Public Health* 88, no. 11
(November 1998): 1715–18.

Madison, James. "The Federalist No. 46." In *The Federalist,* edited by Sherman
F. Mittell, 299–300. Washington, DC: National Home Library Foundation,
1938.

Maharajh, Hari D., and Petal S. Abdool. "Cultural Aspects of Suicide." *Scientific
World Journal* 5 (2005): 736–46.

Malcolm, Joyce Lee. "The Supreme Court and the Uses of History: *District of
Columbia v. Heller.*" *UCLA Law Review* 56 (2009): 1377–98.

Manchin, Joe. Appearance on *Face the Nation*, September 22, 2013.

Martin, Jonathan. "Obama Careful on *Heller.*" *Politico*, June 8, 2008. http://
www.politico.com/blogs/jonathanmartin/0608/Obama_careful_on_Heller
.html.

Martin, Susan Taylor, Kris Hundley, and Connie Humburg. "Race Plays Complex Role in Florida's 'Stand Your Ground' Law." *Tampa Bay Times*, June 2, 2012. http://www.tampabay.com/news/courts/criminal/race-plays -complex-role-in-floridas-stand-your-ground-law/1233152.

Martinelli, Michelle. "Crossroads' $175 Million Strikeout." *OpenSecrets Blog*, November 8, 2012. http://www.opensecrets.org/news/2012/11/despite -dropping-millions-crossroads-strikes-out.html.

Mathiesen, Peter B. "Calibers That Hunt." Military.com Outdoor Guide. http:// www.military.com/entertainment/outdoor-guide/ar-hunting/calibers-that -hunt.html.

Maybury, Kelly. "Most Americans Favor Tougher Drunk Driving Law." Gallup, October 26, 2000. http://www.gallup.com/poll/2395/Most-Americans -Favor-Tougher-Drunk-Driving-Law.aspx.

Mayors Against Illegal Guns. http://www.mayorsagainstillegalguns.org/html/ home/.

McCalmont, Lucy. "Michael Bloomberg Plans $50M Gun Effort." *Politico*, April 16, 2014. http://www.politico.com/story/2014/04/michael-bloomberg -nra-gun-effort-105745.html.

McClurg, Andrew J., David B. Kopel, and Brannon P. Denning. *Gun Control and Gun Rights.* New York: New York University Press, 2002.

McCombs, Maxwell E., and Donald L. Shaw. "The Agenda-Setting Function of Mass Media." *Public Opinion Quarterly* 36 (1972): 176–87.

McDonald v. Chicago 561 U.S. 742 (2010), slip opinion.

McDowall, David, and Brian Wiersema. "The Incidence of Defensive Firearm Use by U.S. Crime Victims, 1987 through 1990." *American Journal of Public Health* 84 (1994): 1982–84.

Metcalf, Dick. "Let's Talk Limits: Do Certain Firearms Regulations Really Constitute Infringement?" The Backstop, *Guns & Ammo*, December 2013.

"Michael Bloomberg." *Forbes*, 2014. http://www.forbes.com/profile/michael -bloomberg/.

Miller, Emily. "Guns Blazing since Election: Obama's Second Term Driving Firearms Sales to New Heights." *Washington Times*, November 13, 2012. http://www.washingtontimes.com/news/2012/nov/13/guns-blazing-since -election/.

Miniter, Frank. "What the Left Won't Tell You about the Boom in U.S. Gun Sales." *Forbes*, August 23, 2012. http://www.forbes.com/sites/frankminiter/ 2012/08/23/what-the-left-wont-tell-you-about-the-boom-in-u-s-gun-sales/.

Moms Demand Action for Gun Sense in America. http://www.momsdeman daction.org/about/.

Mothers Against Drunk Driving. "About Us." http://www.madd.org/about-us/.

Muskal, Michael "NRA Apologizes for Calling Texas Open-Carry Gun Demonstrators 'Weird.' " *Los Angeles Times*, June 4, 2014. http://www.latimes .com/nation/nationnow/la-na-nn-nra-apologize-texas-long-gun-open-carry -20140604-story.html.

Nagourney, Adam. "Baffled in Loss, Democrats Seek Road Forward." *New York Times*, November 7, 2004. http://www.nytimes.com/2004/11/07/politics/campaign/07dems.html.

Nagourney, Adam. "Democratic Leader Analyzes Bush Victory." *New York Times*, December 11, 2004. http://www.nytimes.com/2004/12/11/politics/11dems.html.

National Shooting Sports Foundation. http://nssf.org/.

National Shooting Sports Foundation. "Our Freedoms Face Serious Challenges." Election flier, 2012.

Neal, Terry M. "Election Reflections." *Washington Post*, November 4, 2004. http://www.washingtonpost.com/ac2/wp-dyn/A24733-2004Nov4.

Newport, Frank. "NRA has 54% Favorable Image in U.S." Gallup Politics, December 27, 2012. http://www.gallup.com/poll/159578/nra-favorable-image.aspx.

Nieto, Michael. "The Changing Landscape of Firearm Legislation in the Wake of *McDonald v. City of Chicago*. 130 S.CT. 3020 (2010)." *Harvard Journal of Law and Public Policy* 34 (2011): 1117–30.

NRA–Civil Rights Defense Fund. "About Us." https://www.nradefensefund.org/about-us.aspx.

"The N.R.A. Crawls from Its Hidey Hole" (editorial). *New York Times*, December 21, 2012. http://www.nytimes.com/2012/12/22/opinion/the-nra-crawls-from-its-hidey-hole.html.

NRA Foundation. "About Us." http://www.nrafoundation.org/.

NRA–Institute for Legislative Action. "2012 Election Recap." November 9, 2012. http://www.nraila.org/news-issues/articles/2012/2012-election-recap.aspx.

NRA–Institute for Legislative Action. "About NRA-ILA." http://www.nraila.org/about-nra-ila.aspx.

NRA–Institute for Legislative Action. "Courts Reject Lawsuits against Gun Makers." Fact sheet. http://www.nraila.org/news-issues/fact-sheets/2003/courts-reject-lawsuits-against-gun-make.aspx.

NRA–Institute for Legislative Action. "Gun Laws." http://www.nraila.org/gun-laws/state-laws.aspx.

NRA–Institute for Legislative Action. "Gun Laws, State Gun Laws, New York." http://www.nraila.org/gun-laws/state-laws/new-york.aspx.

NRA–Institute for Legislative Action. "Senate Passes NICS Improvement Act, House Concurs." December 19, 2007. http://www.nraila.org/news-issues/news-from-nra-ila/2007/senate-passes-nics-improvement-act,-hou.aspx.

NRA–Institute for Legislative Action. Statement on S. 1805. http://www.nraila.org/news-issues/news-from-nra-ila/2004/nra-statement-on-S1805.aspx.

NRA–Institute for Legislative Action. "Taxpayer Funded Reckless Lawsuits against the Firearms Industry." Fact sheet, April 25, 2004. http://www.nraila.org/news-issues/fact-sheets/2005/taxpayer-funded-reckless-lawsuits-again.aspx.

NRA–Institute for Legislative Action. "Who's the Right Team to Restore Our Freedoms—and Rebuild Our Future?" Election flier, 2012.

NRA–Political Victory Fund. "About PVF." http://www.nrapvf.org/about-pvf .aspx.

NRA–Political Victory Fund. "If John Kerry Thinks the Second Amendment is about Photo-Ops, He's Daffy." NRA–Political Victory Fund print advertisement. 2004.

Obama, Barack. State of the Union address. January 28, 2014.

"Obama in 2008: 'I Am Not Going to Take Your Guns Away.' " RealClearPolitics video, posted December 27, 2012. http://www.realclearpolitics.com/ video/2012/12/27/obama_2008_i_am_not_going_to_take_your_guns _away.html.

"Obama's Gun Ban?" FactCheck.org. http://www.factcheck.org/2008/12/ obamas-gun-ban/.

" 'Obama Supports Gun Rights': 2008 Campaign Ad Ran in Rural PA 10-13 -2008." YouTube video, 0:29. http://www.youtube.com/watch?v=qmWhta TdqB4.

O'Brien, Michael. "Obama's Gun Plans Spark Little Enthusiasm with Key Lawmakers." First Read, NBCNews.com. January 16, 2013. http://firstread .nbcnews.com/_news/2013/01/16/16546691-obamas-gun-plans-spark -little-enthusiasm-with-key-lawmakers?lite.

O'Keefe, Ed. "Congress Reauthorizes Ban on Plastic Guns." *Washington Post: Post Politics*, December 9, 2013. http://www.washingtonpost.com/blogs/ post-politics/wp/2013/12/09/plasticguns/.

OpenSecrets.org. "Lobbying, Ranked Sectors." http://www.opensecrets.org/ lobby/top.php?indexType=c&showYear=2012.

OpenSecrets.org. "National Rifle Assn." http://www.opensecrets.org/ outsidespending/detail.php?cmte=National+Rifle+Assn.

OpenSecrets.org. "2012 Outside Spending, by Group." http://www.opensecrets. org/outsidespending/summ.php?cycle=2012&chrt=V&disp-0&type=U.

OpenSecrets.org. "2012 Overview: Top Overall Donors." http://www.open secrets.org/overview/topcontribs.php.

Pace, Julie. "Obama Announces Gun Violence Task Force, Presses for Policy Changes after Shooting." *Huffington Post*, December 19, 2012. http:// www.huffingtonpost.com/2012/12/19/obama-gun-violence-task-force_n _2331238.html.

Pacheco, Julianna. "Trends—Public Opinion on Smoking and Anti-Smoking Policies." *Public Opinion Quarterly* 75, no. 3 (Fall 2011): 576–92.

Palmer, Brian. "Why Is the NRA So Powerful? How the Gun Lobby Leverages Modest Resources into Outsized Influence." *Slate*, December 18, 2012. http://www.slate.com/articles/news_and_politics/explainer/2012/06/eric _holder_charged_with_contempt_how_did_the_nra_swing_the_votes_of _so_many_democrats_.html.

Parker v. District of Columbia, 311 F.Supp. 2d 103, 109 (2004).

Parker v. District of Columbia, 478 F.3d 370, 401 (2007).

Peters, Jeremy W. "Bloomberg Plans a $50 Million Challenge to the N.R.A." *New York Times*, April 15, 2014. http://mobile.nytimes.com/2014/04/16/us/bloomberg-plans-a-50-million-challenge-to-the-nra.html?referrer=.

Petzal, David E., and Phil Bourjaily. "Meet the American Hunters and Shooters Association." *Field and Stream,* September 7, 2006. http://www.fieldandstream.com/pages/meet-american-hunters-and-shooters-association.

Pew Research Center. "Gun Homicide Rate Down 49% since 10093 Peak; Public Unaware." May 7, 2013. http://www.pewsocialtrends.org/files/2013/05/firearms_final_05-2013.pdf.

Pew Research Center for the People and the Press. "Broad Support for Renewed Background Checks Bill, Skepticism about Its Chances: Gun Rights Proponents More Likely to Vote on Issue." May 23, 2013. http://www.people-press.org/2013/05/23/broad-support-for-renewed-background-checks-bill-skepticism-about-its-chances/.

Pew Research Center for the People and the Press. "Gun Rights vs. Gun Control." May 23, 2013. http://www.people-press.org/2013/05/23/gun-rights-vs-gun-control/#total.

Pew Research Center for the People and the Press. "In Gun Control Debate, Several Options Draw Majority Support." January 14, 2013. http://www.people-press.org/2013/01/14/in-gun-control-debate-several-options-draw-majority-support/.

Pew Research Center for the People and the Press. "Mixed Reactions to Senate Gun Vote." April 24, 2013. http://www.people-press.org/2013/04/24/mixed-reactions-to-senate-gun-vote/.

Pew Research Center for the People and the Press. "Political Polarization in the American Public." June 12, 2014. http://www.people-press.org/2014/06/12/political-polarization-in-the-american-public/.

Pew Research Center for the People and the Press. "Public Takes Conservative Turn on Gun Control, Abortion." April 30, 2009. http://people-press.org/report/513/public-takes-conservative-turn-on-gun-control-abortion/.

Pew Research Center for the People and the Press. "Timeline: Top News Stories of 2012." December 20, 2012. http://www.people-press.org/2012/12/20/timeline-top-news-stories-of-2012/.

Pew Research Center for the People and the Press. "Why Own a Gun? Protection Is Now Top Reason." March 12, 2013. http://www.people-press.org/2013/03/12/section-3-gun-ownership-trends-and-demographics/.

Pew Research Center for the People and the Press. "Why Own a Gun? Protection Is Now Top Reason: Section 2: Perspectives of Gun Owners, Non-Owners." March 12, 2013. http://www.people-press.org/2013/03/12/section-2-opinions-of-gun-owners-non-gun-owners/.

Pierce, Charles P. "What George Zimmerman Can Do Now." *Esquire: The Politics Blog*, July 14, 2013. http://www.esquire.com/blogs/politics/The_End_Of_The_Daily_Trayvon.

Planned Parenthood. "Planned Parenthood: Extreme 20-Week Abortion Ban Takes Personal Medical Decisions Out of the Hands of Women and Their Doctors." November 7, 2013. http://www.plannedparenthood.org/about -us/newsroom/press-releases/planned-parenthood-extreme-20-week-abortion -ban-takes-personal-medical-decisions-out-hands-wome-42160.htm.

Planty, Michael, and Jennifer L. Truman. "Firearm Violence 1993–2011." *Bureau of Justice Statistics*, May 2013. http://bjs.gov/content/pub/pdf/ fv9311.pdf.

Plumer, Brad. "Here Are the Questions about Gun Violence the CDC Would Study—if It Could." *Washington Post*, June 8, 2013. http://www.washington post.com/blogs/wonkblog/wp/2013/06/08/here-are-the-questions-about-gun -violence-the-cdc-would-study-if-it-could/.

Pogrebin, Mark R., Paul B. Stretesky and N. Prabha Unnithan. *Guns, Violence and Criminal Behavior: The Offender's Perspective*. Boulder, CO: Lynne Rienner Publishers, 2009.

Pratt, Erich. "A Truly Plastic Gun Ban: Opposing View." *USA Today*, December 3, 2013. http://www.usatoday.com/story/opinion/2013/12/03/plastic -guns-gun-owners-of-america-editorials-debates/3863917/.

"President Obama's Remarks at the Memorial Service for Navy Yard Victims." September 22, 2013. http://www.wjla.com/articles/2013/09/full-text-president -obama-s-remarks-at-the-memorial-service-for-navy-yard-victims-94350 .html.

Presser v. Illinois, 116 U.S. 252 (1886).

Preston, Scott R. "Targeting the Gun Industry: Municipalities Aim to Hold Manufacturers Liable for Their Products and Actions." *Southern Illinois Law Journal* 24 (Spring 2000): 596.

Rafferty, Ann P. "Validity of a Household Gun Question in a Telephone Survey." *Public Health Reports* 110, no. 3 (May–June 1995): 282–88.

Raju, Manu, and Anna Palmer. "Gabrielle Giffords Guns Group Raises $11 million." *Politico*, May 8, 2013. http://www.politico.com/story/2013/05/gabrielle -giffords-guns-group-fundraising-91074.html.

"RC Poll: Virginians' Views on Ethics, Mental Health Reforms, Medicaid Expansion Plus Warner vs. Gillespie for US Senate." Roanoke College, January 21, 2014. http://roanoke.edu/News_and_Events/News_Archive/ RC_Poll_Jan_2014.htm.

Redmond, Ian. "Legislative Reform: The Second Amendment: Bearing Arms Today." *Journal of Legislation* 28 (2002): 343.

Reynolds, Glenn H. "A Critical Guide to the Second Amendment." *Tennessee Law Review* 62 (1995): 461–512.

Ridgeway, Greg. "Summary of Select Firearm Violence Prevention Strategies." National Institute of Justice memo, January 4, 2013. http://www.nraila .org/media/10883516/nij-gun-policy-memo.pdf.

Roanoke College Poll, Rutgers-Eagleton Poll, and Siena New York Poll. "Majority in Three States Favorable on Hillary Clinton; Give Former Sec. of State

2016 Lead over Christie, Paul and Ryan." March 4, 2014. http://roanoke
.edu/News_and_Events/News_Archive/Roanoke_Rutgers_Siena_Poll
_0314.htm.

Roos, Leslie, Jitender Sareen, and James M. Bolton. "Suicide Risk Assessment
Tools, Predictive Validity Findings and Utility Today: Time for a
Revamp?" *Summary Neuropsychiatry* 3, no. 5 (October 2013): 483–95.

Rosenthal, Lawrence, and Joyce Lee Malcolm. "*McDonald v. Chicago*: Which
Standard of Scrutiny Should Apply to Gun Control Laws?" *Northwestern
University Law Review* 105 (2011): 85–114.

Rosenwald, Michael J. "Calif. Store Backs Away from Smart Guns after Outcry
from 2nd Amendment Activists." *Washington Post*, March 6, 2013. http://
www.washingtonpost.com/local/california-smart-gun-store-prompts-furious
-backlash/2014/03/06/43432058-a544-11e3-a5fa-55f0c77bf39c_story.html.

Rosenwald, Michael J. " 'We Need the iPhone of Guns': Will Smart Guns Transform the Gun Industry?" *Washington Post*, February 17, 2013. http://www
.washingtonpost.com/local/we-need-the-iphone-of-guns-will-smart-guns
-transform-the-gun-industry/2014/02/17/6ebe76da-8f58-11e3-b227-12a4
5d109e03_story.html.

Rostron, Allen. "Protecting Gun Rights and Improving Gun Control after *District
of Columbia v. Heller.*" *Lewis and Clark Law Review* 13, no. 2 (2009):
383–418.

Rovner, Julie. "Debate Rages on Even as Research Ban on Gun Violence Ends."
NPR. February 6, 2013. http://www.npr.org/blogs/health/2013/02/06/
170844926/debate-rages-on-even-as-research-ban-on-gun-violence-ends.

Ruhl, Jesse Matthew, Arthur L. Rizer, and Mikel J. Weir. "Gun Control: Targeting Rationality in a Loaded Debate." *Kansas Journal of Law and Public
Policy* 13 (Winter 2004): 13–83.

Rushforth, Norman, Charles Hirsh, Amanda B. Ford, and Lester Adelson.
"Accidental Firearms Deaths in a Metropolitan County (1958–1975)."
American Journal of Epidemiology 100 (1975): 499–505.

Saad, Lydia. "Americans Fault Mental Health System Most for Gun Violence."
Gallup Politics, September 20, 2013. http://www.gallup.com/poll/164507/
americans-fault-mental-health-system-gun-violence.aspxU.

"Schieffer: NRA the Lobby Most Feared by Congress." CBS News, December 15,
2012. http://www.cbsnews.com/news/schieffer-nra-the-lobby-most-feared
-by-congress/.

"School Confiscates Third-Graders Cupcakes Topped with Toy Soldiers." *Daily
Caller*, March 8, 2013. http://news.yahoo.com/school-confiscates-third
-grader-cupcakes-topped-toy-soldiers-215018982.html.

"Senate Dems Hesitant on Obama's Gun Control Plan." Fox News, January 18,
2013. http://www.foxnews.com/politics/2013/01/18/senate-dems-noncommittal
-on-obama-gun-control-plan/?test=latestnews.

Shaiko, Ronald G., and Marc A. Wallace. "Going Hunting Where the Ducks Are:
The National Rifle Association and the Grass Roots." In *The Changing*

Politics of Gun Control, edited by John W. Bruce and Clyde Wilcox, 155–71. Lanham, MD: Rowman & Littlefield Publishers, 1998.

Shalhope, Robert E. "The Armed Citizen in the Early Republic." *Law and Contemporary Problems* 49 (1986): 125–41.

Shalhope, Robert E. "The Ideological Origins of the Second Amendment." *Journal of American History* 69 (December 1982): 599–614.

Shalhope, Robert E. "To Keep and Bear Arms in the Early Republic." *Constitutional Commentary* 16 (Summer 1999): 269.

Shear, Michael D., and Peter Baker. "In Gun Bill Defeat, a President's Distaste for Twisting Arms." *New York Times*, April 22, 2013. http://www.nytimes.com/2013/04/23/us/politics/in-gun-bill-defeat-a-president-who-hesitates-to-twist-arms.html?nl=todaysheadlines&emc=edit_th_20130423&_r=0.

Shevory, Kristina. "Bullet Blitz: Demand from Public, Government Leave Ammo Shelves Empty." Fox News, May 12, 2013. http://www.foxnews.com/us/2013/05/12/bullet-blitz-demand-from-public-government-leaves-ammo-shelves-empty/?test=latestnews.

Shrum, Robert. "For Obama, Romney, and America, Gun Control Is Dead." *Daily Beast*, July 24, 2012. http://www.thedailybeast.com/articles/2012/07/24/for-obama-romney-and-america-gun-control-is-dead.html.

Siegel, Reva B. "Comment: Dead or Alive: Originalism as Popular Constitutionalism in *Heller*." *Harvard Law Review* 122, no. 1 (2008): 191–245.

Simpson, Steve. "We Don't Need a 'Media Shield' Law for Fox and AP; We Already Have the First Amendment." *Forbes*, June 19, 2013. http://www.forbes.com/sites/realspin/2013/06/19/we-dont-need-a-media-shield-law-for-fox-and-ap-we-already-have-the-first-amendment/.

Smith, Aaron. "Guns and Ammo Sales Spark Jobs Boom." CNN Money, March 25, 2013. http://money.cnn.com/2013/03/25/news/companies/guns-ammo-jobs/index.html?hpt=hp_t2.

Smith, Aaron. "Gun Shops Face Massive Ammunition Shortage." CNN Money, March 12, 2013. http://money.cnn.com/2013/03/12/news/companies/guns-ammo-shortage/index.html.

Smith, Ben. "Obama on Small-Town Pa.: Clinging to Religion, Guns, Xenophobia." *Politico*, April 11, 2008. http://www.politim/blogs/bensmith/0408/Obama_on_smalltown_PA_Clinging_religion_guns_xenophobia.html.

Smith, Erica L., and Alexia Cooper. "Homicide in the U.S. Known to Law Enforcement, 2011." Bureau of Justice Statistics. December 2013. http://www.bjs.gov/content/pub/pdf/hus11.pdf.

Smith, Kevin B., and Alan Greenblatt. *Governing States and Localities*. 4th ed. Washington, DC: CQ Press, 2014.

Smith, Tom W. "A Call for a Truce in the DGU War." *Journal of Criminal Law and Criminology* 87, no. 4 (1997): 1462–69.

Smith, Tom W. *1999 National Gun Policy Survey of the National Opinion Research Center: Research Findings*. April 2000. http://www.consumerfed.org/pdfs/survey99.pdf.

Snyder, James M., and Tim Groseclose. "Estimating Party Influence in Congressional Roll-Call Voting." *American Journal of Political Science* 44, no. 2 (April 2000): 193–211.

Sobel, Stacey L. "The Tsunami of Legal Uncertainty: What's a Court to Do Post-*McDonald*?" *Cornell Journal of Law and Public Policy* 21 (2012): 489-524.

Sonzinsky v. United States, 300 U.S. 506 (1937).

Southwick, Lawrence, Jr. "Self-Defense with Guns: The Consequences." *Journal of Criminal Justice* 28, no. 5 (2000): 351–370.

Spitzer, Robert J. *The Politics of Gun Control*. 5th ed. Boulder, CO: Paradigm Publishers, 2012.

Steinhauer, Jennifer. "Gun Control Effort Had No Real Chance, Despite Pleas." *New York Times*, April 17, 2013. http://www.nytimes.com/2013/04/18/us/politics/despite-tearful-pleas-no-real-chance.html?nl=todaysheadlines&, memc=edit_th_20130418&_r=0.

Steinhauer, Jennifer, and Charlie Savage. "Pro-Gun Democrats Signaling Openness to Limits." *New York Times*, December 17, 2012. http://www.nytimes.com/2012/12/18/us/politics/pro-gun-democrats-signal-openness-to-limits.html?ref=todayspaper&pagewanted=all&_r=0.

Stern, Ray. "The Anti-Gun Culture: Irresponsible, Phobia-Driven, and Just Plain Wrong on the Facts." *Phoenix New Times Blogs*. January 14, 2011. http://blogs.phoenixnewtimes.com/valleyfever/2011/01/the_anti-gun_culture_irrespons.php.

Stolberg, Sheryl Gay. "Looking Back and Ahead after Senate's Votes on Guns." *New York Times*, March 4, 2004. http://www.nytimes.com/2004/03/04/politics/04GUNS.html.

Stolberg, Sheryl Gay. "Senate Leaders Scuttle Gun Bill Over Changes." *New York Times*, March 3, 2004. http://www.nytimes.com/2004/03/03/politics/03GUNS.html.

Stolberg, Sheryl Gay. "A Swing to the Middle on Gun Control." *New York Times*, March 7, 2004. http://www.nytimes.com/2004/03/07/weekinreview/07stol.html.

"Suicide Rates by Country." *Washington Post*, 2014. http://www.washingtonpost.com/wp-srv/world/suiciderate.html.

Sullivan, Eileen, and Jack Gillum. "US Gun Industry Is Thriving during Obama's Term."

Associated Press. October 19, 2012. http://bigstory.ap.org/article/us-gun-industry-thriving-during-obamas-term.

Sunstein, Cass R. "Comment: Second Amendment Minimalism: *Heller* as *Griswold*." *Harvard Law Review* 122 (2008): 246–74.

Surette, Ray. *Media, Crime, and Criminal Justice: Images and Realities*. Pacific Grove, CA: Brooks/Cole, 1992.

Swanson, Jeffrey W., Allison Gilbert Robertson, Linda K. Frisman, Michael A. Norko, Hsiu-Ju Lin, Martin S. Swartz, and Philip J. Cook. "Preventing

Gun Violence Involving People with Serious Mental Illness." In *Reducing Gun Violence in America*, edited by Daniel W. Webster and Jon S. Vernick, 33–52. Baltimore: Johns Hopkins University Press, 2013.

Third Way. "About Us." http://www.thirdway.org/about_us.

Todd, Chuck, Mark Murray, Domenico Montanaro, and Brooke Brower. "First Thoughts: Why the Gun Measure Went Down to Defeat." First Read, NBCNews.com, April 18, 2013. http://firstread.nbcnews.com/_news/2013/04/18/17809775-first-thoughts-why-the-gun-measure-went-down-to-defeat.

Toppo, Greg. "10 Years Later, the Real Story behind Columbine." *USA Today*, April 14, 2009. http://usatoday30.usatoday.com/news/nation/2009-04-13-columbine-myths_N.htm.

"Trayvon Martin Shooting Fast Facts." CNN Library, August 29, 2013. http://www.cnn.com/2013/06/05/us/trayvon-martin-shooting-fast-facts/.

Tushnet, Mark. "*Heller* and the Perils of Compromise." *Lewis and Clark Law Review* 13, no. 2 (2009): 419–32.

Ungar, Rick. "Here Are the 23 Executive Orders on Gun Safety Signed Today by the President." *Forbes*, January 16, 2013. http://www.forbes.com/sites/rickungar/2013/01/16/here-are-the-23-executive-orders-on-gun-safety-signed-today-by-the-president/.

United Nations. *Global Study on Homicide, 2013: Trends, Context, Data.* Vienna: UN Office on Drugs and Crime, 2013. http://www.unodc.org/documents/gsh/pdfs/2014_GLOBAL_HOMICIDE_BOOK_web.pdf.

United States v. Cruikshank, 92 U.S. 542 (1876).

United States v. Miller, 307 U.S. 174 (1939).

U.S. Census Bureau. "Changing American Households." November 4, 2011. http://www.census.gov/newsroom/pdf/cah_slides.pdf.

U.S. Fish and Wildlife Service. *2011 National Survey of Fishing, Hunting, and Wildlife-Associated Recreation*. Revised February 2014, 21–33. http://www.census.gov/prod/2012pubs/fhw11-nat.pdf.

U.S. Fish and Wildlife Service. "Historical Hunting License Data." http://wsfrprograms.fws.gov/Subpages/LicenseInfo/Hunting.htm.

U.S. Geological Survey. Information and Technology Report USGS/BRD/ITR—2002-0002. "Americans' Attitudes toward Wolves and Wolf Reintroduction: An Annotated Bibliography." April 2002. http://www.fort.usgs.gov/Products/Publications/949/949.pdf.

U.S. House of Representatives. "Final Vote Results for Roll Call 534." October 20, 2005. http://clerk.house.gov/evs/2005/roll534.xml.

Van Dorn, Richard, Jan Volovka, and Norman Johnson. "Mental Disorder and Violence: Is There a Relationship beyond Substance Use." *Social Psychiatry and Psychiatric Epidemiology* 47, no. 3 (March 2012): 487–503.

Vittes, Katherine A., Daniel W. Webster, and Jon S. Vernick. "Reconsidering the Adequacy of Current Conditions on Legal Firearm Ownership." In *Reducing Gun Violence in America*, edited by Daniel W. Webster and Jon S. Vernick, 65–76. Baltimore: Johns Hopkins University Press, 2013.

Vizzard, William J., *Shots in the Dark: The Policy, Politics, and Symbolism of Gun Control.* Lanham, MD: Rowman & Littlefield Publishers, 2000.

Volokh, Eugene. "The Commonplace Second Amendment." *New York University Law Review* 73, no. 3 (1998): 793–821.

Volokh, Eugene. "Implementing the Right to Keep and Bear Arms for Self-Defense: An Analytical Framework and a Research Agenda." Symposium: The Second Amendment and the Right to Bear Arms after *D.C. v. Heller.* *UCLA Law Review* 56 (2009): 1446–47.

Weinger, Mackenzie. "Mitt Romney's Stance on Gun Control." *Politico*, July 20, 2012. http://www.politico.com/news/stories/0712/78767.html.

Weisberg, Herbert F., Jon A. Krosnick, and Bruce D. Bowen. *An Introduction to Survey Research, Polling, and Data Analysis.* 3rd ed. Thousand Oaks, CA: Sage, 1996.

Wellford, Charles F., John V. Pepper, and Carol V. Petrie, eds. *Firearms and Violence: A Critical Review.* Washington, DC: National Academies Press, 2004.

The White House. Office of the Press Secretary. "FACT SHEET: New Executive Actions to Reduce Gun Violence." August 29, 2013. http://www.white house.gov/the-press-office/2013/08/29/fact-sheet-new-executive-actions -reduce-gun-violence.

Wilgoren, Jodi. "Kerry on Hunting Photo-Op to Help Image." *New York Times*, October 22, 2004. http://www.nytimes.com/2004/10/22/politics/ campaign/22kerry.html?_r=0.

Williams, David C. "The Unitary Second Amendment." *New York University Law Review* 73, no. 3 (1998): 822–30.

Wills, Garry. "To Keep and Bear Arms." In *Whose Right to Bear Arms Did the Second Amendment Protect?* edited by Saul Cornell, 65–88. Boston: Bedford/St. Martin's, 2000.

Wilson, Harry. *Guns, Gun Control, and Elections.* Lanham, MD: Rowman & Littlefield Publishers, 2007.

Wilson, Harry. "RC Poll: The Opinions of Virginians on Guns, Gun Policy, and Gun Violence." January 28, 2013. http://roanoke.edu/News_and_Events/ News_Archive/RC_Poll_Jan_2013_Guns.htm.

Wilson, Harry. "RC Poll: Virginians' Views on Ethics, Mental Health Reforms, and Medicaid Expansion Plus Warner v. Gillespie for US Senate." January 21, 2014. http://roanoke.edu/News_and_Events/News_Archive/RC _Poll_Jan_2014.htm.

Winkler, Adam. *Gunfight: The Battle over the Right to Bear Arms in America.* New York: W. W. Norton & Company, 2013.

Wintemute, Garen J. "Broadening Denial Criteria for the Purchase and Possession of Firearms: Need, Feasibility, and Effectiveness." In *Reducing Gun Violence in America*, edited by Daniel W. Webster and Jon S. Vernick, 77. Baltimore: Johns Hopkins University Press, 2013.

Wintemute, Garen J. "Comprehensive Background Checks for Firearms Sales: Evidence from Gun Shows." In *Reducing Gun Violence in America*, edited by Daniel W. Webster and Jon S. Vernick, 95–108. Baltimore: Johns Hopkins University Press, 2013.

Wintersteen, Kyle. "9 Ways Gun Owners Can Lose in the 2012 Election." *Guns & Ammo.* February 27, 2012. http://www.gunsandammo.com/2012/02/27/how-gun-owners-can-lose-in-the-2012-election/.

Workman, Dave. "Ricker Deposition 'Without Foundation.'" *Gun Week,* February 20, 2003. http://www.gunweek.com/2003/ricker0220.html.

Wright, James D., and Peter H. Rossi. *Armed and Considered Dangerous: A Survey of Felons and Their Firearms.* New York: Aldine de Gruyter, 1986.

Yang, Min, Stephen C. P. Wong, and Jeremy Coid. "The Efficacy of Violence Prediction: A Meta-Analystic Comparison of Nine Risk Assessment Tools." *Psychological Bulletin* 136, no. 5 (September 2010): 740–67.

Yourish, Karen, Wilson Andrews, Larry Buchanan, and Alan McLean. "State Gun Laws Enacted in the Year since Newtown." *New York Times,* December 10, 2013. http://www.nytimes.com/interactive/2013/12/10/us/state-gun-laws-enacted-in-the-year-since-newtown.html?emc=edit_tnt_2013 1211&tntemail0=y.

Zimring, Franklin E., and Gordon Hawkins. *The Citizen's Guide to Gun Control.* New York: Macmillan, 1987.

Zimring, Franklin E., and Gordon Hawkins. "Concealed Handguns: The Counterfeit Deterrent." *Responsive Community* 7 (1997): 46–60.

Index

About the Author

Harry L. Wilson is director of the Institute for Policy and Opinion Research and professor of Political Science at Roanoke College, Salem, Virginia. He is the author of *Guns, Gun Control, and Elections*, published by Rowman & Littlefield, and an editorial board member of ABC-CLIO's Guns in American Society and ABC-CLIO's Enduring Questions online essay series. Wilson earned a PhD in political science at Rutgers University and a BA in journalism at Penn State University.